BREAKING CADENCE
ONE WOMAN'S WAR AGAINST THE WAR

ROSA DEL DUCA

Breaking Cadence: One Woman's War Against the War
2nd Edition

Originally Published in 2019 by Ooligan Press
© Copyright November 2021 by Rosa del Duca

Paperback ISBN: 9780997808612
Audiobook digital ISBN: 9781667924731
Ebook ISBN: 9780997808629

All rights reserved. No part of this book may be reproduced for the purposes of sale by anyone but the publisher, Rosa del Duca. If you are using parts of this book for educational purposes, you are free to photocopy chapters, play parts of the audiobook in class, and post on educational websites, granted you include information about the book and author. Pictures may not be reproduced or posted in any way.

No part of this book may be reproduced or transmitted for resale in any form or by any means, electronic or mechanical, including photocopying, recording, or by any information storage and retrieval system, without permission in writing from the publisher, Rosa del Duca.

Reach Rosa del Duca through breakingcadence@gmail.com or rosadelduca.com

Library of Congress Cataloging-in-Publication Data:
Names: Del Duca, Rosa, author
Title: Breaking Cadence: One Woman's War Against the War / Rosa del Duca.

Printed   in   the   United   States   of   America

PRAISE FOR BREAKING CADENCE

"It's hard to believe that a 17-year-old who can't vote or drink can go to war. Del Duca's experience as one of those teens—who joined the National Guard to pay for college and then finds herself on the verge of being sent to fight a war she thinks is morally wrong—is as harrowing as they come. I was riveted by her story and her strength." — Julia Scheeres, author of NYT bestseller *Jesus Land* and *A Thousand Lives*

"Rosa has employed grace and strength to tell a much-needed story about the costs of the military industrial complex on one woman's life. She is a beautiful storyteller as she unravels the ugly truths about good intentions twisted and used by the violent and careless system. Reading her book is the seed of inspiration we all need as we learn about the systems we live within and how violent they can be to others. It is time to divest from war and invest ourselves in a culture of peace. Rosa lays the bread crumbs for us to follow." — Jodie Evans, co-founder and director of CODEPINK

"*Breaking Cadence* is a page-turner, a gripping blow-by-blow account of how Rosa del Duca's immersion in military culture comes to a crisis point when her conscience awakens. This is a deep and compelling exploration of the bridge into adulthood, complete with the nuts-and-bolts of Army training and the hard times of a small-town Montana upbringing, but most of all a savvy warts-and-all self-portrayal, which arrives with a deep understanding of what personal responsibility actually is, and how it can be exploited by the war-making machinery. This is a vital read for anyone wrestling with the ethics of what being in uniform—or frankly being a person—means." — Glen David Gold, author of *Carter Beats the Devil*

"From track star to soldier, from cadet to conscientious objector, Rosa del Duca maps a riveting account of military life and her uneasy metamorphosis in a book that's impossible to put down." — Marilyn Abildskov, author of *The Men in My Country*

"*Breaking Cadence* is honest, beautifully-written, and immensely compelling. Among many other things, it is a vital chronicle of military service, and of the young Americans who volunteer into it. It is a window into a world most civilians know little about, but must, if we are to reckon with the actual human costs of war. Step by painful step, the narrator becomes the person she was destined to be: a conscientious objector, an artist, and a writer who looks honestly at herself and the world, and who tells, in unflinching detail, the truth. The irrefutable evidence of her destiny is this compelling, moving, essential story." — Matthew Zapruder, author of *Why Poetry* and *Sun Bear*.

"*Breaking Cadence* traces Del Duca's forced march into the light of self-confidence. It is the tale of escape and deprogramming from patriotism-as-religious cult. It is a masterful deconstruction of the process of government exploitation of young people too green to know they are being used and too cornered by barren lives to do much about it." —Joel D. Eis, author and conscientious objector

"This book stands as an example of what it takes for someone in the military to stand up for justice, act on their morals, and become a conscientious objector. This story of Rosa del Duca's spirit and her tenacity to follow it is a beacon to shine the light for others who choose not to be the cannon fodder of empire." —Dahr Jamail, Iraq war reporter and author of *The End of Ice*

"A tribute to the notion that dissent is the highest form of patriotism. In her intense, revelatory and liberating transformation from teen military recruit to conscientious objector, we follow del Duca as she navigates contradictory emotions that put her on a collision course with the most powerful institution in the world. Her determination not to fight in an immoral war will hopefully serve as a warning and an inspiration for young Americans across this country. Bravo!" — Medea Benjamin, co-founder of CODEPINK

Dedicated to Itasca and River—the future.

AUTHOR'S NOTE

I've always found catharsis in writing about things that bother me. The events in this book are not only based on my memories, but bolstered by journal entries and letters. In later chapters, some wording is taken straight from official military documents. That being said, the opinions that follow are mine alone and do not represent any past or present organization or employer.

Some of the characters portrayed in this book have granted permission for their real names to be used. Other names have been changed either because it's the polite thing to do or because several people have been combined into one character. In a few cases, names have been changed in order to protect people from their own bad behavior (you know who you are).

Some minor details have been changed in the interest of clarity and narrative honesty.

Some major details have not changed, and, unfortunately, are left for the next generation to contend with.

CONTENTS

PART I: TRUST YOUR MASK

1. Turning Traitor — 1
2. Trajectory — 3
3. The Pied Piper — 12
4. The Responsible Thing to Do — 19
5. Unlikely Chameleon — 24
6. Initiation — 27
7. Trust Your Mask — 36
8. Second Chance, Last Chance — 45
9. Homecoming, Homeleaving — 49
10. Terror — 53
11. Suspension of Disbelief — 60
12. Keeping Up Appearances — 66
13. Now You See the Cage, Now You Don't — 71
14. The Golden State — 87
15. California Love — 105
16. One of the Guys — 111
17. The Script — 123

PART II: END OF INNOCENCE

1. Love and Band-Aids — 144
2. The Call — 153
3. Panic — 156
4. The Pitch — 162
5. One of These Cadets is Not Like the Others — 166
6. The Secret — 172
7. Fifteen Minutes of Fame — 177
8. Wearing the Lead Flak Jacket — 187
9. Girlfriend Points — 191
10. Surrender — 197

PART III: SUMMER CAMP

1.	Claustrophobia	213
2.	Oh Lord, I Wanna Go	222
3.	Summer Camp	226
4.	Reevaluation	231
5.	Navigation	235
6.	This Is My Rifle	243
7.	The Budding Saboteurs	248
8.	Disorientation	255
9.	How Do You Feel Now, Cadet?	259
10.	Fighting the Current	273
11.	Cover Me While I Lie to You	277
12.	Body Double	290
13.	Vortex Time	295
14.	Patriots	306
15.	The Perpetual Periphery	318

PART IV: WAR AGAINST THE WAR

1.	Directive	325
2.	Admissions	336
3.	Citizen Soldier	345
4.	Quandaries	352
5.	Declaration	359
6.	Writing, In and Out of Uniform	363
7.	Battle Plans	370
8.	Investigation	376
9.	Code Pink	394
10.	Code Red	398
11.	The Long Wait	410
12.	Habeas Corpus	420
13.	Orders	425

14.	Messages in the Wind	432
15.	Aftermath	437
16.	Perception, Assumption, Affirmation	451

Acknowledgements	464
About the Author	465
Student Readers Guide	467

PART I

TRUST YOUR MASK

1. TURNING TRAITOR

October 2005, San Luis Obispo, CA

"Are you here to make my life more difficult, Ms. del Duca?" Major Taulk asked, leaning against the doorjamb to his office.

I froze, electricity running up my spine. He *knew* already. He was toying with me, waiting to see if I'd go through with it.

No, he couldn't know. I'd been very careful. I forced myself to swallow. "Actually, sir, I am."

I had the attention of everyone in the main office now—Taulk, the two captains, the secretary, even some delivery driver with a clipboard. "I really need to talk to you," I said, flicking my eyes past the major to his desk and chair.

Taulk studied my stiff posture, clenched hands, and set face and waved me into his side office. He closed the door behind us, dropped into his swivel chair, and gestured for me to sit. I hesitated. What I had to say felt too important to be said without my feet planted, my body stretched to its full height. The words had been festering for years, knots of betrayal and bravery twisting in on themselves.

But now that the moment was here, insisting on standing felt melodramatic. I pulled out the chair and sat like a soldier was supposed to sit—feet shoulder-width apart, hands resting on my knees, back straight, head raised.

"Sir, you're not going to like what I have to say, and I'm sorry I couldn't tell you earlier but I was advised not to." I sucked in a deep breath, wrangling the next sentence. No combination of words seemed right. Only two were necessary: *conscientious objector.* But I didn't know anyone in uniform who would hear those two words in a positive light. They wouldn't feel the conviction I felt: my scrappy conscience not just objecting, but sprinting alongside my boxcar, screaming for me to jump off the moving train while I still could. They would only hear, and see, a coward. A traitor.

"Advised, huh?" Taulk's jaw clenched. His whole body seemed to harden.

The barrier slammed into place. Me vs. Them. I was expecting this, but all the same, it made my ears ring, my skin smart.

The major stared at me. I stared back, then dropped my gaze, feeling like a cockroach. I saw a flicker of myself staring into the bathroom mirror at eight, ten, thirteen, fifteen years old—straining to receive messages from my future self, trying to send messages to my past self. If only things were that easy. If only I could find the exact moment this trajectory had begun and intervene.

But there was no going back. I opened my mouth to speak.

2. TRAJECTORY

November 1998: Outside Fromberg, MT

I was bludgeoning a block of coal with the back of an axe when my mother threw open the trailer door.

"Rosa," she yelled. "Come inside. Family meeting."

Through clumsy gloves, I filled the coal bucket with chunks I'd managed to chip off and lugged my haul inside. I stacked the pieces near the stove, wondering again why we couldn't heat the house like normal people instead of like Old West homesteaders. It was 1998, for Chrissake.

"Are we waiting for *Wayne*?" I asked, drawing out the name in a mocking tone.

"Not this time." My mother leaned over Leila, who was sprawled on the floor, drawing, her golden-brown hair obscuring her face. "Could you stop what you're doing?"

Instantly more comfortable knowing it'd just be the three of us, the real family, I dropped onto the couch and stretched my lanky legs out. Leila made a show of dragging herself up next to me, knocking my knee in the process. I meowed at her. She hissed back. I poked her in the stomach. "Boop on you."

"Don't boop *me*, you," she said, going for my sides. I struggled to fend her off, screeching, before determining the best defense was a counter-attack.

Leila twisted into contortions, howling warnings.

"Girls. *Girls.*" Mom pointed her imaginary remote control at us. "I'm pressing the pause button for the next five minutes. Beep!"

Leila and I shrunk back to our spots, snickering.

"How would you two feel about Wayne adopting you?"

We choked on our giggles. Leila's look of hurt confusion mirrored two-thirds of what I was feeling. The missing third was anger. *Adopt?* I was fifteen years old. No one could adopt me. That was a word for orphans. For kids young enough to want or need parents.

"Wayne and I are married now. Your father has never really—"

"Whose idea was this?" I demanded. "Wayne's or Dad's?" I actively hated Wayne and tracked his offenses in my journal. There was a clear trend these days. Fleeting creepiness had given way to all-out tyranny. As for my dad, at least it seemed like he was trying on the rare occasions we saw him.

"Your father's, at first," Mom said.

Not what I was expecting. My throat started to ache. Who did Dad think he was, bartering us off without even talking to us? Then again, he'd always been an anomaly. I'd heard both sides of the breakup story and I still didn't understand how a guy could abandon his two kids and pregnant wife so abruptly, so completely.

"What, so he won't have to pay child support anymore?" I asked.

"That's part of it. And Wayne wouldn't mind adopting you. He loves you girls..." My mother trailed off.

"Not interested," I said.

Leila hesitated and I glared at her, willing her to follow my lead. With our older sister Alura off to college across the state, Leila was my only ally in the war against Wayne the Pain.

"What would change?" Leila's dark eyes were uncertain. "Isn't he already our new dad?"

My mother frowned. "He'd still be your stepdad. It's more of a legal thing."

"Would we have to change our last name?" Leila asked.

"Not unless you wanted to."

Leila stared out the window at the frozen prairie—dead wheatgrass and sagebrush brambles sticking up out of the blanket of snow. "I don't want to be adopted," she finally said.

Mom was doing her clenched-jaw, pursed-lip thing. I wondered if my sisters and I would inherit the mannerism, just like we'd inherited her wide, full mouth—just like I'd inherited her loud cackle of a laugh and her instinct to gasp dramatically at the smallest mistake, like forgetting to put salt in the pancake batter. And I thought about how passing on Leila's and my rejection to Wayne would not be pleasant.

"You don't even want to think about it?" she asked.

I shook my head. Man, did Wayne have my mother fooled. This wasn't about love. It probably had something to do with taxes. "I have a question," I said, clutching the edge of the couch cushions. Since we were having a family meeting, I might as well ask what was really on my mind.

Okay, it was more than a question. It was a plea that might redefine my relationship with my mother forever. I ground my heels into the carpet so I wouldn't start jiggling my legs. "Can I move in with Heather during the school week? Her parents told her it's okay. They have tons of room in their basement."

My mother's voice lowered half an octave. "Why?"

"To be closer to school," I said. "So I can be on the volleyball team and play in pep band and actually hang out with my friends instead of being stuck out here. You guys never let me borrow the car, never give me a ride, and don't want me accepting rides from other people. That basically leaves me a prisoner."

"How do you plan on eating?"

I sat up straighter. I had everything worked out. "I can buy cereal and milk for breakfast. Lunch is free for me at school. And if you want, I can cook for them sometimes. Or help with groceries." I had over a thousand dollars saved up from working at McDonald's the past summer in Missoula, the gorgeous mountain town we'd had to leave when Wayne got a job across the state at a platinum mine.

Watching her mull this over, I imagined what a luxury it would be to eat what I wanted to. Wayne had instituted a food rationing system soon after the move. At first it was cheese, fruit, peanut butter, eggs. Then, one day, he'd caught me eating a graham cracker and accused me of cheating, lying, and sneaking around. *I got mirrors and I seen you.* We fought. I lost. Wayne instigated a new rule: he had to okay every single thing we ate.

"And I'll do chores," I said, seeing my mother needed more convincing.

"You'll come back on the weekends to help here?"

"Yeah," I lied.

Leila sat quiet and still between Mom and me, studying her socks. *I'll be okay. I don't hate them as much as you do*, she'd said when I told her about my plan.

"Just for the rest of the school year," I added, giddy my mother hadn't said no yet, and heavy with guilt that I wouldn't be around to stand up for her when Wayne made her cry, to remind her that she didn't have to put up with his asshole ways, let alone feed into them. Watching their marriage thrash around in quicksand was like watching my mother be hijacked by some harsh, parallel-universe version of herself who cared nothing for self-preservation. Poor Leila. I planned on jailbreaking my little sister as often as I could.

"I guess you could stay with them," my mother said.

Rocket fuel poured into my bloodstream. I waited for my mother to declare the family meeting over, then raced to pack. True, sweet freedom within my reach! I crammed my two favorite stuffed animals into a garbage bag, followed by my two good pairs of jeans and my best Goodwill finds: the black velvet T-shirt, the hoodie sweatshirts, the mismatched soccer shorts and jerseys I wore to practice.

Brain whirring, I stuffed my journal and my favorite outdoor-adventure and fantasy books into my backpack. When school let out in June, I'd work another summer in Missoula and earn enough money to get my own car. Then, who knew? Maybe I could even move in with Alura and transfer to a high school there and get my friends back! I'd heard you could petition for legal emancipation at sixteen. Not that I wanted to put my mother through that too... but maybe she'd be on my side for once. Maybe she'd even let Leila move in with us. Maybe, with all three of her kids living back in Missoula, she'd wake up and leave Wayne in his dumb trailer in the boonies with its kitchen that smelled like the hot sauce he was always dumping over Mom's food and its creepy root cellar out back and its water tank you had to fill by taking weekly trips to a huge faucet outside some cowpoke town that looked just like all the other towns around here—one main street, three bars, three churches, one school, and a basketball court on a tilted patch of cracked asphalt.

That night as I was doing the dishes, water working its way into a hole in the finger of one of my yellow rubber gloves, I heard Wayne and my mother's voices reach argument pitch—a near-nightly occurrence. But this time, a double dose of anxiety mixed with my typical flood of discomfort and curiosity. I stole past the bathroom and the mudroom to their closed door.

"I provide for them kids more than he ever has," came Wayne's muffled voice.

"I know, but he is their father…"

"Deadbeat dad. Don't even call them but once a year."

"You haven't been very fatherly yourself lately."

"Oh really. How about puttin' food on the table, payin' for the land and this trailer you live in? Hauling water and coal and wood? Takin' your daughters in? I been doing everything around here."

I fumed. He'd spent six years mooching off my mother while she struggled to get off welfare, raise three kids, deal with a long-standing back injury, and earn her bachelor's degree. Now he acted like we were charity cases.

"What do you think about Rosa moving out?" she asked.

"If she's ready to move out, then she's ready to help pay bills."

"I don't think I should have said yes. I'm going to tell her before she calls Heather."

An explosion of panicked defeat clouding my vision, I scurried back into the kitchen. My mother's stomping footsteps followed. I turned around innocently when she said my name.

She was in a worn flannel nightgown and booties I'd knitted her one Christmas. "I know you really want to move in with your friend, but you are part of this family, so until you're eighteen, you'll live here, in our family's home."

"Is there any reason other than that?"

She sighed.

"What if I don't want to be part of this family?"

"Too bad," she said. "What did you tell Heather was going on here? What did she tell her parents?"

"What I told you earlier."

She nodded her head slowly. "I bet it never occurred to you how embarrassing that would be for me."

I turned my back on her and finished the dishes, rehearsing a speech. Later, I knocked on their door. My mother slipped out, casting a worried look toward the bed, where Wayne lay flipping through a tool magazine. He went to sleep at 8:30 because he got up at 4 a.m. to make it to the mine by 6 a.m. But it was only 8:00, so I had time.

"If it's about Heather's, I'm not changing my mind," she said, leading me back into the kitchen.

My hands fidgeted, working my thumb ring around and around, wedging it on harder, then nudging it over my knuckle. "I can't stand living here anymore, Mom." I took a breath. "I get really down. I get—" I couldn't look at her. The speech dissolved. The ring popped off and bounced on the carpet.

"*What?*" she asked, exasperated.

"Sometimes I want to hurt myself."

"Hurt yourself how?"

I stared down at the ring—a silver dolphin, its tail and one flipper melted together. "Like *hurt* myself," I said again, hoping she would ask me to explain and dreading the very same thing.

My mother released a loud burst of air and let her arms fall from her hips to her sides. "You know what I think? I think you're a manipulative bitch when you don't get what you want."

Tears welled. It was the first time she'd called me a bitch. And I suppose I had told her to get what I wanted, or at least some attention, concern. I felt a part of me break off and crumble—a childlike limb encoded with the belief that to solve any problem, all I needed to do was bare my heart to my mother.

• • •

In bed, I stared up at the ceiling, listening to the relentless wind pound and flex the trailer's metal roof. The house trembled, hollow-seeming now that everyone but me was asleep. With new cuts on my arms radiating heat, I imagined the walls bulging inward, the air thickening to tar, the trailer hurtling toward the side of a mountain. I darted out of bed and jammed my feet into ratty sneakers.

A biting gust of freezing air met me as I opened the window, pushed out the screen, and maneuvered outside. Java, Wayne's brown-and-white hound dog, trotted around the corner as I hit the ground. "Come here, girl. Keep me company."

The hound stared at me, then retreated into her doghouse. I stumbled past Wayne's workshop, which I was forbidden to enter, to the empty horse pen. I'd dug all the postholes for that enormous pen, swooning at Wayne's promise to get a colt and help us train it. The whole family was moony for horses. And Wayne did bring back a shy, brown colt. But then he forbade us to go inside the pen, and then he forbade us to coax the horse to the fence, and then, a month later, when I looked out the window and said, *Oh my God, where's Jake?* Wayne smirked and said, *I was wondering how long it would take you to notice. I sold him yesterday.* Imagining Wayne's face, I gave the gate a sideways karate kick, the wind whipping my short hair, stinging my wet face.

I charged across the snow-filled irrigation ditch to the road, grateful someone had driven through the drifts and I could follow the tracks. I tried to ignore the gusts that knocked me off balance and cut through my sweats. There was malice and intelligence behind those blasts—like the wind wanted to see if it could force me back inside. No coat, no hat, no gloves, I stomped on, blinking hard to keep my eyelashes from frosting, a sense of defeat building in my stomach—spilling, spreading—because I knew I couldn't keep walking away. It was five pitch-black miles to Fromberg, a hilly route of rangeland too barren to even support cattle, bordered by sandstone ridges rising out of the landscape like giant teeth. And what would I do if I made it to town? Throw rocks at Heather's window? Try to break into the school and warm up? The wind had already won. At some point I would have to turn around and retrace every step, ending up right back inside what increasingly felt like a cage.

3. THE PIED PIPER

March 1999: Outside Fromberg, MT

Leila and I were outside, wrestling sticks from Wayne's new black Lab puppy before bringing in a load of wood. He'd decided Java wasn't a good hunting dog and given her away. It was still cold, the ground a mess of slush and mud.

Wayne appeared with a boom. He'd thrown open the door so hard it bounced against the side of the trailer. "Don't fuck with me, you guys."

Leila and I looked at each other, startled.

"Don't fuck with me. I told you not to fuck with the dog. I saw you put a stick in its mouth, I already told you not to play fetch with it, he's a hunting dog and you'll fuck him up!"

We'd never heard Wayne say fuck so many times in a row.

"He chews on sticks anyway," Leila started. "And we weren't playing fetch. We were just taking the stick—"

"Damn women always screwing things up. Glad I had boys. Just get out of my fucking house. And stay out!" He stormed inside. Leila and I shared another look. We were already outside. How long were we exiled?

We fooled around, bashing Wayne. I'd just learned the word *misogynist* and was thrilled to be able to use it with such accuracy. After a while we loaded the wheelbarrow and trundled it to the front steps. I led the way through the kitchen to the wood-and-coal box in the living room, our arms stacked high. Wayne was sprawled in his recliner, watching some cowboy movie he'd rented. We didn't get TV reception out here. Leila and I were on our way out for another load when he said, "Now I know why your dad left you."

The implication hit the back of my head like an arrow. I froze, my breathing loud in my ears. Leila's pinched face launched another arrow, this time to my chest. Pain bloomed. Then anger. But then came triumph. This was what I'd been waiting for. Something my mother couldn't ignore. There was way too much complicated baggage attached to this insult, and a level of cruelty Wayne was usually smart enough to edge instead of breach.

"He said *what*?"

I was right. Mom was pissed. And instead of making excuses for Wayne like she normally did, she let something slip: "I wasn't going to tell you girls yet, but I've been looking for a place in town. As soon as I sign a lease, I'm telling Wayne I want a divorce."

Within a few weeks we were carrying boxes past Wayne, who watched us from his recliner throne with a mask of superior amusement fixed on his pudgy face. He could smirk all he wanted. Victory was ours.

Our new trailer in Fromberg was paradise. Out from under the thumb of Wayne the Pain, we could all eat whatever we wanted, take normal showers instead of worrying about the dwindling water in the tank, and make noise past eight. We stopped looking at the floor so much, stopped watching our backs, stopped holding our breath. I made the most of our new location and the most of the rest of high school, hyperaware that soon my life would drastically change. Education would cost money, as would housing. Sports teams would host tryouts and cut small-town stars like me. My graduating class of twenty-three would drift apart, no matter how many promises we made to one another. It was probably for the best. A growing number of kids at Fromberg High were starting to inherit the small-town small-mindedness of their parents and were already parroting Rush Limbaugh on top of talking smack about anybody who deviated from their warped view of "normal." The emergence of these prejudices came as a surprise, like roiling thunderheads overtaking a clear, blue sky. *Where was this coming from,* I wondered. *Who wanted to be normal anyway?*

A ravenous anticipation for independence swelled as the months passed. I was determined to go to college in Missoula, where Alura was finishing her degree. My older sister had advised me to become "well-rounded" so I'd stand out come admission time. The result was overdrive. I piled the yearly musical onto pep band, honor band, choir, FFA, and student government. I wrote articles for the school paper and the weekly Fromberg-area paper and tutored a foreign exchange student. I played basketball and volleyball and ran track. Whenever I got called into the principal's office for streaking my hair blue, purple, or orange, I would remind him of my 4.2 GPA. I was getting out of here and into college if it killed me, goddamn it.

There was just one problem: paying for it. They put a limit on loans and stuff, right? All I knew was Alura had gotten straight A's too, and while she'd gotten some financial aid, she still had to take on debt and work two jobs to pay her bills. If she of all people was struggling, I wasn't sure how I was going to pull this off.

October 2000: Fromberg, MT

The recruiter was young and hot, unlike the other uniformed stiffs who had made the rounds. He was one of the hottest guys I'd ever seen in person—walking into our American Government class with catlike precision, his shoulders filling out his pressed uniform. He had an angular jaw, bright blue eyes, and dark hair he fixed with some kind of gel. None of the Fromberg guys would dream of using gel. I was fascinated.

"Good morning. I'm Sergeant Lamson." He waited for our mumbled "morning" back. "Now, I know the Marines and Navy and full-time Army guys have already been through here. And they probably told you their branch is a great choice for college and you'll get excellent job training and it's fun and all that good stuff. Well." He raised his eyebrows and leaned toward us, a hand by his mouth like he was telling us a secret. "They all wish they were in the National Guard."

We laughed.

"I'm serious. The Guard is the best branch by far. We're not asking you to go full-time military. This is a chance to be a citizen soldier. One weekend a month, two weeks during the summer. See, the Guard doesn't make you put off college. It's set up to help you succeed in college. It's a win-win. You get 75 percent of your tuition paid for, and we get highly educated soldiers."

The thought of delaying college and being ordered around like an automaton just when I'd won total freedom was exactly why I had tuned out the other recruiters. This time, I scribbled in my notebook, doing the math. "One weekend a month, two weeks a year" translated to about 10 percent soldier, 90 percent civilian. Barely a part-time job!

There was a catch, of course. I knew, because I was a cynic, or at least liked to think of myself as a cynic because I was in love with words and *cynic* sounded badass and meant something badass too. As a cynic, I observed that Lamson did not say one word about going through boot camp first.

"If you're interested in hearing more, I'll be in the counselor's office upstairs," he said, backing toward the door. "And one more thing. We're offering six-thousand-dollar bonuses for signing up this year."

My brain clicked into overdrive. I heard my mother reminding me three times in the last six months that if I planned on going to college she couldn't help with tuition or rent or books, as much as she wished she could. She'd had to declare bankruptcy because Wayne had bought a bunch of tools with their credit card and then filed for bankruptcy during the divorce, leaving her with bills she couldn't pay.

I saw myself escaping Fromberg and writing rent and tuition checks with that $6,000. I saw shopping carts full of food. I saw a car with a heater to defrost the windows and an engine that could handle trips longer than ten miles at a time, unlike the junker I'd bought off the neighbor for fifty bucks.

The teacher announced that if we weren't following Sergeant Lamson we should turn to page 196. I crammed my books into my backpack and stood up, along with John R. and John S.

On my way out, Heather and Ember shot me disapproving looks. I knew what they were thinking—that the military was authoritarian rah-rah bullshit. A big part of me agreed. But this National Guard thing appeared to be a very tolerable means to an end.

In the hall, the recruiter's boots squeaked with every step like new high-tops on the basketball court. "So y'all took the Armed Services Vocational Aptitude Battery test this year. You remember your scores?"

"Eighty?" John S. said.

"Ninety-three," I said.

Lamson turned, his action-star eyebrows raised. "You'll qualify for just about any job you want with that score. What about you, big guy?"

John R., who stood a good six inches above us all, scratched his head of shaggy brown hair. "About that. Are we allowed to take it again?" John S. and I knew he was joking, but Lamson turned serious, explaining John R.'s options.

In the counselor's office, the recruiter handed us folders with a picture on the front of soldiers climbing a rope ladder. "That's got some information about all the Army jobs available. It's got pay scales matched with rank and—"

"Don't you have to go to boot camp first?" I interrupted, holding up the folder and pointing to the picture. "There's no way out of it, is there?"

Lamson smiled, tapping a pen on the desk, running his eyes over my worn sweatshirt with homemade thumb holes in the cuffs, my green skater-girl pants that were

17

actually off the men's rack, and my hiking sandals. "You *do* have to complete basic training and your specialized job training first. But you can do what's called a 'split option.' Go to boot camp this summer, do your first year of college, and then knock out the rest of your training next summer. After that, it's one weekend a month."

"And what exactly do you do in boot camp? Scale walls and roll around in mud?" I was pretty sure boot camp was one long obstacle course, which, for a tomboy, was tempting in its own right. But I was playing the cynic here. I needed him to admit it was abusive and sexist and half the recruits didn't pass.

Lamson slapped his hands down on the desk and laughed. "Where does she come up with this stuff? Is she always like this?"

"Yup," said John S. and John R.

I couldn't help but crack a smile too. And with my defenses down, I forgot all about being a cynic.

4. THE RESPONSIBLE THING TO DO

November 2000: Fromberg, MT

Sergeant Lamson stood framed by our trailer door, looking like a soldier from parades and history books in his dark green uniform with little bars of color pinned to his chest. He'd dressed up for the occasion, I realized, embarrassed that I hadn't thought to put on something nicer than jeans and a basketball jersey.

"I have some questions about this contract," my mother said through the screen door. Because I was seventeen, I'd had to ask her to cosign. Now, she looked like she expected Lamson to barge in and kidnap me.

As another wave of embarrassment washed over my head, Lamson smiled his charming smile and swiped his hat off. "Of course, ma'am. And we don't need to sign anything today. I'd like you both to be as informed as possible before we put pen to paper."

The fight fell out of my mother's body and she offered him a seat at our kitchen table—an aluminum table from the '50s with a Formica top that squeaked and jiggled. One leg was held on with duct tape. I'd eaten just about every meal of my childhood at that table. I'd made Valentine's Day cards and dyed Easter eggs and opened birthday presents there. I'd solved thousands of math equations and mixed up countless batches of chocolate chip cookies on that table. Once, I'd jumped on the rickety top with my hysterical mother because a mouse was running around the kitchen. Today the table would serve a much different purpose. An adult purpose. I found myself feeling embarrassed of the table, wishing we had something dignified, something at least solid wood for Lamson to sit at.

"Would you like some tea or juice?" my mother asked the recruiter.

"Just water, ma'am."

"Are you sure? I'm making some huckleberry tea for myself. I wouldn't want you to catch a whiff and regret not having your own."

"Huckleberry tea?" he said, managing to look like an overjoyed five-year-old. "Well, I might have to try some of that." He raised his eyebrows at me. I blushed.

I sat across from my mother and Lamson took Leila's spot as he walked us through the deal: I would join the supply unit in Billings as a fueler. (While my ASVAB score was good enough for pretty much any job, the local unit only had openings for fuelers or supply specialists.) I'd "drill" one weekend a month in Billings all year, then do boot camp in the summer, then go off to college, transferring to Missoula's Guard unit. The next summer I'd be trained as a fueler. After that, I'd be a regular citizen soldier.

"You see, the Guard follows you, unlike the regular Army and Coast Guard and Marines," he said. "You're not stuck where you're stationed. You can move from Billings to Missoula. Heck, you can move anywhere in the country."

"Every time I move I just have to make sure they have a slot I could fill, right?" I asked. The plan was to start as a fueler and then transfer into a press corps job as soon as one opened up. I wanted to write, both in and out of uniform.

Lamson nodded. "And you know, just about every unit needs a public affairs person."

My mother, who until now had been taking slurping gulps of her tea, set her mug down and pulled her hands into her lap. "What are the chances Rosa will be called up?"

Lamson cleared his throat, those beautiful eyebrows furrowed. "That's a very important question. Now, we do get called up to help fight wildfires in the summer sometimes."

I envisioned dragging a hose to a fire line, walls of flame tonguing into an orange sky. The glee I was feeling must have splashed across my face because my mother shot me a look of skepticism.

"She'll be out there fighting forest fires without any training?"

Lamson laughed. "It's not like that, ma'am. Mostly we transport the real firefighters to the staging area. Or the Guard pilots help drop water from above. We're a support force."

I watched my mother rearrange herself, only half comforted. "What about her getting called up to fight in a war?"

Lamson lay the documents he was holding on the table and clasped his hands on top. "The first thing you should know is that women are not allowed in the infantry. They are never on the front lines. And war?" He studied his hands. "I suppose the United States hasn't been in a declared war in decades. Not since Vietnam. Actually, scratch that. Even Vietnam wasn't a declared war, although I believe everyone considers it one."

At the word *Vietnam*, an unspoken understanding rippled through the kitchen. The war there had been a quagmire, a disaster, a horrible mistake the country had learned from. I was seventeen and even *I* knew that. No one would ever let Vietnam happen again. We were smarter, more sophisticated. Evolved.

"What about that Desert Storm thing?" my mother asked. "That seemed to come out of nowhere."

"Yes, there was the Gulf War about ten years ago. But that was never a declared war. I suppose you could call it a short-term operation since it was over in a few months."

"Is it possible that she could be called up to serve in something like that?" My mother's disapproving look was back, mouth between a purse and a frown, eyes unblinking.

Lamson fiddled with the papers. "Well, it's *possible*. Anything's possible."

"I understand that hypothetically something could come up," my mother pressed. "But you're in the military. I'm just wondering if you're aware of something the rest of us aren't."

"Oh no," he said, shoulders relaxing. "No ma'am. I mean, I'm not a general, I'm not in Washington, but we haven't been told about anything like that."

My mother shifted in her seat but didn't say anything more. Lamson took the silence as a signal to slide me the first page of the contract. I plucked a pen from the chipped owl mug on the table, uncapped it, and pictured *Future Rosa*. At twenty-four years old, Future Rosa was done with the military and a cub reporter at some paper. She was strong and lean and full of stories from the fire line, from college, from training trips to Germany with her unit. She had her own apartment and a fiancé and no debt. She was oh-so-grateful to have made the mature, responsible choice to join the National Guard as a teen. What foresight! What guts!

"If you need more time to think about it—" my mother started. Agitation tightened my scalp. She'd insisted I spend two weeks thinking "long and hard" before she would agree to cosign. Perhaps she was having second thoughts.

In answer, I scrawled my name and slid the paper across the table to her. She squinted, reading the entire page before choosing her own pen from the mug and placing her signature next to mine. I let out the breath I'd been holding. Lamson passed me page number two, launching a regimented, triangular choreography, weaving a web, a net, another cage. I just didn't see it that way yet.

5. UNLIKELY CHAMELEON

December 2000: Billings, MT

When I showed up for my first drill at the Billings armory, a supply sergeant issued me the Battle Dress Uniform (BDU)—pants, jacket, and cap in woodland camouflage, a brown cotton undershirt, black wool knee socks, black belt, and black boots dull from neglect, molded to fit someone else's feet. I put everything on in the bathroom, feeling like I was playing dress-up, wondering if I was doing it right.

In the hallway, confronted with dozens of camouflaged strangers, I spotted Sergeant Lamson and made a beeline.

"You made it," he exclaimed, like I'd shown up to some hard-to-find house party. "Looking good. Just button your cuffs on the third hole. I'll show you how to shine your boots up next time." The toes of his own boots shone like glass. "The secret is panty hose," he said, pulling a nylon sock out of his pocket.

"You and those panty hose, Lamson. Is there something we should know?" A burly, bald man winked at me.

"Don't ask, or he might tell us," said his lanky companion.

Lamson laughed and rolled his eyes. "Watch this." After a few seconds of buffing, his boots were so glossy they looked wet. Whistles rose from the guys around us.

• • •

I wasn't planning on stopping on my way home from that first drill, but my mom's Ford Festiva was under a quarter tank. Climbing out of the driver's seat at the gas station, I kept my eyes on my boots, self-conscious, a chameleon stuck on the wrong color. So much for wearing camouflage. The short walk to the convenience store felt like a half-mile march.

Hearing the bell on the door jangle, the cashier turned toward me. I watched his back straighten and his face transform from slack acknowledgment to sharp attunement. The two other men in the store looked at me with a similar mix of interest and... *something* I'd never seen before.

They were *impressed* with me, I realized. Like I was some kind of badass. I slapped ten dollars on the counter, trying to play the seasoned soldier role. "I'm on number four."

"Yes ma'am. Ten dollars on number four. Anything else I can do for you?"

"Naw, that's it." I squared my shoulders and tromped out, listening to the commanding sound of my boots on the pavement, straining to appear comfortable in this new skin, to live up to the ideas those men paired with the uniform—strength, conviction, maturity, patriotism. I met the eyes of other drivers filling up, reveling in the attention.

At home, I wandered around the living room, getting used to the swish of canvas sleeves on canvas pants, practicing moving from "at ease" to "attention" to "parade rest," the treads of my boots catching on the shag carpet.

Now that I was a member of the military, an adult, I needed to make some changes. No more doing homework last minute. No more dying my hair crazy colors. No more riding on the roof of Ember's Jeep out past the old cemetery. No more chugging hard alcohol on a dare and then seeing quadruple. And no more cutting myself for some emo reason or another. Time to get a grip before I got scars, not just scratches that healed in a few weeks.

My mother brought out the camera and snapped the first picture of me in an Army uniform. Spilling out of my small smile is youthful pride, adventurous optimism, and a deep anticipation for full independence. Ironic, considering that I'd just made a commitment to an organization with perhaps the least amount of that coveted component—*independence*.

6. INITIATION

June 2001: Ft. Jackson, SC

Two weeks after graduating high school and riding the high that soon I'd be a Freshman at the University of Montana, I was back on a school bus—not in Montana, but in muggy South Carolina—and the mood was anything but celebratory. I had gone through three days of "in-processing" with hundreds, if not thousands, of other teenagers—enduring vaccinations and exams and lectures, waiting in countless snaking lines, the sweltering sun pounding down on us as we were forbidden to sit, to talk, to move, to act anything but robotic. And now we were being delivered across base to begin Day One of boot camp.

"Get off my bus!"

I flinched. The two drill instructors that had been joking with the bus driver were now on their feet, their Smokey Bear hats nearly touching the ceiling, their faces hard and angry.

"I *said*, get off my bus!"

Scrunched against the window, wearing a backpack crammed with my civilian belongings, hugging an Army duffle stuffed with all the gear and uniforms I'd just been issued, I could do no such thing. Anxiety racing up my backbone, I watched a line of guys charge for the door, which was still closed, and which the drill sergeants were blocking like Doberman Pinschers.

"Back off, private!"

"Where the hell you think you're going?"

"I said get off my goddamn bus *now*."

The guys tried to shuffle backward. One of them cleared his throat. "Sir, we need to get past you to get off the bus."

"Sir? *Sir?*" The closest drill sergeant swelled, the brim of his hat bumping into the bill of the private's BDU cap. "Do I look like a fucking *sir* to you? I earn my living. Don't you ever call me sir."

I stared at the back of the seat in front of me, the worming lines in the synthetic leather like the underside of bark. At drill back in Montana they had warned me: Never look a drill sergeant in the eye. Never look at them period unless you have to. Fly under the radar. Bring duct tape, natural colored hair clips, and Band-Aids. Don't bring anything you don't absolutely need. They'd stopped there, a half-voiced understanding that they couldn't make things *too* easy for me. I shouldn't be too prepared. They had suffered. I needed to suffer. That was how initiation worked.

"Are you dense? Do you see anything shiny on his collar, private? Jesus H. Christ," the taller drill sergeant said. Every time either of them said "private" it came out in a southern "*pry*-ut."

The drill instructors turned to each other and shook their heads before the shorter bellowed, "Move your asses and get off our bus!"

Finally, someone thought to open the emergency door in back, triggering the alarm. "Move, move, move!"

I shimmied out of my seat and hobbled to the door, someone pushing on my back, and almost fell from the jump down. I joined hundreds of other teenagers struggling to run across a field to the barracks, drill sergeants charging random victims. Guys whizzed past me, trotting like they were carrying pillows instead of heavy duffels and backpacks. I strained to catch up but even with my bare-bones packing the best I could manage was a fast walk.

Halfway across the field, a bear of a drill sergeant blocked my way. "You wearing *lipstick*, pry-ut?"

The question was so bizarre that I glared over the top of my duffle at him. "No, Drill Sergeant."

"You lyin' to me?"

"No, Drill Sergeant."

"Wipe your mouth."

I wiped my mouth hard on the back of my hand and held it out to him.

He frowned from my skin to my face. "Why's your mouth look red?"

I remembered myself and jerked my eyes to the ground. "I don't know, Drill Sergeant. I'm wearing ChapStick, but it's the plain kind."

"Lemme see it."

I pulled the stick from my cargo pocket, uncapped it, and thrust it toward him.

He shoved it back. "Get out of here. Move, move, move!"

The delay made me look like a straggler. I heaved the duffel onto my front and broke into a lumbering run. When I reached the huge slab of concrete everyone was headed for, a female drill sergeant stopped me.

"You there. What's your last name?"

I snapped to an awkward parade rest. "Del Duca, Drill Sergeant."

"Where'd you learn that?" she asked, looking at my feet, my elbows.

"I'm National Guard, Drill Sergeant."

"You go on over to Third Platoon and volunteer when they ask for squad leaders. You got a leg up on most of these pry-uts."

"Yes, Drill Sergeant."

But I did not volunteer. I kept my "leg up" a secret, a tight ball of conceit. I was going to very quietly kick boot camp's ass. Which meant I should let my lips dry out and crack. I didn't want them drawing any more attention.

• • •

Three days later I was still managing to fly under the radar. I hadn't done anything stupid enough for the drill sergeants to learn my name. I paid attention and didn't ask questions. In the barracks, I bit my tongue when other girls complained or got into barbed catfights or lost important things or screamed for people to hurry up in the shower. I marched in time, ran as fast as the boys, refrained from whispering in formation, polished my boots, and never dropped to my knees when we were ordered to "beat our faces"—i.e., do push-ups until further notice.

But a lot of the rules were pointless—rules just for the sake of more rules. Like having to call the bathrooms "latrines" and being forced to chug water every time a drill sergeant yelled in a sing-song way, "Drink—water!" and not being allowed to look at members of the opposite sex unless you had to (not that they were much to look at). We were banned from talking at all times, even in the chow hall. We had to point to food we wanted dumped on our tray, like cavemen. In the gigantic "bays" we slept in, most of the floor was boxed off into a "kill zone" and if you stepped inside, even to make room for someone passing, you were in deep shit. While I was careful to play along with the rules in front of the drill sergeants, I began to use some discretion when they were out of sight. Take my upcoming fireguard shift at two o'clock in the morning. It seemed fireguard had three purposes: (1) to make sure we got shitty sleep, (2) to provide cleaning time without taking away from training time, and (3) to get us ready for pulling guard duty out in the field, where there would actually be something to guard against.

I was paired up with Greene that night for a fireguard shift. She was a mousy girl with long brown hair, bad posture, and a drag to her movements. Like several of the girls there, she'd been a cheerleader in high school. I didn't understand how one made the leap from cheerleader to soldier. Even my own leap from athlete to soldier was proving difficult.

Considering nighttime was our only time away from omnipresent drill sergeant wrath, and considering each fireguard shift was two hours long, I made what I saw as a common-sense suggestion to Greene.

"Sweeping and mopping will take us half an hour at the most," I told her. "How about the first hour one of us sweeps while the other goes back to sleep? Then we'll trade off and the other person will mop."

Greene looked like I'd suggested we strip naked and run through the guys' barracks.

"There's no reason we both need to lose two hours of sleep," I said, buttoning up my camouflage BDU jacket. The uniform for fireguard shift was BDUs, which meant we lost even more sleep changing from gray T-shirts and black nylon shorts (PTs), which was the uniform for sleeping, into BDUs for fireguard, and then from BDUs back into PTs at the end of the shift. *Don't let me catch anyone sleeping in their boots*, our female drill sergeant had warned us. *Good way to rot y'alls feet off.*

"I don't know," Greene said. "Shouldn't we just do what they told us?"

"They'll never know. They don't come in at night."

Greene calculated the risk, eyes roaming the dark bay—fifteen bunk beds and thirty wall lockers on each side, the bathroom in back, the desk under glaring fluorescent lights up front. "What if we fall asleep and forget to wake up the next fireguard?"

"I have a little alarm clock we can use."

She let out a long-suffering sigh. "If we get in trouble, I'm blaming you."

I shoved down the impulse to roll my eyes. "Go right ahead."

Greene opted for the first shift. I went back to my bunk, slipped off my boots, and lay down, my back turned against the light from up front. An arm flung over my ear, I listened to my breathing and the muted sounds of Greene bumping into things with the wide dust broom.

I jerked awake when Drill Sergeant Evans barked, "Hey, you, come here." I saw Greene running for the front and sprang into action, swinging off my bunk and darting behind my wall locker, grabbing my boots on the way. Cramming my feet and the bottoms of my pants inside my boots, I jerked the laces up and jammed the ends down the back, no time for tying.

"Where's your battle buddy?" I could hear Evans ask Greene.

"I don't know," Greene said.

"You don't *know*?"

"Maybe in her bunk?"

"Show me."

I grimaced. She couldn't have stalled for one second? I stole to the bathroom while Evans prowled to my bunk.

"This here's hers?" Evans said.

"Yes, Drill Sergeant."

"So where is she?"

"I'm not sure, Drill Sergeant."

"Then why weren't you up at the desk?"

"I was cleaning, Drill Sergeant."

"Then why wasn't *she* up there?"

I took a deep breath and gave the bathroom door a shove, hoping that if Evans was looking into the shadows at the back of the bay, the light would make it seem like I'd just come out of the latrine.

"You find her right now," Evans barked at Greene.

I trotted toward the front as Greene trotted toward the back. She turned around when she saw me and we faced Evans together at parade rest—legs stiff, arms locked behind our backs.

"What were you doing back there?"

"Getting another mop, Drill Sergeant," I said.

Evans scrutinized me. "Fix your collar."

My hands whipped up to comply.

"This is how fireguard works," she said, strolling to the front. We followed. "One of you stands your ass here at this desk. The other cleans. When you're done cleaning, you both stand your asses up here. No sitting. No writing letters. Huah?"

"Huah," I echoed, heart waterlogged at the thought of my journal waiting for tonight's entry, the letters to my mother and sisters that needed scribbling down.

"Now what's your head count?"

Greene and I shared a look of concern.

Evans slapped her notebook down on the desk. "You two are royally chewed up. What's your *head* count. How many people are here, braindead?"

"Well, there's twenty-eight in Third Platoon and thirty in Fourth, so fifty-eight," I said.

"Are you sure? Have you counted everyone?"

Why in the world would we count? No one had left the room. We were locked in.

"Go count!"

Greene took the right side. I took the left. We came up with fifty-six. Evans's nostrils flared. "What are you standing there for? I don't want to see your faces until I get my fifty-eight *head* count."

This time we checked the stalls in the bathroom. Fifty-seven. Banks had been peeing.

"That's it!" Evans flipped on all the lights to the bay, her voice loud as a bullhorn. "Toe the line! Rise and shine, get on the line. Now! You too, braindeads." She waggled a hand at Greene and me.

We scurried to the line of red paint boxing off the forbidden "kill floor."

Fifty-seven startled and groggy girls stood at attention, awaiting punishment.

"Count—off!"

We screwed up the count three times before getting all the way around the circle, Greene ending on the dreaded "fifty-seven." Jesus, where the hell was fifty-eight? Hiding in a wall locker? Evans stalked the line, whipping two girls' colorful bandanas from their heads. "What the hell's this?"

"A do-rag, Drill Sergeant," said one girl.

"I know what it *is*. Why you wearing it? This needs to get locked up with the rest of your civvies." She flung the bandanas, then attacked the three girls caught sleeping in BDUs.

"Drop," Evans finally barked. "Y'alls excuses are making me tired."

We dropped to the front leaning rest, careful our fingers didn't cross into the glossy kill zone.

"The push-up!"

"The push-up!" we echoed.

"One, two, three," Evans sang.

We pumped down and up, down and up, ending in a thunderous, "One!"

"One, two, three."

Down and up, down and up, "Two!"

Our elbows bent to the rhythm of Evans's cadence. Before long, knees started to hit the floor. We sounded strangled, counting "Fourteen! Fifteen! Sixteen!" Arms trembling, I gave up trying to do any more push-ups and locked into a sagging front leaning rest. Greene flopped to the floor next to me. And that's when Lin crept out of the bathroom in shower shoes and PTs, her hair up in a towel. She scrambled to a front-leaning rest, the end of her towel flopping into the kill zone. I closed my eyes, dreading Evans's reaction. Maybe it would be easier to follow the rules after all.

7. Trust Your Mask

June 2001: Ft. Jackson, SC

Three weeks into boot camp, I woke up with a swollen face for the third morning in a row. In the bathroom at the end of the bay I waited for a chance to wedge myself in at a sink and stared at my squinty-eyed reflection, brushing my teeth. I looked like the girl in *The Exorcist*. I wondered if the green wool blankets were responsible or if it was because I was sick. I'd had an excruciating sore throat for the past week and a half, pounding headaches in the sun, and I couldn't tell if my muscles hurt from all the physical exertion or from a fever. On Sick Call they'd given me a measly twelve Aspirin, long gone by now.

We had one addition to our uniforms that day: gas masks. Mine was packed perfectly, the hood inside-out, straps inside-out, tucked into its lunch box–size bag, so at the warning "Gas, gas, gas!" I could flip open the case, jam the mask onto my face, whip the straps over the top of my head, tighten them, and jerk the hood down over the straps.

With the case strapped around my hips and one leg, I took a few practice steps. The way the bag hung made me feel like a gunslinger in the Wild West—like I was about to spend the day threading my horse through sagebrush and cacti, a bandana around my neck, cowboy hat pulled low. My walk turned to a swagger.

"Oh my God I'm so nervous. I'm not eating anything at breakfast," Pickerillo said in her low-pitched rush as I sauntered past her bunk. "You guys are all skipping breakfast, right?"

"I'm not," said her bunkmate. "It's a long time before lunch. If I puke, then I puke."

My stomach twinged. I threw up pretty easily. But more than that, I knew the poison would make my throat feel even worse. Then again, it would make for a genuine boot camp horror story. Of course, I wouldn't tell it like a horror story back home. I'd wait for people to pry, then downplay the whole gas chamber experience, treating it like a bit of trivia on par with how, in the Army, you aren't supposed to say "nine" but "niner."

In the chow hall I shoveled in hot grits, cold Jell-O, and lukewarm applesauce, wincing at each swallow but thankful for food that slid down easy. The drill sergeants prowled for a chance to ridicule. "Whoa-ho-ho, Steiner's got milk *and* cottage cheese. Remind me to watch you come out today, Steiner." (The rumor was that the gas would curdle any dairy in your stomach.)

We marched out to a bunch of classrooms in the South Carolina woods and practiced donning our masks in nine seconds. In the real world, they said, if you couldn't get your mask out of the bag and suctioned onto your face in nine seconds, you'd be dead. In practice, I was dead every time.

Sweaty and nervous, I took my place in a long, long line—single file, no platoon divisions anymore, just 240 teenagers, except for that 34-year-old guy in Second Platoon everyone called "Grandpa." With my mask sealed on my face and adrenaline churning through my body, I waited for one of the drill sergeants to come down the line and check me.

"Is your mask sealed? Cover your canister and suck in," a heavyset female drill sergeant said. I obeyed. She wasn't satisfied and yanked the bottom straps as tight as they would go. "You leave it like that. You had a leak before." I was almost choking, the straps gouging into the swollen lymph nodes under my chin.

I waited like that for half an hour. The taut pain was all I could think about. I imagined tearing the mask off, hurling it into the woods, walking away. But I knew if I moved from parade rest to loosen the straps I'd be reprimanded and my mask would be retightened.

Finally, it was my turn to enter the chamber, along with about twenty others. We filed into the cave-like room, the air an artificial green from glow sticks in the corners. The instructors, in full protective gear, closed the door and broke open a "chem pill," sending out a slow, neon-yellow cloud of concentrated gas.

They had us breathe through our masks for a minute, letting us get used to the environment, saying things like, "See? You gotta trust your mask. You're getting clean, filtered air now."

The skin on my exposed hands and neck simmered.

"Break the seal," an instructor ordered.

I took a deep breath and tried to worm my fingers under the bottom edge of my mask. It was too tight.

"Let's go, pry-uts!"

I fumbled to loosen the straps.

"Let's go, let's go, let's go!"

I wrestled the mask off, ripping out a chunk of hair in the process. The air on my face felt gritty and dry. My eyes burned. I scrunched them shut and held my breath.

"Reseal your mask."

I pressed the rubber to my face and fought to get the straps over my head. They were too tight. I opened my eyes to claw and pull at the clasps until they loosened, slapped the mask back on, and took a gulp of contaminated air. It dropped like a smoldering coal to the pit of my stomach. Shoving down nausea, I raced to clear and reseal. Within four or five breaths, the burning subsided and the air was clean again.

We were ordered to take our masks off one last time before they released us outside. As I stumbled out the door and down a gravel walkway, retching, snot running down my face, stomach doing flip-flops, I thought, *That wasn't too bad. As long as I never have to do it again.*

• • •

Two days after the gas chamber, I lay spread-eagle in my bunk, tears rolling from the corners of my eyes into my close-cropped hair. Every time I drifted off to sleep I woke up wheezing and choking, sure my swollen throat was closing all the way this time. And with each stretch of my legs, cramps gripped my calves and feet. I knew it was from dehydration. The only time I forced water down anymore was after dinner chow, crouched between lockers, banging my head against the wall with each swallow, using the new pain to distract myself from what felt like a throat packed full of barbed wire.

That night, I couldn't stand it anymore. I swung my legs over the side of my bunk and jumped to the floor. A cockroach skittered away from my tennis shoes as I slid them out from under the bed. Too exhausted to be disgusted or squeamish, I slammed a shoe down on the bug and tied my laces.

"I want to go to the hospital," I told the girls on fireguard, my voice a thick whisper. The clock above their desk read 12:24 a.m. Their eyes widened, no doubt picturing the tall, hard-faced Drill Sergeant Rims downstairs losing his shit at such a request.

"You can go on Sick Call in the morning."

"Try to go back to sleep."

"No one can do anything now anyway."

I crossed my arms. "If you don't want to use the intercom, I will."

"Don't do that!" Mathis, the shorter, blonde girl leapt to her feet. She skittered to the intercom mounted on the wall, hesitated, hesitated, and then haltingly explained the situation to Rims on the other end.

"Send her down here, and one of you come with her," the speaker blared, cracking. "Hurry up. I'm locking the door again in thirty seconds."

Mathis descended two flights of cement stairs with me to the platoon area. The air was warm, wet, and heavy with an earthy scent. A flash of how luxurious a South Carolina night might be if we weren't in boot camp darted through my brain. But then we were up against the wall in the office, standing at parade rest while the towering Rims surveyed me. The sound of my breath scraping in and out of my windpipe filled the room.

"Are you having an allergic reaction or something?"

"I'm really sick. My throat is so swollen I'm having trouble breathing." The words came searing out.

"Did you go to Sick Call?"

"Last week. They didn't do anything."

"We'll send you back to Sick Call in the morning."

The pain of swallowing sent fresh tears to the corners of my eyes. "Drill Sergeant, I want to go to the hospital." I burst into coughing that my mother would have dubbed "seal barking."

Rims watched me, waiting for me to cave. There was a layer of fatigue under his disgust. "I don't think you're that sick," he said. "I think you're making a big deal 'cause you wanna go home."

Rage coursed through my gut. All I wanted was some goddamn painkillers and antibiotics. I was no quitter.

"You think all this is too hard," Rims mocked. "You want to go back home to mommy. You've been up there crying and feeling sorry for yourself 'cause you caught a little cold."

The humiliating tears kept coming, making my throat tighten and the fire line inside me flare hotter still.

Rims pulled his desk chair out, dropped into it, and leaned back, hands behind his head. "They're gonna give you some cough syrup and send you back. You gotta buck up, soldier."

I broke parade rest to gulp in air, hands on my knees. I knew Rims wanted me to turn around and go back upstairs, but instead, I pulled myself straight and stared at the picture of George W. Bush on the wall.

"How long has she been sick?" Rims asked Mathis.

"A while. I know she doesn't mean to, but she keeps us up at night coughing and snoring really loud."

This detail mortified me further.

"Why didn't you go to Sick Call earlier?" Rims accused. "You got to nip these things in the bud."

The fire in my throat met an indignant fury rising from my chest. I gritted my teeth. "I thought I could get over it."

"Mathis, go get your bay's CLB."

In two minutes she was back with the Combat Lifesaver Bag and I had a thermometer sticking out of my mouth. Looking at the little digital screen that read 101.9, Rims heaved a sigh and reached for his drill sergeant hat. "Pack a Sick Call bag."

Riding in the back of an SUV nicer than any car I'd ever been in, my laundry bag of toiletries and extra PTs in my lap, I watched Drill Sergeant Rims drive the abandoned streets of the base. The radio was low, but I could make out Train's "Drops of Jupiter," and I stayed absolutely still to hear better, realizing it had been more than three weeks since I'd heard music. "Drops of Jupiter" slid into Alicia Keys's "Fallin'." God, no wonder everyone was so snippy and wound-up and depressed. We didn't have music! I wondered if Rims had chosen this station, whether all the drill sergeants secretly listened to music in their office to relax after us pry-uts had driven them crazy all day. Seeing Rims look both ways at stop signs, his hands at ten and two, it seemed laughable that I was normally so afraid of him.

"Sorry if I gave you a hard time," he said at a light, glancing at me in the rear view. "I had to make sure you were serious."

I started to say "that's okay," but caught myself. That would imply I had some kind of power over him—moral authority, or the power of forgiveness, which might trigger a tirade. "I understand," I said instead, feeling like I had won some kind of victory.

It didn't cross my mind that in any other occupation, not only would I have been immediately *allowed* to see a doctor, but I would have been encouraged to. In any other occupation, I would not have been locked in a room without a phone in the first place, forced to ask for help like a petulant child. No, I was years away from recognizing that the military has a funny way of stripping you of basic rights and then acting like you're being unreasonable if you ask for them back.

• • •

I spent my first eleven hours at Ft. Jackson's hospital shivering on an exam table in a tiny, dark room as nurses pumped bags of cold saline solution into my veins and drew blood. Twelve hours in, I was taken to get an X-ray. And fifteen hours after arriving, I was informed that I had mononucleosis and an enlarged spleen that could rupture if I continued training. They were sending me upstairs, by wheelchair, and putting me on an IV and liquid diet. And then they were sending me home. *Better luck next time.*

The word *no* ricocheted from one side of my brain to the other—a scream, then a whimper. No, I was not leaving! Another year dreading boot camp? Another year standing around at drill, a useless dumbass? I already felt like the tagalong kid sister. And how was I ever going to train for an Army writing job if my original fueler training was two years away? In a year, the few battle buddies I'd managed to make would be gone. The physical stamina I'd built up would be gone. I'd have to figure out the pet peeves of new drill sergeants, ferret out who I could trust and who would get me into trouble, memorize new rules and new platoon slogans and new chains of command. I'd have to throw my self-respect out the window all over again. Didn't they understand what I'd been through the last month?

I sat in bed and composed speeches in my head, in my journal, ready to rattle them off the minute I saw one of my drill sergeants. I'm sure I looked like a madwoman doing it, gesturing and muttering to myself. But I never saw one of my drill sergeants. Instead I was fed the line, "They'll be by tomorrow," and at the end of my fourth day at the hospital, with nothing to do but nap and stare out the window in the room I had all to myself because I was highly contagious, the words shriveled, dried, and drifted out the door. The cadre would never let me back in the barracks to breathe my mono germs into the air—mono that never would have been discovered if I hadn't insisted on getting help. I should have kept my mouth shut. Now I was going home with nothing to show for my time but an illness known as "the kissing disease." Fantastic.

8. SECOND CHANCE, LAST CHANCE

July 2001: Ft. Jackson, SC

On my fifth day at Ft. Jackson's hospital, they pointed me toward a bus stop with instructions to catch a ride across base to a building where they'd give me a plane ticket home. There were small bleachers set up at the bus stop and privates were pawing through paper bags of medication they'd just been given. A girl in Army sweats pulled cough syrup out of her bag and started unscrewing the cap. Her battle buddy was reading the back of a bottle of pills. A specialist in BDUs at the end of a bench checked his watch.

"Why are you wearing that mask?" a guy in PTs asked me.

"I have mono. I'm contagious."

"Don't you get that from kissing?"

I scowled under my mask. "Apparently that's not the only way you can catch it."

"So you get to go home?"

A breath blasted out my nose. "They're *making* me go home. In a year I'll have to come back and finish."

"Or you could not come back at all. I'm going home too, but there's no way I'll ever step foot on a base again."

Heads swiveled. Eyes widened.

"What do you mean?" asked Cough Syrup. "You can't just decide to go home."

45

"That's what they want you to think. All you have to do is say you refuse to train at boot camp and they'll terminate your contract."

"But you have to do what they say," said the girl, dubious. "They'll give you an Article 15 if you don't. They'll call the military police on you."

An Article 15 was serious. It could come with a reduction in rank or docked pay or extra work and loss of privileges. Worst of all, it stayed on your Army record forever.

"Again, that's what they want you to think. If you stop what you're doing and say you refuse to train, they have to let you go. I kept saying it for three days and now I'm going home. This bull isn't for me."

Holy shit. I'd never heard that. How could that be true? And if it was true, how had he uncovered this little secret?

The rebel leaned back and crossed his feet on the bench in front of him. "I'm not going to be one of their robots they don't give a fuck about, and y'all shouldn't either."

Deep down, part of me let out a guttural "yeah" and pumped my fist. A lot about boot camp and the Army was screwy and even creepy in how it seemed they wanted us to be the same factory-assembled person. And if there was a way out for people having second thoughts, then it was pretty damn shady no one knew about it. I was sitting next to a true rebel, a traitorous folk hero!

But on the surface, like a common mercenary, I was focused on The Deal. If I wanted that signing bonus and tuition money, I needed to put up and shut up. Now more than ever I had to keep to the track I'd chosen. I'd gotten into the University of Montana and they were expecting me to pay that first semester's tuition in a matter of weeks. And as for me being a rebel too? Hell no. I might have it in me to backtalk jerks like Wayne the Pain and confront kids at school when they said idiotic things, but I cringed at the very thought of refusing to train, demanding they rip up my contract. What a scene this guy must have caused—multiple scenes, ongoing scenes—and instead of troubled, he looked cool and collected.

• • •

That moment at the bus stop is cemented in my memory because of how many times I've wished I was back on that metal bench. I wish I would have listened to the skeptic and pressed him for details. I wish I would have listened to my heart, which saw the conflict clearly: I was good at going through the motions, marching in time, parroting on cue. But I did not believe in blindly following orders, or in the cruel treatment of people caught making miniscule mistakes or in the hyperpatriotic fervor. I did not belong.

The universe had dropped a second chance, a *last* chance, directly into my lap in the form of that kid. Turns out he was right. He knew his stuff. Years later, some research revealed that the best chance of backing out of a National Guard or Reserves contract without consequences was to either (1) not show up for boot camp, or (2) refuse to train in the middle of boot camp. You'd get shit for it. You'd get badgered. But people who regretted things this early were usually discharged under "failure to adjust." If I'd had the gumption to check out the rebel's story back then, I could have swallowed my pride and admitted that I had made a mistake too. I could have diverted the train to another track—skipped five years of lying and hiding and fighting paper battles.

Instead, when a blue-line bus pulled up, I climbed aboard, took one last backward look at the rebel, and faced forward.

9. HOMECOMING, HOMELEAVING

July 2001: Billings, MT

"Don't pick that up," my mother said, shooing me away from my fat Army duffle trundling toward us on the baggage claim. We were in the tiny Billings airport, surrounded by the dozen or so other passengers who had shared my flight in.

"Mom, it's way too heavy for you."

She grabbed a strap and wrestled the bag to the floor. "What do you have in here, bricks?"

"I told you it was heavy." I ducked my head, my face growing hot. Everyone must be wondering why I had an Army duffle in the first place. I certainly wasn't acting like a soldier.

"Well you can't carry it," she said. "Your spleen. You're not supposed to lift anything."

I hovered over the bag. "Well *you* can't carry it. It's bad for your back."

"You take one strap and I'll take the other. We'll carry it between us."

In the car, my mother pulled out an assortment of plastic containers. Instead of actual Tupperware she used old yogurt and margarine tubs. "Are you hungry? I've got strawberries, cheese, chocolate chip cookies, and some pretzels."

Immediately brightening, I collected the containers into my lap. "You're the best."

She made a sound of satisfaction, then put on her sunglasses like a surgeon positioning a scalpel, checked all of her mirrors, and cautiously pulled out of the parking space. Ordinarily, this would have driven me nuts. Today it was a comfort.

"How was the food there?" she asked.

"Pretty good until the swill at the hospital. The trick is eating a whole meal in three minutes." I finished a handful of strawberries and went for a cookie.

"That can't be healthy. What else did they make you do?"

"Stand for hours at a time without moving. Tons of push-ups. You get used to being screamed at. They only let you use the pay phones on Sunday, and then only for ten minutes at a time before you have to get back in line. You have to measure two finger widths between all your hangers and roll your shirts into little tubes. There's this whole diagram for how your wall locker and bunk should look."

"And did yours look like the diagram?"

"Of course, Mom. You couldn't *not* look like the diagram."

We passed the Boys and Girls Ranch, where my mother worked. It was a school that threw together troubled kids and kids who'd gotten in trouble. She'd had to take self-defense classes to teach math there.

"What are your plans now that you're home?" she asked. Her tone let me know this was not a question simply to make conversation.

I slouched in my seat and stared at the farmland whizzing by. I'd already told my friends goodbye, that I wouldn't see them until Thanksgiving or Christmas. The plan was to go straight from boot camp to Missoula for college. With that plan in the toilet, I wasn't sure what to do. I was too embarrassed to let anyone know I was home. I couldn't get a job—not contagious and with orders to take it easy and warnings that I might feel an overpowering need to take a nap at any time. And while it felt nice to be home at the moment, in a few days I knew I'd be all wound up in small town angst—stir crazy, frustrated, and hollow.

"I guess I'll buy a cheap car and move to Missoula early," I said.

My mother stared hard at the road. "I was hoping you were going to stay home for a while."

There's nothing here, I wanted to say, picturing Fromberg's one blinking traffic light, its boarded-up cafe and no gas station and one store called The Store. But that wasn't true. She was there, and Leila too, who was much more of a best friend than anyone from school. It struck me that this was the last time I would ever come home in quite the same way. By Thanksgiving I wouldn't belong, and by spring break I'd be completely estranged, an outsider disrupting their two-person routine.

This was the beginning of a slow and steady drift away from my mother. I could feel it, like a cusp, like the rise in the road ahead—a stretching before the pull of downhill momentum. And in another three years, Leila would pull the same disappearing act.

I pictured my mother eating dinner alone, waking up alone, watching movies on the sagging couch alone, driving an empty car, grocery shopping for one. For a moment, *to get out of Fromberg, to start my own life* seemed like an awful thing to want.

"There's no rush," I said. "Maybe I'll start looking for a car in a week or two."

10. TERROR

August 2001: Missoula, MT

Rather than move into the dorms, I told the University of Montana I would be living with Alura just outside of Missoula, but rented an apartment a few miles from campus with a friend from middle school instead.

"I'm so glad you came back. You should have never left. You know, we should paint this place," Jill said, clasping her hands together. Standing 5'11", Jill was two inches taller than me and a little overweight, but she moved with the doe-like grace of a child fresh out of charm school. She had a hint of a lisp, a soft, musical voice, and a self-deprecating sense of humor. "The best part is that since I am a giantess, and since the ceilings are so low, we won't even have to borrow a step stool. Whatever you do, don't let me pick a color just because I like the name. No 'daffodil' or 'dusted crimson.'"

After we painted the walls a bright turquoise, I hung an immense picture of an empty sailboat in the living room and went to Goodwill to hunt out matching dishes, some curtains, and even a welcome mat. Next, I adopted a kitten, who I imagined would be a cuddly addition to our family, but who promptly declared war on the potted plants, climbed up the clothes in our closets, and refused to be pet or held.

Barring "Devil Cat," I was thrilled by my new responsibilities. I loved writing rent and utility checks. I reveled in things like buying groceries and calculating when I would next need an oil change and deciding which drawer would be for silverware. I made large mugs of herbal tea. I listened to NPR in the car and in the houses I cleaned for extra money.

On September 11, 2001, I warned Devil Cat to "be good" on my way out. Even though I was regretting my decision to sign up for a 7:30 a.m. class, I enjoyed driving to school as the mountains blossomed into a glow, backlit by the rising sun. My radio was set to NPR, of course.

I had just crossed over the Clark Fork River, which separated the downtown area from the university area. I was driving past the new campus fitness center, about to troll for parking on the maple-lined side streets, when Bob Edwards reported that a plane had crashed into a building in New York. He sounded serious, but he didn't have anything else to relay. He repeated that a plane had crashed, several people were believed dead, and he would report more information as the story unfolded. At least, this is how I remember it.

I pictured a small, private plane. Probably one or two people on board. I wondered why the anchor had made it seem like such a big deal. It was sad, but there were far worse things going on in the world. *Well*, I thought, *it was New York City*. It wasn't like a plane crash in a remote marsh. I parked, silenced the radio, forgot about the accident, and went to class.

It wasn't until nine o'clock Montana time that I started to piece together that something grave and terrible had happened. My second class was canceled "due to the tragedy in New York."

"What happened?" a guy in a beanie asked. The room fell silent. The professor, who had come in fifteen minutes late, made some feeble reply like, "It's not for me to say," and strode out.

In the student union, they had wheeled out televisions on metal stands. Dozens of students stood or sat around them, hands in their pockets, hands over mouths, hands holding other hands. I overheard conversations about relatives in New York. Someone's uncle worked in that building, someone's brother wasn't answering his cell phone.

Not knowing a single person who had ever been to New York, let alone anyone who lived there now, I felt like I was intruding. I still didn't know what had happened, but the newscasters and reporters weren't helping, and everyone around me was so fixated on the televisions I didn't want to ask. I left to work my campus job at a testing center for disabled students and then went home, made a plate of pasta, and did my homework.

How strange, was my reaction to the school paper the next day. The front page featured a huge photo of grim-faced students watching the news in the student union. We were so far from New York it seemed like another country to me. But reaction to a crash there was on the front page of our little paper?

I was that oblivious. That young.

"Have you been following what's going on?" Alura asked over the phone that night, a full thirty-six hours after the attack.

"A little bit. I read the article in the *Kaimin* today. And I caught some of it on NPR."

"That's right. You don't have a TV. Do you want to come over and watch the news?"

Half an hour later I was on her couch, legs drawn up in front of me, eyes wide, drinking in the barrage. I saw the planes shearing through the towers, the buildings collapsing, streets full of people with pinched and determined and terrified faces. I watched a blurry form falling against a blue background and realized with a shock that I was watching a man jump to his death. This man, this human being, was falling and falling, knowing he was going to die, and now I was watching, knowing he was already dead. Then *another* figure hurtled through the air—a person reduced to a speck on the screen, a ghost. Stomach twisting, I pressed a hand over my mouth, tears running down my face. How could they show something this sickening and invasive? Alura reached over and squeezed my shoulder.

No, I thought. This was the truth. People should see it. And we did see it. Again and again, in a loop, a wave, that numbed one minute and jolted the next.

For a moment I wondered if my Guard unit would be called up to help clear the rubble and... do whatever else needed to be done. This wasn't a natural disaster, but it was definitely a disaster. And then I thought, *Of course not. That's what the New York National Guard is for.*

• • •

In the weeks that followed, I made a habit of going to Alura's to watch the news. She lived at the base of a mountain a few miles outside town, in a small complex that looked like it had been a motel at some point. She shared the place with her boyfriend, Eric, and the miniature collie she'd adopted when the pet store she used to work at determined the puppy might have brain damage, and couldn't be sold. (Turns out the dog was fine.) On nights Alura didn't have to work at the diner down the street, she cooked us chimichangas or enchiladas or stir-fry, the veggies always undercooked. I told her about my classes and the escapades of Devil Cat and about Aaron, the lanky, sandy-haired jokester I'd started dating. She told me about the random discussions she got into with Eric, who was twelve years older than her, the doldrums of being a waiter at the local greasy spoon, and how she would probably have to move away to get a job when she graduated in the spring. It was all pretty lighthearted until we turned on the TV.

I remember the October night when the US and its allies launched a ground assault into Afghanistan, aided by air strikes. The night-vision video was eerie and lurid—glowing green rounds jet-tailing across the screen, accompanied by a dramatic soundtrack. It made me mad, that music. They were treating the attack like it was entertainment, not real violence in real time.

"So what happens to you now?" Alura asked. "Will you have to report somewhere?"

We were on the floor, backs against the couch, an untouched bowl of popcorn between us. My body stiffened at her question. It took effort to peel my eyes away from the television and look at her.

"We're basically at war," she said, her large blue eyes searching my face. "Does that mean you're called up?"

I hadn't considered this. *Were* we at war? Alarm leeched into my pores. The air in the room grew darker and the light from the screen surged brighter until rationality overtook panic. "I'm pretty sure they have to actually call you on the phone. It's not automatic," I said cautiously, hoping Jill wasn't back at the apartment taking a message for me: *Report to the armory at 0600. We are at war.*

"Plus, I'm not fully trained. I don't think they can send me over until I graduate boot camp and then Advanced Individual Training. I won't be done with that for almost two years."

"It's a good thing you got mono this summer then," Alura said, plunging her hand into the popcorn.

She was right. Being sent home suddenly seemed like a stroke of luck instead of a disaster. "Although... I wonder if they'll rush me through training because of what's going on," I said, the panic starting to encroach again. In a war, everyone was an infantry soldier first, no matter what your official military job was. That detail was one of the first little surprises the Drill Sergeants had sprung on us in boot camp. Everyone was infantry when needed, despite whether you'd been planning on fighting forest fires, despite your expectations of going to college.

Alura chewed her bottom lip, gathering her thick brown hair over one shoulder and clutching it like a rope. "Has anyone told you they're going to speed up your training?"

"No, but I think that's what would happen. If they need people to go..." I trailed off and shrank down into myself. I didn't know what I was talking about, and like a deer paralyzed in the path of oncoming headlights, I had no clue how to react, what to think, what to say, what to ask. Maybe if I just stayed frozen in place, it would all blow over.

A few miles away, on campus, the other students tossed Frisbees as the sun went down, dumped vodka into orange juice bottles for a night at the arcade, updated their MySpace pages, and rounded up friends to cruise the strip or catch a movie.

Across town, Aaron was making pizzas and Jill was tidying the racks of clothing at the Bon Marche. Tomorrow Alura would work her campus job, then her waitressing job. Until now, I'd had similar jobs—babysitting, McDonald's, Dairy Queen, monitoring tests, housework—jobs that didn't instill a dread of answering the phone, jobs where I knew what I would be doing, and where, and for how long. Jobs that if I decided weren't for me, I could quit without anyone batting an eye.

Watching the missiles, listening to that orchestrated soundtrack, I felt a gap between me and my sister, between me and everyone I knew, open and grow.

11. SUSPENSION OF DISBELIEF

November 2001: Missoula, MT

I spent the rest of the fall and all winter convincing myself that the "military conflict" we were involved in would end long before I finished my training—long before the newscasters, Congress, the president, named it War. I needed to believe this because to even think about backing out of my contract now that we were in a "military conflict" would be unforgivable.

Alongside the convincing and avoidance, something else was brewing that winter. It was more than typical bouts of what my family and I had always dubbed "moodiness." *Moods* could strike any time of the year, and if they spiraled, they often ended in little cuts up and down my arms. But that winter there was a darker feeling of deadness and weight that descended and rose without rhyme or reason—like my insides were as cold and lifeless as the plants buried under the snow and ice, and soon I'd be under there too, so what was the point?

I did not connect these feelings to the brewing war that I could soon be ordered to play a role in. I assumed I just needed the kind of constant stimulation I'd had in high school, so I tried to stay as busy as possible. I drove to school early to pick up coffee from the student union snack store, even though I didn't like coffee yet. I soaked up journalism, philosophy, anthropology, and psychology. I wandered around campus between classes, scoping out good study nooks. When I didn't have to work at the testing center, trips to the fitness center to lift weights or play basketball with Aaron kept the dark moods at bay.

I'd met Aaron as soon as I'd moved to Missoula—a blind date set up by Jill. He was a tall, pale beanpole who liked to hike and gently tease and talk about music, and who asked with adorable shyness on our third date if he could kiss me. Aaron unwittingly derailed more than one plunge into moodiness, but as another student with a full-time job, he could only distract and protect me so much. And as a bit of a pothead, he had a single suggestion when I couldn't shake a mood: pack a bowl. Aaron rarely found a problem that couldn't be resolved with a little weed and a little time. The effect of a few hits on me, however—especially if I was already depressed— was an overpowering need to go to sleep, even if it was 8:00 p.m. and I had a pile of unfinished homework.

So unlike Aaron, I didn't get high often. I saved it for when I was in a good mood and could stave off fatigue long enough for us to hang out and enjoy the mind-expanding effects. Maybe once a month we'd clamber onto his roof and share a teeny bowl while looking out at the town below us, sprinkled with white and gold and blue lights. Up there, wrapped in a slow-motion blur, I let my guard down and let the giggles rise, let my mouth blurt out whatever came to mind instead of judging whether it was worthy enough to say.

January 2002: Missoula, MT

"You will not leave until everyone has taken a piss test. And I mean *everyone*," my First Sergeant announced one drill, walking the length of formation in giant strides, glaring into the ranks. "The doors have been locked and I've stationed soldiers at the exits to make sure no one slips out. Now, if any of you have something to confess, own up. Best to be up-front than have us learn about something stupid through the results. If you have any inkling whatsoever you might fail, let your squad leader know. If you were at a party and you were exposed to something secondhand, let us know. It's that serious. Huah?"

"Huah," the platoon echoed.

"Fall out."

My squad leader—a short, pear-shaped woman with dark hair—motioned us into a huddle. *Fuck.* I thought random drug tests were reserved for training and medical exams! My brain ticked through everything I'd heard about marijuana: That it took at least three weeks to leave your system. That the only way to mask it on a piss test was to drink a gallon of cranberry juice. That you could lose rank and pay and get slapped with an Article 15 if you tested positive.

"No one has anything to tell me, right?" Sergeant Hoff asked. "Everyone's going to pass with flying colors?"

The rest of the squad nodded, cracked jokes, muttered about being treated like a pack of criminals. I waited until everyone wandered off, then sidled up to Sergeant Hoff, clutching my BDU cap in clammy hands.

"I don't know if I'm going to pass," I said.

Her eyebrows rose and I could see the recalculations being done in her head. She'd pegged me as a quiet, reserved, goody two-shoes. Now I was a troublemaker.

"What did you do?"

"I smoked some pot."

Her eyebrows lowered a fraction. "How many hits did you take?"

"Hits?"

"How many times did you inhale?" The calculations shifted again. More goody two-shoes than troublemaker.

"Maybe three?"

"How long ago? Is this a regular thing?"

"Almost two weeks ago. And no, it's not a regular thing at all."

She took a deep breath and shook her head. I could tell she didn't think this was serious. That she'd probably smoked her own fair share of weed. But we were in an organization that cared very much. Getting drunk off our gourds was fine, but pot was like any other drug, a cardinal sin.

"Are you going to report me?"

"I have to. Sorry. Just hope you pass the test. If it's clean, we'll forget the whole thing. If it's not, we'll go from there."

I started downing water, imagining it diluting my urine, my blood, knowing it didn't work that way. *Shit.* This would be on my record. Word would spread. I'd lose my bonus, if not rank. And I'd still be stuck in uniform for another five years. *Shit!*

Feigning nonchalance, I picked up a cup, wrote my info on the sticker curving around the orange plastic, and got in line. All the water I'd drank sat heavy in my stomach as I waited for the eleven women in front of me to enter and exit the female latrine, one by one.

"Next." A frizzy-haired sergeant held open the bathroom door for me.

I barely met her eyes.

Frizz Hair took my cup and unscrewed the lid. "So you know that you have to pee in front of me, right sweetie?"

"I know."

"Do you need the water running? I can turn on a faucet."

"Sure," I said, scuffing into a stall. I undid my belt and sat down, camo pants around my ankles. Frizz handed the cup back to me and I peed as she leaned against the stall door, swung one boot behind the other, and crossed her arms. With a rush of glee, it struck me that the toilet was full of water. And Frizz wasn't really watching. I carefully tipped out half my pee and scooped in some water. Taking a deep breath, I held the sample out to her.

She reached for the cup. "Thanks, hon. I got it from here."

• • •

Looming worries about the unfolding War on Terror were instantly eclipsed by the pot drama. For the next month I wavered between assuring myself I had successfully sabotaged my sample and suspecting I was doomed. I braced myself every time I answered the phone. The weeks ticked by until the next drill. No word. I certainly would have heard by now if I were in trouble, right? Then again, this was the Army, which loved to humiliate offenders. A few drills before, they had dragged in two guys and made them stand up front while the officers berated them for being AWOL. One of the guys had claimed he was sick at the last minute and couldn't make drill. The other hadn't bothered to call his leaders with an excuse at all. So the platoon leader had sent a couple sergeants to track them down and inform them they could either get their asses to the armory and clean latrines all day, or they'd get the military police sicced on them. Maybe they were waiting for first formation to make an example out of me too.

I arrived at the armory early and made small talk with the other privates, keeping an eye out for Sergeant Hoff. She showed up with a group of sergeants, but once she saw me, she excused herself. I met her halfway and followed her to a corner of the drill floor.

"We got the results back," she said, "and you passed the piss test. But I would not recommend taking that chance again."

She tried to look stern and long-suffering. I tried to look indebted and earnest. Those were our roles. And after a briefing downplaying our potential deployment to Afghanistan—*You'll know something as soon as we know something; word from top is keep doing what we're doing; no need to alarm your families*—I slipped right back into clinging to the formula I had worked up: 90 percent civilian, 10 percent soldier. I turned my attention to tests, essays, work, fending off moodiness, solo road trips, hikes, and, after Aaron and I lost our virginity on New Year's Eve, sex, sex, sex.

It all worked for a month or two. But the closer Boot Camp #2 crept, the more sandbags I had to stack against the floodgates of unease.

12. Keeping Up Appearances

June 2002: Missoula, MT

The night before I shipped out to Boot Camp #2, Aaron threw me a party at his house up in the south hills. His roommates Keith and Quinn were there, as well as Keith's girlfriend Wren. Keith and Wren were so dopey and inseparable we called them the Keiren Entity. In the kitchen, we gathered around two-liter pop bottles, six-packs of beer, and sugar cookies someone had snagged from the grocery store.

"Tomorrow's the big day, huh?" Keith said, pulling Wren into a smothering side hug.

"Don't tease her," Wren said. "It's not going to be fun. Right?"

"*Fun?*" You could drink the sarcasm dripping off my voice. I didn't want a makeshift party. I wanted Aaron all to myself on this last night of freedom.

"Do you get to shoot a machine gun?" Keith asked. "Throw grenades?"

"Yes on the grenades. No on the machine gun, unless you count the M16. It can only shoot three bullets in a row on the burst setting."

"Fuck, that was creepily specific," said Keith.

"Are you gonna come back and show us how to kill people with your bare hands?" Quinn asked.

I shot him a perturbed look. Didn't they understand that training was for real now? A year ago I never would have dreamed I could be fighting in a war. Now the odds seemed very high. As idiotic as it sounded, that wasn't what I had signed up for. I didn't know if I could kill people if the time came. Not up close. Not unless it was in self-defense and I was sure he was a "bad guy." That was the whole problem with this war. Nothing was simple like with the Nazis. I could kill a Nazi. But what about a guy who looked like he was either planting an IED or tying his shoe?

"She doesn't need her hands, look at that death glare," Keith said. Wren punched him on the shoulder.

"I'd like some hand-to-hand combat training," Quinn said wistfully, eyes rolling to the ceiling. "I've seen pictures. It's like wrestling, and I like to wrestle." Quinn was openly gay, and often bragged about his goal to sleep with 100 men before he hit twenty-five years of age. We listened intently to his escapades, half scandalized by his ambition, half in awe. At twenty-one, his tally was already in the forties.

Quinn grabbed a cookie and announced, "I'm off to puff the dragon. Anyone?"

Eyes, heads, shoulders perked.

"I'm going to hold off tonight," Aaron said. "Rosa can't smoke. They're going to test her."

"God, sucks to be you," Quinn said, turning and sauntering down the hallway. Keith and Aaron looked after him, looked at each other, then the table.

"I'm gonna honor your sacrifice, Rosa," said Keith. "Just beer tonight." He tossed a silver can to Aaron, then poured a can into a glass with a beer cozy for Wren. I uncorked the half bottle of wine I'd left there the night before, replaying Quinn's cheerful *sucks to be you.*

In the living room, I watched the boys play video games and horse around and talk about their plans for the summer—camping and fishing trips, barbeques, and working enough to buy beater motorcycles.

"Can we go on the roof?" I asked Aaron.

The house stood on a steep slope so getting to the roof was easy. All we had to do was go into the back yard and take a high step up. We walked to the roof's peak, the chill of the night sharpening our senses, and sat facing the valley Missoula filled, mountains on all sides. We watched the traffic lights wink from green to yellow to red, pointed out the fairgrounds and the university and the river to each other.

I spotted McCormick Park, where I'd grown up ice skating in the winters and swimming in the summers before the move to Eastern Montana. Seeing it in the dark from this distance, like it was unattainable, reminded me of stopping there a few months back. I'd taken a wrong turn and instead of turning around I'd kept going and found myself pulling into the park, excited to see it again. But after enduring stares from the kids fishing in the pond, finding the Olympic-sized swimming pool covered with a dirty tarp, and looking at the playground and realizing that of course I couldn't go tearing around on it—I was an adult, that would be weird, idiot, freak, *what-were-you-thinking*—I strolled back to the car, pretending I was enjoying the lovely spring day, pretending that the adventure and bliss I'd felt as a kid wasn't gone for good. Driving home, a familiar heaviness settled back onto my shoulders—the weight of troops in Afghanistan, the anxiety that my Missoula unit would be headed there soon, the incomprehensibility of how the world had changed so quickly.

Now, hours from a second stab at boot camp, I knew I wasn't ready to be an adult in the way the Army wanted me to be—a blind, unquestioning grunt.

"I don't want to go," I said, the words coming out tight and raspy.

Aaron put an arm around my shoulders. "I know. I wish you didn't have to."

"It's sweltering and humiliating. Half the recruits act like jackasses," I said, avoiding what I was really upset about. "You're at their mercy twenty-four seven, all for a measly thirty-five bucks a day. I don't even know how that's legal." I sat ramrod straight, muscles tensed under Aaron's arm, head down. If I looked at him I'd lose it. "I feel like some kind of prisoner, even when I'm here. Even right now."

"I wish I could go in your place," he said.

My head jerked up.

"I mean it. If they'd take me in your place, I would go. I know how much you've been dreading it all year."

Had it been that obvious? My shoulders softened from rocks back to flesh and I turned to hug him, my face pressed into his chest. He smelled like beer and cotton and the incense he burned in his room.

"See how they like trying to order me around," he said, his voice high and playful. "Drop and give you fifty? Screw you Mr. Drill Sergeant. Get up at 5:00 a.m.? I would like to see you try. Target practice, okay. And if they have climbing courses and stuff, that would be fun. But screaming about blood making the grass grow green? Yes sir, no sir? Fuck that shit."

"I think I made a mistake," I said into his shirt. It was the first time I'd said it out loud. "I don't belong in the Army."

"So don't go."

I closed my eyes and bit back a tirade. I was angry at myself, not Aaron. "I signed a contract."

"So what? Don't show up."

I pulled away from him, thinking about the rebel at the bus stop. It was way too late for me to back out now. I'd been in the Guard a year and a half. "You don't understand. I took oaths. They come after people who go AWOL."

"Let them come after you. You don't have to go if you don't want to."

I roughly wiped the tears from my cheeks. "Are you kidding me? This is the federal government. They'll court-martial me and throw me in jail. I have to do everything they say for the next five years."

Aaron cautiously squeezed my shoulders. "Sorry."

My throat ached from trying to keep my composure. "Why did I think I needed them to pay for tuition? All I needed was a part-time job, especially at the U of M. It's not worth fighting a war for. I don't even understand how going after one group of terrorists turned into a war."

We watched the lights below flip from red to green, block by block. Headlights crawled closer. Taillights shrunk to pinpricks and disappeared.

"Let's go back inside and pretend we're a normal college couple," I said. "I'm not in the Guard. September 11 didn't happen."

"Deal."

13. Now You See the Cage, Now You Don't

June 2002: Ft. Jackson, SC

Standing at parade rest, fresh off the bus from the airport, I told a bored-looking sergeant at Ft. Jackson my story—how I could skip all this preliminary mumbo jumbo and join a company starting week four. I had everything I needed in the duffle by my feet. *I'll be damned if I go through that gas chamber again,* I thought.

"You came back?" the sergeant asked.

A slow comet flared and detonated like a firework. *What?* "Of course I came back," I said, searching his face, feeling like my body was draining through the floor.

He shook his head and puffed out air in a little scoff. "Wow. Don't know if I would have."

A dozen questions gathered on the tip of my tongue. *Is that even possible? Can I still leave? Who do I tell?* I opened my mouth, then snapped it shut. He was screwing with me. That's what they loved to do here. *The contract. The contract. The six-year contract.* There was no *choice* about any of this.

"I don't know who said we could put you with a company a couple weeks in," the sergeant said. "But that's not going to happen."

"The month I was here doesn't count for anything?"

"At least you'll know what to expect," he said.

"What about starting at week two? Or even one?"

"You'll start back at the beginning. Right here at in-processing."

I felt like screaming. "But I have everything I was issued last year. It's right here," I said, breaking parade rest to point at my bag.

The sergeant gave me a sharp look, one that said *shut the fuck up, pry-ut*. The time for having an opinion, being treated like a person, was over. I returned to parade rest, dulled my eyes, and imagined I was a fire-breathing dragon razing the room, busting outside and taking flight, turning the cheerful, green treetops to clouds of ash.

• • •

My fury died, of course. Because boot camp has a way of forcing you to live a narrative that goes a little like this: be stripped of everything, suffer, fume, strive, surrender, bond, fail, commiserate, fight, fight, fight, redeem yourself, succeed, get pats on the back, feel like a champ, go home.

The narrators of this story are your drill sergeants, your Army parents. The first three weeks they revel in pushing your body into muscle failure and your mind into despair. They are the agents of perpetual discomfort, strain, embarrassment, and dread. If they can't make an impression on you with push-ups, they order you to skip around the company area singing nursery rhymes, or call you a dumb piece of shit in front of the whole platoon. They say things like "I joined the Army because of Rambo." While you're out training, they destroy the barracks, tipping the bunk beds like dominos, spilling cleaning products on the floor, and tying different-sized boots together and flinging them. If you are a woman, they ban you from plucking your eyebrows, make snarky comments about the fine hair on your upper lip, and threaten to chop off your hair if it falls below your collar. Drill sergeants decide whether you can go to the bathroom or not, whether you get a phone call on Sunday, whether you get five minutes to eat a meal or thirty-seconds. So when the drill sergeants pull out the cadence that goes: "Here we go again / Same old shit again / Marching down the avenue / Eight more weeks and we'll be through / I won't have to look at you / Ugly, ugly, ugly you," you slam your boots with each step and belt the words back at the top of your lungs. Everyone else is stomping and shouting too. You are not alone in this slice of sleep-deprived hell. You have brothers and sisters. Not one of you would dare break cadence.

Then, what I like to call the "children of gruff parents syndrome" sets in. Because it's so hard to please the drill instructors, you crave their approval. For weeks, like starving kittens, you lap up scraps as small as "So you're not useless after all."

You start to get letters back. *It sounds pretty wild,* Alura wrote. *A lot of guard duty. What the hell do you guard against? Werewolves? The sane people in your platoon who are trying to escape? Or, perhaps, ALIENS? I also have a question about the going to church thing. Is it mandatory? You should be so glad I never went to boot camp. I would have made such a stink about stuff like that, and their supreme sexism, that I probably would be public enemy number one right now and our whole family would be in danger of CIA assassinations. Was there a reason that you had to down a whole canteen of water? If you do that in the middle of battle does it save your life? I'm sorry. I just get so pissed off at the thought of pointless crap being pulled on my little sister.*

Rolling your eyes at such letters, composing arguments you can't wait to send back—in my case: *Going to church gets you out of cleaning the barracks, plus you can sing there. What's sexist about doing everything the guys do? Hydration is very important. Most everything here has a point*—marks the start of a gradual shift. You now believe in the narrative. Breaking cadence wouldn't just trigger drill sergeant rage, it would be traitorous. And you are rewarded for this belief. The drill sergeants seem less and less pissed with each passing day until, at times, you can almost describe them as friendly. Meanwhile, you're passing tests left and right. Obstacle courses, ropes, first aid. You qualify on your M16, memorize the soldier's creed, memorize the entire soldier's manual. You throw a live hand grenade, get gassed, wriggle under barbed wire while live rounds whiz overhead, and run screaming through the bayonet assault course, stabbing tires nailed to trees. At some point your drill sergeants start bragging about you to the other platoons' drill sergeants. They laugh. Sometimes they go out of their way to make *you* laugh. You feel like a phoenix—forged by fire into something stronger, older, wiser—a version of yourself that makes you stand a little taller. And then you come to the end.

The morning before graduation we scrambled out of bed as Reveille blared over the speakers. The drill sergeants walked in and we toed the line at attention, ready for our usual bout of push-ups and overhead arm clappers. But the instructors beamed at us, joked around, and told us to get dressed; there was a lot to get done before our parents arrived that afternoon.

August 2002: Ft. Jackson, SC

Family greeting time was set for 4:00 p.m. Stuck across base, getting tickets for my flight home, I kept thinking about how my mother had said, hesitantly, during one of our ten-minute Sunday conversations: *I got a letter from your commanders about your graduation. Would you even want me to come?*

Maybe it was the deprivation of familiar faces, the absence of kind words, the industrial sense of the base, or the feeling that years had passed, not just three months, but the thought of seeing my mother at graduation had set off a yearning that choked me up. Now, trying to sit still and not glare at the gum-smacking civilian woman botching my tickets, I pictured my mother back at the company area, watching everyone else hug sons, daughters. She was probably in a corner or backed up against a wall, waiting with that tight, expectant smile she wore when she was uncomfortable. Even though she was with my Aunt Bev, she'd be feeling like an outsider, which I imagined she'd felt like most of her life, and her back would be killing her and she'd need to walk around but she wouldn't let herself because what if she missed me? She'd come so far and spent so much money just to see me shake someone's hand and get a piece of paper.

The bus dropped me off at 4:45 and I sprinted to Echo Company, winding my way through clots of civilians and soldiers. It was strange, seeing bright blues and yellows and reds mixed in with our woodland camos. Sisters and girlfriends in heels and makeup, their hair tumbling down their backs, looked like a different species. I found one of my drill sergeants and checked in. "Have you seen—"

"Your family's out by the picnic tables, soldier."

My mother's back was to me. Aunt Bev sat next to her. They were both in sleeveless shirts and knee-length skirts, their short dark hair and the straight-backed way they were planted on the bench declaring them sisters.

"Mom!"

She turned around and struggled to extract herself from the table. I barreled into her, wrapped her in a hug and held on, even though we'd been ordered to give only "a short hug hello and a short hug goodbye." She seemed smaller and softer than I remembered, and the familiar feeling that she was a fragile bird I needed to protect flared. The smell of her rose perfume and piney deodorant triggered an avalanche. I wanted to tell her a transformative summer's worth—how much I loved and admired her, how much I regretted giving her a hard time in high school, how it killed me that Dad and Wayne had obliterated any chance of her letting someone get close again.

"Good grief," she said. "You haven't hugged me like that since you were five years old. Why are you crying?"

"I'm just glad you're here." I blinked furiously but kept churning out tears. I realized this was the first time in three months someone had touched me on purpose, not an accidental collision in line or someone pushing and tugging on bits of my gear.

My aunt moved in for a hug, looking up at me with a mix of curiosity and confusion. "Hey there, Army gal. I'm proud of you. The whole family is."

"They were telling us what you all had to go through. You're one tough cookie," my mom said.

"And you're getting some award?" Bev asked.

Behind my back, I pinched my arm hard and twisted. The tears stopped and I blotted my face with a BDU cuff. "Two actually. Leadership and Iron Woman. I've been Platoon Guide for the last three weeks and I maxed the PT test."

Bev exclaimed. My mom thrust her nose in the air in mock snobbishness. "Well of course you're a hot shot. Didn't they know who they were getting?" A second round of hugs ensued. The drill sergeants roared "fall in," and I went running back to the company area, where we yelled mottos and creeds, beat our faces, and did drill and ceremony while our families watched and applauded.

"Family time is over, huah," they announced. "Platoon guides, take 'em to chow."

I stepped in front of formation. "Platoon, *attention!*" The ranks snapped straight on my command. "Right *face*." Fifty-nine bodies turned as one. "Counter-column, *march*." My feet rose and fell in rhythm to the tramping of my battle buddies, weaving between each other. "*Left*, right on, *left*, right on, *left* right *left*. Forward, *march*." I could feel my mother's gaze on my back. It felt like the sun.

• • •

That night, I clambered into my bunk and daydreamed about eating a Snickers bar at the airport on my way home. Salvarado, who slept one bunk over, was gossiping with Ellis, who slept under me. Salvarado had spent most of boot camp complaining or trying to draw attention to herself. For instance, the first week, when the drill sergeants were constantly punishing her for putting her hands on her hips, she had lamented how being a model in civilian life had given her bad habits. "Hands on hips is just such a natural pose for a model. I can't help it." Because Salvarado had the body of a ten-year-old, the poise of a hyena, and was stuck wearing Army-issue Basic Combat Glasses, nicknamed Birth Control Glasses, none of us believed the model claim until she had her parents mail some headshots as proof. Ellis was her opposite—nearly six feet tall, quiet, friendly, and no-nonsense.

"Did you hear about the list the guys made?" Salvarado asked Ellis in a whisper.

"What kind of list?"

"A list of the hottest females in the company."

I rolled my eyes at the ceiling. What a juvenile *boy* thing to do.

Ellis let out a snort. "The guys do that at my high school." I felt Ellis sit down on the bed and heard her unlace her boots.

"Don't you want to know who's on it?" Salvarado pressed.

"No. I know I'm not. I'm bigger than half the guys here." In addition to her height, Ellis was a solid, big-boned person. She'd been the only girl I couldn't knock around when we had pugil stick training. "Are you on it or something?"

"Number *nine* in our platoon. These boys have no idea. Put me in civilian clothes and no question I'd be number one."

Thrilled at Salvarado being taken down a notch, my mouth curled into a smirk. I knew people like her in the civilian world. Tedious, self-absorbed people whose parents bought them cars (or modeling careers) and who were most confident when they had new things to show off. Here, no one had anything. No one could wear makeup or jewelry or spend hours fixing her hair or tweaking her outfit. We were more raw, honest versions of ourselves, at least physically.

"Guess who's number one for our platoon?" Salvarado said.

I could hear Ellis slip on her shower shoes and rummage through her toiletry bag. "Hawn?"

"She's number two."

"Yoshira?"

"No."

"Del Duca?"

"*Yes*," Salvarado hissed. "Del Duca."

Whoa. I couldn't help but grin up at the ceiling. For three months I'd dressed like a man. I'd rolled around in sand and mud and sweat through my uniform and hocked up phlegm so I could breathe and gulped down food like a cretin and yelled guttural yells and dug holes out in the woods to bury my shit. Yet while I'd been feeling ugly and crude and masculine, a bunch of boys had conferred and agreed that I was a sexy girl. Holy crap.

I stretched out and allowed myself to inhabit my hips, my breasts, my thighs, my lips. Ever since reaching base

I'd ignored them. Mentally sheared them off. Then I started to wonder why I was taking so much stock in this list. It was a very Salvarado thing to do.

"What?" said Ellis. "Del Duca's pretty. And she's a way better platoon guide than Westfield. I don't know why you hate her so much."

"She's cute, not hot," Salvarado mumbled. "She's *okay*. Like I said, after graduation, the guys' jaws will hit the floor when they see me."

That was why. She was right. The next day, she'd undergo this incredible transformation: makeup, clothes, hair, skin, contacts instead of glasses. Meanwhile, I'd be the same—lucky if I could apply mascara and eyeliner correctly, my jeans tight, yes, but not cool or suggestive like jeans Salvarado likely had in her civvy bag. Come to think of it, she was probably saving a cute little dress for the occasion—not that I resented her or any of the girls who would undergo similar makeovers. No, even when I returned to default, low-key Rosa the next afternoon, I'd be reveling in the miraculous discovery I could be strong *and* pretty, maybe even beautiful, in this organization designed to quash any semblance of femininity and individuality. How ironic that boot camp could me feel like more of a woman.

• • •

It was overcast and misty the morning of graduation, but that didn't dampen our spirits. The entire battalion marched onto the field, chins held high through the color ceremony and patriotic songs and speeches, and then we were marching past the bleachers, saluting the officers, snapping our heads at the command "eyes, *right*." Soon Aunt Bev was taking pictures of me with my arm around my mother, my green Class A's blending in with the lush green Ft. Jackson fields behind us.

"You raised one remarkable young woman," a general said to my mother. We were standing under a special awning where the award winners had been invited for refreshments.

"I certainly did," she answered. "You don't have to tell *me* that."

I cringed, but then remembered that my mother was not a soldier. She could be informal.

"But thank you very much for saying so," she added, perhaps realizing my discomfort. "I'm very proud of my daughter."

"Is there a Mr. del Duca I should be congratulating?" The general scanned the tent.

My mother hesitated, then said, "No, I'm a single mom. Their dad wasn't really in the picture. But all three of my girls turned out wonderfully."

Now it was the general's turn to be uncomfortable. "History of military service in your family?"

Bev spoke up this time. "Our dad served in the Navy in World War Two. He was an engineer with the Seabees."

"The Seabees, huh? I had an uncle in the Seabees." The general smiled, then turned to me. "They give us officers coins to present soldiers who make an impression. Soldiers with a great amount of potential. Do you have one yet?" He pulled a coin, painted gold, white, and blue, from his pocket.

"No sir."

"Let this be your first." He passed the coin to me and shook my hand.

August 2002: Missoula, MT

The day after I got back to Missoula, Aaron threw me a welcome home party at his house. The same crew was there: Quinn and the Keiren Entity. The TV was nattering away in the living room and ska music was playing in the kitchen, but fresh off the constant buzz and chaos of Echo Company, the house felt like the rest of the civilian world: small, quiet, and sterile.

"Did you bring us souvenirs?" Keith asked.

I gave him a wry smile and thought about everything I'd brought home—thick certificates, my coin, muscular shoulders, a taut stomach, calluses on my heels and hands, and the knowledge I had sex appeal a man's uniform couldn't hide. I'd brought home power. And I'd developed a renewed confidence in my role in the Guard. I would land a press corps job, and then, if my unit got called up, so be it. I would serve my country as a writer. After all, we were fighting terrorists. They deserved to be hunted down.

"Whoa, look at that. She's about to kick your ass, Keith," said Wren.

"So you *did* learn hand-to-hand combat!" Quinn pointed a finger at me.

"I did. But I probably forgot everything by now. It's all these weird wrestling moves for when you're pinned under someone."

"Mmmm, sounds interesting," said Quinn. "Do they let people audit hand-to-hand combat class?"

I laughed.

"Did you wrestle guys or girls?"

"Both."

"Wait a minute," Aaron broke in. "They let you wrestle guys?"

"What do you mean 'they let you'?" I said, poking a finger into his chest.

He held up his hands and made a show of stammering excuses and apologies.

Keith laughed and passed Aaron the bottle opener. "The Army's been co-ed for a while now, dude."

"So what's it like?" Wren asked. "Everything I know about the Army I know from movies."

"Well, it sucks," I said. "But it's fun too. I think everyone should have to go through at least a couple weeks of boot camp."

"*What?*" Quinn shot sidelong glances at Keith and Aaron. "Why?"

"Americans are so spoiled. Having everything taken away makes you appreciate the little things. Like sitting down when you're tired, waking up when you want—being able to choose what you eat, what you wear, when to talk to someone, when to leave the room. You forget what a luxury it is to listen to music and watch movies and... everything. We have so much choice, so much freedom. People take it for granted because they don't know anything else."

The group nodded, heads bowed, eyes downcast. They'd all spent the summer goofing off, doing exactly what they'd wanted. "Not that I think you guys take stuff for granted," I rushed.

"No, you're right," Keith said. "I don't think about any of that."

"Plus, there's no racism in the military," I went on, my privilege speaking for me. "And no materialism. It's kind of socialist if you think about it. Nobody has anything, so there's no social ladder to climb."

"What about rank?" Aaron asked.

"That comes into play later. Boot camp is all about everyone working as a team on the same level. You have to get along. And most people end up pretty good friends." I thought about the list of names and emails I'd brought home.

"Wait a minute," Quinn said. "I'm still stuck on no racism in the Army. You've got to be kidding me."

"I'm serious," I said, feeling my shoulders rise in defense. "I never saw or heard anything remotely racist, even though it was so diverse. I've never been around so many different kinds of people. But when you're in uniform, everyone's the same. You have to rely on each other and get over your differences fast or you'll all be in deep shit. This one girl said she'd never spoken to a white person in her life before she got assigned a white battle buddy."

"Oh my God, that is so crazy," Wren said, then frowned into her beer. "But you know, now that I think about it, I don't know if I've ever actually talked to a black person. Montana is so white."

"Just because you didn't see any racism doesn't mean it doesn't exist," Quinn said.

I rolled my eyes. "Of course not, but you're missing the point."

Quinn stroked his chin and, for some reason, launched into a German accent. "Vat about sexist? Surely ze Army es very sexist."

"Maybe a tiny bit," I admitted.

"Ah ha! And vat about all ze screaming, ze yelling, ze push-ups?"

"They do it for a reason. They break you down to build you back up stronger. Everything has a purpose. The drill sergeants are hard on you at first so that—"

Quinn made a buzzing sound like I'd answered a question wrong on a game show. "I'm not buying this utopian bullshit. Sounds like you were brainwashed after all."

I shrugged, dismissing the idea. Then came a rising tide of unease. *Was I brainwashed?* The things coming out of my mouth sounded like slogans. But I believed them. I did a quick mental assessment. No, I was still me. Still that cynic. Still on the alert. Was it a crime to agree with aspects of the Green Machine?

I stared at Quinn until he looked up from his beer. "That's a cliché thing to say," I said. "Being brainwashed."

He stared back. "Clichés are just truths that are so true they're boring."

I felt my face grow hot, and a sharp recognition dawned. It wasn't just quiet and sterile away from the platoon—it was lonely with the nostalgia of knowing I'd never see any of them again—the pseudo brothers and sisters I'd shared the roller coaster of a summer with. And no civilian would completely understand boot camp. I could try to explain until I was blue in the face, but unless they'd been there, they'd never really get it.

"No more Army talk," Wren said, waving her hands in the air. "Moving on."

"Yeah, what else is new with you two?" Keith asked, making a point to smile at me and Aaron.

"We're moving in together," said Aaron, wrapping an arm around my waist.

The guys whooped and howled.

A shit-eating grin spread across Aaron's face. "Hey now. Quit thinking about my girlfriend like that."

• • •

About a week later, I was unpacking my Army duffle in the basement apartment Aaron and I had found between downtown and the university. Shaking out a pair of wrinkled PT shorts, I felt a sharp slap on my thigh. Something was in the shorts' tiny Velcro pocket. I wormed my fingers inside, touched cool metal, and pulled out a bolt cam pin—a round, stubby bolt with a square head and a hole drilled through the cylinder. Without it, an M16 won't fire.

At first I was confused. Then I remembered. Ellis had found it on the drill floor a few days before graduation. Because I'd been Platoon Guide, she'd given it to me to pass on to a drill sergeant. I'd slipped it into my pocket, and in the pandemonium of training, forgotten all about it.

I wrote a note explaining what happened and slipped the bolt and letter inside an envelope. I still had the company's address memorized. They'd be happy to get it back.

But I never mailed that envelope. And a week later, I finally admitted to myself that I wanted to keep the bolt. It was novel—cool. It was a souvenir no one else had. I took it out of the envelope and put it in the bottom of a plastic, heart-shaped jewelry box Aaron had given me for Valentine's Day.

14. The Golden State

January 2003: On the Road to Morro Bay, CA

The road was sliding out from under me. If you could call it a road. I was driving on a swath of ice, barely doing forty miles an hour, straining to make out Aaron's taillights in the snowy dusk. Aaron was driving a U-Haul crammed with everything we owned and we were headed for balmy, golden California and the alluring Pacific Ocean.

It had been my idea—partly because I thought I might lose my mind if I went through another Montana winter, especially in our cave-like basement apartment. There were more and more days when I felt like I was dragging a chain gang of dark animals behind me, more and more days when I felt like crawling under the covers and pushing the world away for as long as possible. Some days I fell into bed as soon as I got home, woke up for a late dinner of hastily made spaghetti, and then went back to sleep. On rare days, I cut myself.

"You're sad," Jill had said when I'd tried to explain it to her—the lethargy and ennui and general... what was it? Anxiety? Angst? Dejection? Wretchedness?

"I'm not sad," I said. "Just down. I hate winter."

"SAD, Rosa. S-A-D. It stands for Seasonal Affective Disorder. Jessica's mom has it. She put a sun lamp in her basement and goes down there and hangs out for at least an hour every day. Maybe you should try it."

"A sun lamp can't replace the actual sun. I'm afraid if I don't get out of here I'll go nuts." The fear was tangible and encroaching, the teeth of those dark animals snapping at my heels.

Aaron wanted out too—to someplace new and different, away from where he'd lived his entire life. Someplace warm and near the ocean. After a search of affordable schools in California with journalism programs, I'd found Cal Poly, San Luis Obispo, halfway between San Francisco and Los Angeles. So there we were, headed south in the middle of a blizzard. The walkie-talkie in my cup holder fuzzed, and then Aaron's voice came through.

"This is scary as fuck. Should we stop?"

My right hand left the steering wheel and reached for my walkie-talkie in slow motion. Anything sudden and I might sail into the ditch. "I feel like I'm learning how to ice skate all over again," I said, body rigid under my puffy coat. "Should we put on chains?"

"Our chains are for snow, not ice. Do you want to pull over anyway?"

"I guess not. We'll just be cold and stranded. And my dad will think we got in a wreck."

My father was in the middle of one of his I'm-interested-in-my-progeny streaks. He'd achieved a precarious friendship of sorts with my mother, visited Leila a few times, and offered to help me move to California. I was dazzled by the attention.

"What are you listening to?" Aaron asked.

I thought about lying but felt the effort might disturb the equilibrium of the car. "Joni Mitchell. What are you listening to?"

"Rancid. Next up, NOFX." His voice went high and musing, his favorite tone when he was joking. "Good thing I have this truck all to myself. Otherwise I'd be stuck with your wussy fairy folk music."

"Hey now. Be nice."

"I am nice. And I have good taste in music."

"I listened to The Pixies before Joni."

"Good. Now I won't have to shun you the rest of the trip."

"You would never shun me," I said, grinning. The road had lured me deep into the *Golden State*: The state of being between old and new lives. The state of possibility, where the unknown is crisp and sweet, its skin unbroken. Where reinvention is a blank mask on the wall, waiting for your reach.

"I know. You're sexy and smart and beautiful and way too good for me. One of these days you'll figure that out. But until then…" He trailed off.

The Golden State wavered. This was what Aaron said to me every night before we went to sleep—some variation of *you're smart and beautiful and talented and way too good for me*. I loved it, except for the "too good for me." It foreshadowed what we both suspected: that as much as we loved each other now, we wouldn't end up together, and I would be the one to break us up. Aaron was the boy next door. Kind, funny, wonderful and safe. The kind of guy you could meet ten years later and he would be exactly the same guy.

Meanwhile, I was in metamorphosis—struggling and changing and uncertain of what kind of transformation I was undergoing and how long it would last. On some level I hoped it would last a lifetime—not the struggling necessarily, but the *grasping for*. At some point I would have to deeply hurt Aaron, push him away out of selfishness for something different. And when that happened, in his eyes, I'd be fulfilling this cruel destiny of realizing I was too good for him. That's what I hated. The warped reasoning that he was a lucky guy right now and it was only a matter of time before I came to my senses.

"One of these days you're going to put on glasses and realize I'm just as flawed as everybody else," I said, trying to sink back into the golden glow.

"Unlikely. I got forty-forty vision."

• • •

"So you're the man who's been sleeping with my daughter."

We were in the driveway, having just pulled up to my father's rundown apartment on the edge of town. My dad looked like an anachronism in his worn jeans and old sheepskin coat, his hair in two long braids, a beaded necklace hanging down his front. In high school, I'd been told by several people he looked like Willie Nelson. I didn't know who Willie Nelson was at the time, but now I can confirm that yes, the parallel was pretty spot-on, although I can't imagine Willie greeting his daughter's boyfriend the way my dad did.

"Excuse me?" Aaron said, brows furrowed.

"I said it's nice to meet the man who's been sleeping with my daughter." My father offered a handshake, but one very close to his body, elbow against his side.

Aaron stared at the hand, then stepped forward to take it. "Nice to meet you too, I guess."

My dad pulled him into a hug and clapped his back, then gave him a long once-over. Aaron turned to me, questioning. I shrugged and shook my head, shielding my eyes like the sun was blazing down on us.

"Good guy," my dad finally said to me, jutting a thumb at Aaron. "Do you two make each other happy?"

"Yep," I said.

My father wrapped his arms around me. "I'm glad he's your man then." I could feel the vibration of his low voice in his chest. He smelled like sweetgrass.

"Hi there," a woman called. She was walking from the house with an energetic mutt who seemed to want to run right up our legs and into our arms despite the woman pulling at its leash.

"This is Rebecca," Dad said in his deep, slow way, waiting for Rebecca to catch his glance before he flung an arm around her shoulders. "She's my ride, if that's all right with you."

He hadn't mentioned this. "Uh, sure," I said. "Did you tell Alura?" The plan was to reach Las Vegas by midnight and stay with Alura and her husband overnight. Alura had married Eric on the same day she graduated college, at twenty-two years old. They were in Vegas now, where she'd gotten a job at a middle school teaching kids whose main goal, she said, was to graduate eighth grade before going to work in the casinos.

"You might want to give Alura a call and ask if it's all right," Dad said. "I'm sure you're on better terms with her than I am."

I reigned in a sigh. Alura wasn't happy Dad was tagging along. About a year prior, they'd gotten into one of their epistolary spats and he had mailed her a box of stuff she'd given him as a child as "proof she once cared about him" and "reason to repair their relationship." Dad didn't ask for the box back, so Alura threw it out.

"I don't have a cell phone," I said, biting my lip.

"We can always grab a cheap motel if your sister can't put us up."

I nodded, appeased for the moment. Dad was staring at me, an expression of mild pride and surprise in his face, his posture. "You've grown up to be a beautiful woman."

I wondered if he meant it. I remembered him letting slip I looked "unusual" on one of his rare visits. *Not in a bad way. Just different. Interesting.* Not what a self-conscious teenager wanted to hear.

"And brave," he added. "It takes guts to pick up and start over someplace new."

"California," Rebecca broke in. "Nice place. How fun."

I didn't know my father well, but I knew Rebecca was not his type. He liked smart, political women, Native American women, or hippies. Foreign women. Spiritual types. Outdoorsy sorts. Liberal as hell and not afraid to speak their minds. Rebecca seemed ordinary, empty, simple. Still, I was jealous. Dad wasn't interested in me. He was interested in taking a little road trip with the new girlfriend, who had a car.

As if he'd heard my thoughts, he pulled out his wallet. "Here's three hundred bucks for the U-Haul. I'm glad we could be part of this journey."

Dad was looking at me again in that intense way that drove me nuts, making me wonder what he was filing away, what he could see that I couldn't.

"Thank you," I said. "Should we hit the road?"

Dad looked to Rebecca.

She tossed her hair. "I just have to grab my suitcase."

I watched them head back to the house, picturing her hoity-toity matched luggage set. Who brought a *suitcase* on a road trip? I was pretty sure my dad didn't own a suitcase, just like I didn't own a suitcase. So much for spending any time with the dude. I turned to Aaron to complain but he was already halfway to the truck so I hurried to the car. My walkie-talkie fuzzed as soon as I slammed the door.

"What the hell was that?" Aaron said.

"I know," I moaned into the receiver. "I'm sorry."

"I thought he was punking me. 'So you're the man who's been sleeping with my daughter?' Who says that?"

"I told you. He's socially inept. He's always been that way."

"Man, that pissed me off. And I don't get pissed," Aaron said.

"I can't believe he's bringing some random lady and her dog. Alura is going to kill me."

"Let them sleep somewhere else."

"We can't do that. He just gave us three hundred bucks!"

Back on the road, my mind drifted to the few memories I had of Dad. Most of them were similarly screwy. When I was about seven, he'd let me drive his Jeep on the highway, sitting on his lap. He was in town camping with his new wife and their toddler. A few years later I remember him taking me to a vivid, enthralling outdoor pow-wow where I ate five pieces of fry bread in the span of an hour, watching the dancers turn in that enormous, slow circle. He gave me an oblong rawhide pouch he'd made and painted himself with red, blue, and yellow designs. It was so stiff and crude it wasn't really functional, so when he asked for it back the next year, I willingly handed it over, even though I was a little hurt he didn't want me to keep the gift.

One summer, Alura, Leila, and I took a bus across Montana to spend a whole week with Dad and his second family. I'd been about ten. Dad had moved to Crow Agency, a reservation town near Billings just a few miles from where Custer and his men were defeated. We thought it was weird for the Native Americans to let this white family live on their land, but we didn't ask questions. Dad (and Mom, for that matter) had a long history of wanting to fit in with Native cultures. After all, I'd been born on a Navajo reservation, even though neither of my parents had a drop of Native blood.

That summer, my sisters and I slept in a teepee in Dad's front yard, despite there being room in the ramshackle house for us—even with the pack of seven stray dogs they'd taken in. There was no bathroom in that house. Just an outhouse near the horse pen. And every time we used that outhouse we walked past a stinking, rotting piece of buffalo hide hanging from a shed. During our tour of the place Dad had pointed to it proudly, saying he was drying it to make into a medicine bag.

The next year, Alura and Leila decided to stay home while I visited Dad by myself. I got to go horseback riding and swim in rivers and see another pow-wow and mess around with leather decorating tools. One day one of the dogs, Arlo, got into a fight with two of the neighbor's dogs through the fence. When I tried to pull Arlo away, he bit my knee, hard, leaving three puncture wounds. My Dad walked me to the tiny general store and bought me three candy bars as reparation.

The next day he showed me a collection of dirty old glass bottles he'd just dug up in the front yard, excited to discover the property must have been some kind of speakeasy during prohibition. When I asked why he was digging a hole in the front yard, he admitted that he'd shot Arlo and was digging his grave. If he'd bitten me, he couldn't be trusted around my young half-sisters.

About a week after returning home, I'd gotten a letter from Dad and excitedly went to my bunk to read it.

Dear Rosa,

I'm happy that you decided to visit us all by yourself. I enjoyed spending time with you and getting to know you better. So did your sisters. Please talk to your mother about adopting Charlie the dog. We'd love to find a home for him.

Marta and I were talking about your visit after you left. She was happy to have you stay, as I was. But there were aspects of your behavior that concerned us. I don't think you are aware of the impressions you made, so we thought it best to address them with you directly. Improving your attitudes will help everyone have a more enjoyable visit, and help you grow into a fine young woman. But if you are unwilling to work on these behaviors, perhaps you shouldn't come again. Below is a list of what we observed.

You Were:	*You Could Be:*
Selfish	*Generous*
Quiet	*Outgoing*

Closed Off	*Engaged*
Boring	*Interesting*
Aloof	*Caring*
Cold	*Warm*

Alura poked her head over the top bunk. "Are you crying? What's wrong?"

I lifted the letter to her and replayed the entire trip to Dad's over in my head at warp speed. Had I really acted that way? Was I awful and just didn't know it?

"I can't believe this," Alura said. "You're not taking this seriously, are you? You're one of the most caring, generous, interesting people I know."

"Then why would he write that?"

"Because he's an asshole. Why do you think Leila and I didn't go back after last summer? He barely spent any time with us. He segregated us in that mosquito- and tick-infested teepee. He said the reason he left when we were little was because Mom told him she didn't love him anymore, which is bull. This is the last straw. I'm writing my own letter. I'm going to give him a piece of my mind and then I'm never talking to him again."

I wrote him back too, apologizing. And I kept that letter, reading it to feel worse when I was already in a low mood, when I wanted to wallow. Here was proof my own dad thought I was a terrible person.

Sophomore year of high school, Dad picked me up for a drive on the back roads to talk, to get to know me. The main topic of discussion was sex. He wanted to know whether I was having it, whether my classmates were—not because he was a creep, but because he was genuinely curious and hopelessly clueless about how awkward and uncomfortable the topic could make a fifteen-year-old girl.

"Of course I'm not having sex yet!" I answered.

"You know, it would be okay if you were. Some people start exploring their bodies with other people at this age. It's nothing to be ashamed of or embarrassed about."

"I don't even have a boyfriend."

"Who says you need a boyfriend to start having sexual experiences?"

"I'm not that kind of girl," I said, crossing my arms, refusing to even look at him.

"Are there girls like that at your high school? Who have a reputation for... what do they call it these days? Putting out? Being easy?"

"Yep." In a school as small as mine, there were only three of them.

"Well, I hope you don't think less of them for what they chose to do in private. It's really unfair how young women are seen as whores when they're going through a perfectly normal period of awakening and experimentation and discovery."

This was perhaps Dad's one great parenting moment with me. In a roundabout way, he showed me that I was buying into the same slut-shaming attitude everyone around me had. We ended up having a deep discussion about teenage sexuality, agreeing that the norms were misguided and unfair. A fissure opened up in my brain that night. Maybe status quo opinions about a lot of things were screwy.

Junior year, he passed through town again. He insisted we run a 400 on the local track so he could prove he was faster than me, and then gave me a back massage that was way more weird than relaxing. He turned off his motel room lights, lit some candles, busted out some massage oil, and then asked if I would be comfortable taking off my shirt. If not, he could just reach under the shirt. Again, this was not because he was a slimeball, but because it didn't occur to him that giving a young woman you barely knew a sensual massage was inappropriate, whether she happened to be your biological daughter or not. No, after I took my shirt off and tried to get comfortable on the floor, he was completely wrapped up in the intellectual aspect, telling me all the massage tricks he was learning from books.

When my dad announced he was coming to my high school graduation and my mom and sisters acted like this was the scandal of the century, I decided to pursue the real source of Mom's hatred for him. I was tired of the drama, the hour-long Dad-bashing session every time his name came up. So the guy could be a jerk. Couldn't everyone get over it already?

I learned some key details about my parents' early history. I learned Dad had an affair with a gas company worker soon after my mother found out she was pregnant with Leila. Then, he'd left my mother for Marta, a mutual friend of theirs, days before Leila was born.

Because there was no formal custody agreement for years, and because he could be unpredictable, my mother was nervous on more than one occasion that he might kidnap us. The first time, he'd come to Pennsylvania, where we were living with Grandpa and Grandma. I was three or four and have no memory of this. But apparently, he tried to get Alura to lie for him and say he'd come alone—like my mother had asked—when really he'd brought Marta. About a year later, when Mom launched a failed attempt to move back to Arizona, he came to the campsite where we were stuck living one night and refused to get out of the car to see us. He wanted Mom to bring us to the car, where he and Marta were waiting. She was terrified he wanted to snatch us and drive off.

When I was eight, after the move to Montana, my dad sued my mother for full custody of us, claiming that my mother had threatened to kill my sisters and me. In reality, during a fight over the phone my mother had said, "They'd be better off dead than with you." In far less drastic terms, the court agreed with my mother.

Okay, I could see how she didn't want to sit in the same row as him when I graduated.

• • •

"Hey, Ro." Alura padded out of the darkness in sweats and slippers and gave me a kiss on the cheek.

"How did you know we were here?" I asked, setting my backpack down and taking off my sweatshirt. I'd ditched my coat hours before. "Is it always this warm?"

"We could hear Aaron trying to turn around and park. And yes. Welcome to the Southwest. Are you guys hungry?"

I ogled the row of palm trees outside the complex, wondering if they grew coconuts or if that was a different type of tropical tree. Then I spotted Dad and Rebecca getting out of her car. "Alura, there's something I have to tell you."

"I made popovers," she said, grabbing my backpack. "We have fruit too. How was the drive?"

"Really icy all through Idaho, but listen—"

"Hey, hey! Thanks for putting us up," Aaron said, stepping onto the sidewalk.

Alura lit up. She loved Aaron. "Anytime. I'm glad we could help."

Rebecca's dog shot past us, body stretched, head bobbing like a champion racehorse. Alura came out of her hug with Aaron and looked from Dad and Rebecca, who were walking toward us hand in hand, to the dog, to me.

"That's…" I trailed off, forgetting Rebecca's name. "Dad brought a friend. But you don't have to, uh…" I stuttered, watching Alura's eyes narrow, her shoulders square.

"Alura. It's good to see you," Dad said, politely keeping his distance, pronouncing "Alura" like no one else in our family, turning her name into Ah-LEW-rah. "Is it okay to hug you hello?"

Alura shrugged.

The one-sided hug was preempted by a dog yelp from the complex behind us.

"Alura!" I recognized her husband's voice. "Some dog's after Sammie."

Sammie was Alura's miniature Sheltie. My sister bolted. I followed, Aaron on my heels, Dad and Rebecca behind.

"Beaner!" Rebecca shouted. "Beaner, come."

Eric had a half-scared, half-excited Sammie by the collar, trying to keep himself between her and Beaner, who sped and lunged, tongue lolling.

"Is she okay?" Alura asked.

"It didn't break skin," Eric said. "More of a snap than a bite."

Alura rounded on Dad. "You brought your dog?"

"It's Rebecca's dog." The pace of his words was still slow and pronounced. "Is your pup okay?"

"I'm so sorry," Rebecca said, finally grabbing Beaner. "She gets along great with other dogs."

"No, obviously she doesn't," said Alura.

"She's never bitten another dog. She doesn't bite."

"Until now?"

"She's just trying to play."

Alura bent down and cuddled Sammie. The rest of us went through a round of introductions or hugs with Eric before awkward silence descended. *Here it comes,* I thought. But instead of a confrontation, everyone bit their tongues, a silent agreement that we would all try to play nice.

Upstairs, light blaring down on Alura's dining room table, which was barely big enough for the six of us, we struggled to find neutral ground.

"Nice pad," said Dad.

"We like it," said Alura.

"Is your mom settling into that house in Billings? It seems she's doing better lately. She can even have a conversation with me."

Alura bristled. "How are Freyja and Camille? Or don't you see them anymore either?"

Freyja and Camille were our estranged half-sisters. Alura was convinced Dad had abandoned his second family as completely as his first.

"Your sisters are well," Dad said. "It's very nice of you to ask about them."

I scrambled to change the subject. "You know, Leila's going to be a valedictorian when she graduates this year."

Dad smiled. "You all inherited some smarts."

A sigh blasted out of Alura's nostrils. She reached for the knife and the tub of margarine, smeared her popover, and stuffed a hunk in her mouth.

Rebecca gave a meek cough. "So, why California?"

"Why not?" Aaron grinned. He was the only one who didn't seem to notice the bowstring tension in the room. "There's surfing, snowboarding. Fresh produce all year round. All kinds of people and art and stuff to do. What's not to love?"

"And no winter," I said, feeling like I was quoting a fairy tale. "The coldest it gets in Morro Bay is about fifty degrees."

"You're going to try to surf?" Eric asked.

Aaron shook his head. "No trying. We're *going* to surf. First thing I'm gonna do once we unpack is buy a used board."

"What about the National Guard thing?" Alura asked, her mouth half full. "They let you leave Montana?"

The long, nerve-wracking drive caught up to my brain, my body, at mention of the Guard. I glanced toward the futon in the living room, which Alura had made up with spare blankets and pillows. "I can move anywhere in the US. The Guard follows you. Once we get to California, I'll belong to the California National Guard instead of the Montana National Guard."

"What would happen if you kept on moving?" Dad asked.

My eyes narrowed. "Like check in with one Guard unit, but then before drill move to another state?"

"Exactly." It was as if my father and I were the only two people in the room, the way he was boring holes through me.

"First of all, I'd have to sacrifice my college education to become some kind of hobo. And second of all, once they figured it out, they'd brand me as AWOL and throw me in jail."

"Could be a better alternative than war."

I crossed my arms and pushed against the back of the chair. "We're not *at* war."

"Darling, yes we are. We're fighting a war in Afghanistan."

"Barely. We're looking for terrorists, not attacking a whole country."

"And what about Iraq?" Dad asked.

"We're not at war in Iraq."

"Yet," he said, putting his arms on the table and leaning toward me.

"Right. So why would I screw up my life based on what might happen? Besides, if we do go to war, I'll either be writing or fueling trucks and stuff. I won't be killing people."

"So you're saying you'll go fight this president's war?"

I glanced at Alura, Eric, Aaron. They all looked to be on Dad's side. "I don't want to. I don't trust Bush. I think he's an idiot. But, yeah, I might have to fight his war."

"It's quite a dilemma. I hope you can make decisions that you can live with the rest of your life," Dad said, letting out a sigh. "And I wish you would have talked to me before you enlisted."

Underneath my crossed arms, my hands closed into fists. He wished I would have talked to him first, huh? So did I. But not in the way he was picturing. All it would have taken was a few measly birthday cards from him, some regular phone calls and visits for me to believe he gave a shit, for it to even cross my mind to seek his advice, for me to consider getting his permission too. "Thanks for your concern, but I got it handled."

• • •

Of course I didn't have anything "handled." I didn't understand what was going on, and I was starting to think my commanders didn't either. Drill after drill I expected an explanation, an update, but there weren't even any rumors about what the future might hold. The one comfort was that it seemed like the country's thinkers, the experts, had it handled. Influential diplomats were writing editorials about how unwise a war in Iraq would be. The media focused on the inspectors invited by Saddam to comb his country for damning evidence of weapons of mass destruction. Five weeks into their search, they still hadn't found biological or chemical weapons, or evidence Iraq had "reconstituted its nuclear weapons program." And if the inspectors *did* find something, then there were various courses of action to take besides war. Treaties, summits, sanctions. The experts made it seem like that was the only logical, ethical way for a world power to handle things. We needed to serve as an example, not react with threats and violence like we were some authoritarian regime. Besides, Iraq hadn't attacked us. There weren't a bunch of terrorists in Iraq. There was no reason to invade or tamper. Or at least, that's what I believed, safe in my cocoon, safe in the Golden State.

15. California Love

January 2003: Morro Bay and San Luis Obispo, CA

Morro Bay was a fantasy land with its ancient volcanic peak rising from the jetty like a crag imported from Ireland, the fog that rolled off the ocean to tuck the town in at night, the sea glass that washed up on the beach, and the otters that skimmed the marina on their backs. I became obsessed with palm trees. Wherever I went, I kept my eyes peeled for baby palms. I imagined one day I'd find a fat little tree that looked just like an oversized pineapple, dig it up in the dead of night, replant it in a big pot, and drag it up the stairs to our room—a room with its own bathroom, where we could see the ocean if we stood on the toilet!

Aaron stayed true to his word and bought a surfboard immediately—a little six-foot-five "fun shape" that would supposedly be easy to master, but took us three afternoons of wobbling to stand up on. Of course we both became hooked. Aaron would surf after lunch until I got home from school. I'd grab my wetsuit from the house and zip down to the beach, waving to get Aaron's attention. He'd come out of the water, give me a kiss and a progress report, hand the board off to me, and head to the house for a shower before work at a local sporting goods store. (He'd decided to put college on hold.) I'd race into the waves and stay there until the sun sank below the horizon.

February 2003: Camp Roberts, CA

After the move, the California National Guard ordered me to drill at Camp Roberts, about an hour's drive from Morro Bay. To get there, I wound east through the hills and emerged on a flat expanse of rangeland, broken only by the occasional winery, and towns almost as small as Fromberg. The first time, I nearly missed the exit for Camp Roberts. The place was a sprawling ghost town—deep cracks spider-webbing the asphalt, empty buildings flaking white paint, hardly any traffic on the rough roads. I wondered if the post-apocalyptic feel of the base was because most of its troops were in "the Sandbox." I worried they would toss me in a unit due to ship out right after I finished Advanced Individual Training (AIT).

Instead, I ended up in a brand-new Engineering Company, whose mission was to build a rock quarry and then help revitalize the base. Camp Roberts had been a huge military hub, training and shipping out 400,000 men during World War II, and another 300,000 during the Korean War. Most of the facilities dated back to that era and were in need of repair.

"We don't have much need for a fueler," my new squad leader said. "We pump our own gas down at the gas station. How about running the front loader?" Sergeant Morgan pointed to a tractor-looking contraption with a wide bucket in front.

I lit up. "Really?"

A few hours later I was deep in the trance of engine roar, the bounce of tires, the lurch of lowering the bucket, the satisfying collision into a mountain of rock and dirt. I was having a blast.

Don't get used to this, I thought. I kept my optimism in check that whole weekend, that whole month. But soon it was growing back like the stubborn blackberry brambles by our new front door. I decided to do some reconnaissance the next time I saw Sergeant Morgan.

We sat on the ridge overlooking the quarry, a breeze cooling our sweaty faces. My front loader looked like a hulking pet waiting for its owner.

"You really got a knack for that thing," Morgan said. "You move twice the rock anybody else does in a day."

I smiled. I knew. But I also didn't take breaks, preferring to hide inside the machine, lost in motion as long as I could. Remembering my recon mission, I cleared my throat. "If we get called up, will I still be able to run construction equipment?"

"Depends on where we are, whether we need fuel bladders set up."

That wasn't what I'd meant to ask. I took a deep breath. "What are the chances we'll get called up?"

"It'll happen," Morgan said.

My scalp tightened and burned.

"But not anytime soon. It'll be a year at least before we reach capacity. We've picked up a few people here and there, but we're about a hundred people shy of a full unit."

"They can't call us up until we're a full unit?" I asked.

"We have to be somewhat near capacity. Otherwise we can't properly operate."

"And when we do get called up, we'll be helping rebuild?"

"Right. I imagine we'll help with roads, schools, stuff like that."

Nowhere near capacity. We'll be helping rebuild. I repeated the phrases when I needed reassurance. If my sisters or mother asked if I had any bad news, I'd tell them to relax; we were years away from capacity. I felt lucky. Spared. My unit wouldn't be fighting any war. We'd be helping after the bullets stopped flying. It was something to believe in. And so I let complacency envelop me like Morro Bay's nightly fog, diving into the rhythm of school and work at the motel down the street and surfing. The war slipped back into its abstract realm, far from my sleepy beach town and my clean, sunny school, and far from remote Camp Roberts with its tarantulas creeping across the firing range.

February 2003: San Luis Obispo, CA

At school, like a hungry lion, I hunted for my *thing*, something to push the military even further toward the back of my mind, and found it in radio. A few weeks into my first quarter at Cal Poly, my elderly Broadcast Journalism professor led me with his elephant gait to the communications building. Professor Madsen labored up the stairs to the third floor and pointed out a men's bathroom.

"You know Weird Al?" he gasped, his normally slicked-back white hair falling into his eyes.

"Of course."

"He went here. In the 1980s. He was a DJ. That bathroom is where he first recorded 'My Bologna.'"

I was staring at the door, thinking how I couldn't wait to tell Leila, when a guy walked out and gave me an odd look. I jerked toward Madsen, who was across the hall, moving through an open door marked KCPR. The station's long entryway featured a ratty couch with a person sleeping at either end, and walls covered with band posters, stickers, Sharpie doodles, and photos of people looking caught off-guard, red plastic cups in hand.

Further in, the studio split into several nooks and crannies stuffed with records, CDs, and art from bands I'd never heard of. One of the main rooms had computers and tables. The other main room was the on-air studio, where a guy in headphones was hunched over the controls, talking into a microphone. The studio had glass windows on three sides but resembled a murky cave more than a fishbowl.

In the computer room, Madsen took an eternity lowering himself into a chair. "Here it is. Cal Poly's student-run radio station," he said, gesturing with mottled hands. I couldn't believe this guy was still teaching. And I couldn't believe I was the only student who'd followed him after class, wanting to see the station right away.

"You are listening to Electronic Immersion. I'm your host, DJ Sasquatch." The words came from a silver boom box, and, very faintly, from the room next door. I watched Sasquatch grab a CD case and flip it over. "We finished off that set with The Postal Service, 'The District Sleeps Alone Tonight.' Sounds like Death Cab for Cutie, you say? Well, that's because The Postal Service is Ben Gibbard and a few collaborators. Woot, I say. Because you can never have enough—"

Madsen flipped the radio off. "I'd like to try having the class put together a live newscast every night. In the past they've been recorded and played willy-nilly."

"Is he live on the air right now?" I asked, looking through the glass wall at the Jolly Green Giant of a guy who had taken his headphones off and was bopping and dipping to an electronic song that came cartwheeling in the door. I'd never heard anything like it. It was a siren song. The whole place was.

"Yes, he is. Right now it's all music, no news whatsoever. Which, if you ask me, is hogwash considering the size of Cal Poly's journalism department. We need to get the news on here live and daily."

"Could I do that? Read the news on air?"

"Of course. I think you should take the lead. No one else appears interested."

Then DJ Sasquatch was lumbering through the door in hiking boots, cargo shorts, and a T-shirt too small for him. He slouched to hide his height, which must have been around 6'3", but was hard to calculate with his thick brown hair mussed straight up. "Can I help you folks with something?" he mumbled with the same not-quite-British accent I'd heard from the radio.

"We're just visiting. I teach broadcast journalism," Madsen said dismissively.

Sasquatch raised his bushy eyebrows at me.

"How do you get to be a DJ?" I asked.

By the end of the month I was a KCPR trainee, paired up with none other than DJ Sasquatch as my mentor. I read the news on air twice a week and wondered if the Army still had radio jobs like in the movie *Good Morning Vietnam*.

16. One of the Guys

May 2003: Morro Bay, CA

"I think we should break up," I said.

It was five months after the move to California. Aaron and I were in our upstairs loft of a bedroom in Morro Bay.

"What?" He looked up sharply from the shoes he'd just kicked off. "I thought you were happy. We've been doing great."

"I know, I am," I said. "That's what makes this so hard. Nothing's wrong. I just don't think we're meant to be together forever."

Aaron sat on the bed and rubbed his hands over his face. "I don't understand," he finally said. "Is there someone else you want to date? Is there a guy at school?"

"No, it's nothing like that!" My arms were crossed, my hands clutching my elbows in a weird hug. "Not yet anyway. It's bound to happen though. We're going to meet people at work or school or around town. I want us to have the freedom to explore that."

He shook his head, eyes down. "There's no one else I want to date here. Are you sure this isn't about something I did?"

Daggers needled my heart. "No, no *way*." I sat next to him but kept my arms crossed. "Aaron, you're amazing. And I will always love you. Even fifty years from now. But I'm not *in* love with you." There was no good way to express the fact we clearly were not soul mates. Aaron lived in the moment, drifting from surfing to work to starting and abandoning art and cooking projects. What I wanted was an abstract *more*—physically, emotionally, intellectually. I wanted the wild adrenaline rush of out-of-control attraction. I wanted intense, important conversations. I wanted someone to challenge me. And perhaps more than anything, I wanted someone who understood why I was so upset over the escalating War on Terror, someone who thought about it half as much as I did.

Aaron was vaguely against the war in that he thought it was "dumb," and like a true punk rock fan, despised all forms of authority. But because the war didn't affect him directly, it was easy for him to ignore. It was easy for a lot of people to ignore. In March, Bush had given Saddam Hussein forty-eight hours to leave Iraq, and then, in an address from the Oval Office, announced the start of a war in Iraq. Unlike 9/11, there were no horrific scenes you couldn't tear your eyes away from, no climbing death toll to keep track of. There were no inconveniences like grounded air traffic or spotty cell service. At school, there were no crowds around TVs in the student union, no discussions or canceled classes. Just a small "die-in" by student activists on Dexter Lawn, dismissed by most as melodrama. Bush had downplayed the fact that this was a war at all. "Coalition forces have begun striking selected targets of military importance to undermine Saddam Hussein's ability to wage war," he'd said. He'd warned that battles in the *days* ahead could be tough. And of course he hadn't mentioned how the war was not authorized by Congress or the UN, that France and Germany thought we were reckless morons, and that weapons inspectors still maintained there was no justification for war.

"Let me get this straight," Aaron said, hunching his shoulders. "There's nothing wrong with us. But you want to break up. To date other guys."

"Not just me. What if the girl you're meant to marry is here?"

He looked up from the floor to shoot me a glare.

I faltered. "Who knows, maybe it'll be terrible and we'll end up getting back together," I said. The words landed like the bricks of bullshit they were.

Later, in bed, staring at Aaron's bare back, my chest swelled with regret. Watching the microscopic rise and fall of his shoulders, I wanted to snake an arm around his middle and bury my nose in his neck. I wanted to take everything back. This was a guy who'd moved across the country for me. Who'd wished he could take my place at boot camp. Who told me every single night I was smart and beautiful. *Who fucks up a perfectly good thing?*

• • •

Aaron and I ended up living together as friends for another four weeks, which was when I was due to ship out for AIT, where I'd learn my Army job. While I was away, he would move out. When I returned in three months, I would move into the tiny room under the stairs, which rented for four hundred dollars a month.

The closer AIT crept, the more relieved about the breakup I became. I loved Aaron. I hoped we would stay close forever. But now he could find his real true love, and I could go crazy before the Army yanked everything away.

President Bush had given a speech on an aircraft carrier about how the mission in Iraq was accomplished and major combat was over. But the war didn't seem to be winding down. Instead, units across the state were on alert. At drill, rumors flew. Everyone expected to ship out in a matter of months. My little dream state was over, and this time the threat of activation felt different. I could feel myself peeling away from the Green Machine, like I'd gotten onto a switch in the railroad tracks somewhere down the line, and with each passing mile we were farther apart. It was more than not belonging and not believing in the foundation now. The overarching apparatus was highly suspect. Bush and Congress clearly thought they could use us—me—any way they wanted, public sentiment be damned, facts and truth be damned. I understood the original mission in Afghanistan: find the terrorists responsible for 9/11. But I didn't understand how Iraq had managed to end up center stage. Dust devils of panic started spinning in my ribcage every time I caught reports about the unfolding chaos—looting, lawlessness, people being rounded up and sent to "black sites" but never charged, soldiers from the disbanded Iraqi Army roaming the streets, civilians confused and terrified. What the hell had we gotten ourselves into? Why was everyone going along with it? And what was the goddamn rush? It seemed like the worse and more murky things got, the faster we plunged ahead.

The Army panic made me want to do radical things—go places, deviate from the norm. Like maybe, over the summer, I could have a *fling*. A no-strings-attached, heat-of-the-moment, temporary, meaningless romance to distract myself from fueler school.

Yes, what I needed was a fling—preferably with a soldier as angry with Bush as I was, although finding that would be a feat in and of itself. My angst with Bush went beyond what I saw as an illegitimate war. It seemed he was out to inflict as much damage as he could on America—drilling for oil in pristine wildernesses, giving the rich tax breaks, cutting social programs, appointing bigoted people to government posts, enacting wrong-headed programs like the Patriot Act and No Child Left Behind. Every time I heard a sound bite from him on the radio or watched him speak on TV, I cringed. His voice, his mannerisms, his condescending, bumbling choice of words all screamed he was a fool, a criminal, a man with vague, dangerous ideas and far too much power. I couldn't wait to help vote him out of office. Back in the 2000 election I'd been old enough to join the military, but not old enough to vote.

There were multiple levels of absurdity to me being primed for casual sex heading into AIT. Beyond the fact that we were fighting two wars, a fling was something as mythical to me as a unicorn. I had kissed a whopping three boys in my life and had sex with one. And there was the bizarre notion that I would find love in a place where romance was banned, and where I was expected to look, act, and dress like a man.

I knew that I had potential—that the guys didn't think I looked ugly or butch in uniform. After all, I'd made "the list" in Boot Camp #2. But I didn't want to get the wrong reputation. If I played it too feminine, I'd be seen as a weak link, a ditz, a slut. But if I played it pure tomboy, I could be seen as "one of the guys" again. While scoring macho points in boot camp had been rewarding, the guys had gotten so comfortable around me they'd cracked comments like, "I don't trust anything that can bleed for a week and not die." They'd discussed the flavor of their girlfriends' pussies and what girls from other platoons they'd like to fuck while I stared at the ground, feeling like an elephant in the room.

This time, I wanted to be seen as what I was. Not "one of the guys." Not a chick. Not even a girl. I wanted to be seen as a woman.

June 2003: Ft. Lee, VA

Three weeks into AIT at Ft. Lee, I was in formation outside the barracks, ready for the morning march to class, when I heard someone call my name.

"Hey, del Duca."

I turned around and saw a short, muscular guy wearing BDUs so vivid I knew they hadn't gone through ten washings yet. He must have been one of the poor suckers shipped to AIT right after boot camp.

"I got this friend who thinks you're real cute," he said. "You've probably heard of him. Rullen? In Second Platoon?"

"I don't know who that is," I said, glancing at Hohns, who was next to me and listening in on the conversation.

"You don't know who Rullen is?"

I shook my head. Hohns shrugged.

"You don't know who *Rullen* is," he repeated, incredulous.

"Why would I? We're in different platoons."

He held up his hands. "Okay, it doesn't matter. Look over at Second Platoon. See the guy on the end of fourth squad with the blue notebook out? That's him."

Rullen was a hunk. Tall, tan, thick, with a baby face like a young Marlon Brando. And he thought *I* was cute?

"He wants to know if maybe you want to go out next weekend if everyone gets a pass."

"Why doesn't he ask me himself?"

"What can I say? The guy's shy," he said. "But a real good guy. We were buddies all through Basic at Fort Lost in the Woods."

"I guess," I said, playing it cool. "Tell him to come say hi sometime on break." The instructors let us socialize outside and use the vending machines for fifteen minutes twice a day.

"So you'll go out with him?"

"Maybe. It'd be nice to meet him first."

The guy shifted his shoulders and let out a scoff. "Why can't you just say yes?"

I raised my eyebrows. "Because. This matchmaking thing is weird. Like a Jane Austen novel or something."

He scoffed again. "Can I at least tell him you're interested?"

"Yeah. Tell him I think he's real cute too," I said, immediately feeling like a character in *Dawson's Creek* or *My So-Called Life*. So much for Austen sophistication.

The next weekend, I met Rullen at the mall. I felt powerful in my tight jeans and black tank top and lean body, which could kick these mall-rat civilian girls' asses at everything but applying eyeliner and clinging to their boyfriends' arms. My short hair fell down around my face instead of being pulled back in clips and my chest was gloriously free of my sports bra. The only part of the uniform I'd kept were the boots, because, well, they were really comfortable and I preferred them to tennis shoes or sandals.

"You look good, girl," Rullen said, standing up from a bench outside Macy's. He had a low voice and the slow cadence of a surfer or skateboarder.

"So do you."

He wore jeans, white sneakers, and a polo shirt, his muscles bulging out of the short sleeves. We wandered, made small talk, ate a slice of pizza, and then checked into a humid hotel with a bunch of other soldiers. Before long, the booze started pouring in, even though we were all underage. Someone's bathtub became a makeshift cooler. After two beers I felt warm and tingly and not entirely balanced.

In Rullen's room, rumpling the floral bedspread, I thought we'd stop somewhere between kissing and grinding with our clothes on—build up to sex in a few weeks. I wanted a fling, not a one-night stand. Besides, I was on the rag, a detail I let slip after he took my belt off.

"Why don't you just take your tampon out?" he asked, wedging two fingers into my waistband and tugging me closer.

"But... I'll still be bleeding." With Aaron, sex during my period had been taboo. I assumed all guys thought periods were so unsexy the mere mention of them signaled immediate hands-off.

"I don't care."

How mature of him, I thought, watching him pull his shirt over his head and admiring his broad, smooth chest. *How progressive.* I checked in with Future Rosa. I imagined myself the next day. Then the next week. The next month. The next year. Would I regret sleeping with this hot guy? *No,* I concluded. *I am going to enjoy this while I have the chance.* Could alcohol be screwing with my judgment? *Of course not.* Did I remember using this same, mind-blowingly faulty litmus test when joining the National Guard? *Not a chance.*

The next weekend, I was even more confident. I had a "fuck buddy." As someone who had felt awkward her whole life, I'd never imagined myself having a fuck buddy. I felt sophisticated, in control—a cool girl. On Saturday I escaped base with the rest of the horde on pass. Again, we converged at the only place we could think of: the mall. We traveled in packs. My pack eventually met up with Rullen's pack and we piled in cabs and made our way to the same hotel. I cruised from room to room with Rullen, drinking a beer here, a beer there, thinking how we were all Cinderellas, flaunting our civilian sides for a night before being delivered back to Army drudgery. Around midnight, Rullen and I grabbed an abandoned bottle of wine, still half full, and headed back to his room. We peeled each other's clothes off, garment by garment, and reveled in each other's bodies, the smooth slide and grip of skin against skin. His hot, wet mouth traveled from my lips to my breasts and back. We came like polite fuck buddies: me first, then him, no dramatic moans, no cuddling afterward—that would be too intimate.

"Why are you so quiet?" Rullen asked the next morning.

I was standing at the hotel room door, looking out across the parking lot, waiting for him to get ready so we could grab breakfast before returning to base. I shrugged. "I'm just thinking."

"Why don't you watch TV or something?"

I glanced at the cartoons he had blaring. "Because it doesn't interest me."

"You are the weirdest girl I've ever been with." The soft quality of his voice was gone.

I turned around, my arms gripping each other in a strange hug. "What do you mean by weird?"

"This," he waved his arms. "Standing there staring off into space. Always quiet. Is there something wrong with you?"

"Like I said, I'm thinking."

"Why don't you talk?"

"What do you want to talk about?"

"I don't know. Anything."

"I guess I don't talk unless I have something to say."

He grabbed his wallet off the bedside table, and on opening it, shook his head. My eyes traveled over his compact body—a body you got from long hours at the gym and steady doses of creatine. A slow dread crept up my throat as I reexamined his manufactured tan, the way he fixed his hair, his frat boy clothes, his expensive white shoes. I'd been wrong. He wasn't a shy and sweet "good guy." He was an asshole jock who was actually entertained by his shallow and crass platoon buddies and who relied on his good looks to get what he wanted.

I thought about my own body—how in the shower girls sometimes asked me if my breasts were real. How the drill sergeants had singled me out to model the Class

A uniform for the company's officers when we were getting fitted. How Rullen had teased me for my ridiculously long legs, had asked me if my lips were "natural," if they were "always swoll like that." I caught a glimpse of myself in the wide mirror over the sink at the back of the room. I saw the same ungainly, scrappy girl I'd always seen. Slender and a little busty, yes, but with huge hands and feet and a weak chin and small eyes and thin hair. I saw me. Did everyone else see a girl with fake boobs who Botoxed her lips? Did Rullen see a self-conscious fool who'd be an easy lay with a little flattery?

I leaned against the door frame and shrank into myself. "You want me to be all bubbly and flirty, don't you?" I could picture exactly the kind of girls he'd dated in the past. Girls who wouldn't in a million years entertain the idea of joining the Army to pay for school.

Rullen shoved his wallet in a back pocket. "Well, yeah, flirty would be more fun than what you are now. Hey, can you pay for the room like you offered last night? I'm broke."

"Sure." I turned back around and stared past the parking lot to the green swath that was Ft. Lee, for once looking forward to covering myself head to toe in camouflage—marching in rhythm in a sea of green, black and brown. I wanted to hide, to disappear, to be one of the guys again, even though I knew I'd never really been one of them. The guys weren't even "one of the guys." They were caught up in their own struggle to be seen as manly men. That is the lure of the US Army, the Green Machine, its gears clicking and whirring and whispering *almost. Parachute out some planes, see some action, get some scars, watch the great maw of death open and close. Then you'll be one of the guys. A hero.*

Or is it the machine that's doing the whispering? Could be Hollywood or Washington or the news. Could be the ads on the subway or the football game cheerleaders or the boys playing video games next door, racking up virtual kills. Could be everything combined.

And as for me being seen as a woman, it was glaringly obvious I was still a girl.

17. The Script

July 2003: Ft. Lee, VA

One day, soon after the Rullen debacle, we didn't have class for some reason. We spent the morning cleaning, and around 11:30, the females headed outside. We were slated to march to chow at 11:40 a.m. by ourselves, instead of being escorted like daycare kids.

Come 11:40, a few of the males had started to trickle out of the barracks but we were nowhere near ready to leave. We stood and chatted, surveying each other's ironing jobs and boot shines. If one of us looked too sharp at any given moment, the rest would get dropped into the front leaning rest, just as if one of us looked too "ate up," we'd all get dropped. I had a strip of nylon in my pocket in case someone's boots looked dull, a trick I'd adopted from my recruiter. As for ironing, there wasn't much you could do about that last-minute.

"Where is everyone?" I asked Santos. I had grown keenly adept at recognizing the atmosphere of an impending punishment, and we were fast approaching the point of no return. So much for AIT being more lax than boot camp.

He shrugged his thick shoulders. "Buffing the floor, I guess. That's what they were doing when I left."

Drill Sergeant LaMonte sauntered out of the building, hopping down the front steps with a carefree abandon that flaunted his degree of absolute power over us.

Seeing us, he did an exaggerated double take, checking his watch and then posing like Peter Pan, fists on hips.

Part of me liked Drill Sergeant LaMonte, even though he was impossible to please, condescending, conniving, unforgiving, and unforgetting. Maybe it was his theatrics, like he was playing the role of himself through our eyes. Or how he looked like a little drill sergeant doll, standing just 5'4", including the Smokey Bear hat. Seeing him, we all shut up and straightened.

LaMonte took his time walking to formation. He paused to scuff a crack in the cement, bent to examine a dropped pen, whirled to admire the barracks framed against a brilliant blue sky, and finally stopped in front of our gangly platoon leader, who had raced into position moments before. Making a face, LaMonte noisily sucked his teeth. "How's life treatin' ya today, Richards? Do ya feel *gooooood*?"

"Yes, Drill Sergeant," Richards said.

"Yes *what*? I asked you two questions. And one of them was not a yes or no question."

"Yes I feel good, Drill Sergeant."

"So I guess life's treatin' you all right?"

"Yes, Drill Sergeant."

"What about Newman, Banks, Lee, Kirtner, blah blah blah? You think life's treatin' them all right?" By this time Drill Sergeant LaMonte was standing inches from Richards, smiling up at him, his face glowing with amusement. The fact that Richards was a foot taller than him failed to disturb LaMonte. He seemed to enjoy intimidating large people.

"I don't know."

"You don't know *what*?"

"I don't know, Drill Sergeant."

LaMonte backed off. I shifted in my boots, growing more lethargic and irritable by the second in the sweltering Virginia sun. It was a CAT 5 day, the highest heat category ranking the Army has. CAT 5 days are anything over 90 degrees, and regulations stipulate that soldiers should only do ten minutes of hard work per hour. But we all knew that if the Army actually followed these precautions, nothing would ever get done. A drop of sweat worked its way down my spine. I imagined myself back in Morro Bay, diving into the cold waves.

The guys continued to dribble downstairs, but Drill Sergeant LaMonte didn't let them join the regular formation. He siphoned them off to the side and started an all-male formation next to us. It was clear they were in trouble; it was the degree we were unsure of.

After everyone was accounted for, LaMonte trotted inside and reappeared with the big-boned Drill Sergeant Jennings. Unlike her male counterpart, she was not entertaining, just hard. The closest thing to a smile I'd seen on her face was a sneer that played about her lips whenever she thought we were fucking up—a frequent occurrence. I knew she had children, and this fact helped me break down the impressive aura drill sergeants have: that they never need sleep, never utter a term of endearment, never buy things like birthday presents, never fit into the role of wife or husband. As for LaMonte, it was hard to imagine him in any civilian or domestic context.

"What a hard, hard time y'all males are havin," LaMonte began, pacing in front of us in his slow, swaggering way. "Ya can't seem to do the simplest things, like show up on time for a march to chow. Now the females, they got it down. Johnson, what time were all y'all females out here?"

"11:30, Drill Sergeant."

"Richards, did you have a different time than 11:40 written down for formation?"

"No, Drill Sergeant," Richards said, eyes uncertain. I felt sorry for him. He really wasn't cut out to be platoon leader with that cautious demeanor of his.

"Then why didn't you get the males down here on time? Wouldn't that be one of your responsibilities?"

"I must have lost track of time, Drill Sergeant. I told all the squad leaders to make sure everyone got to formation on time."

"Yet you yourself was late. Do you see the problem here? Ya delegated, but ya can't trust the squad leaders, and ya can't trust yourself. So who *can* ya trust?" LaMonte rocked up onto his toes and bounced, looking at us in exaggerated innocence.

"Looks like you can trust the females," said Jennings, covering a yawn.

The sun beat down on us, the heat releasing the stale smell of starch from our uniforms.

"Let's iron this out." LaMonte marched the males across the road and into a field of tall weeds and grass. He didn't waste any time in dropping them. Jennings led the females in single file, our boots clumping on the pavement, then the grass swishing against our pants. She lined us up overlooking the field where LaMonte was smoking the boys. The air blurred with heat. My clothes felt heavier by the minute, clinging to my sweaty skin at every crease and fold. I wanted to take my cap off so badly I settled for lifting it a few seconds while pretending to check my hair clips.

"The bear crawl!" LaMonte shouted, his voice especially nasal from far away.

"The bear crawl!" the boys echoed, taking crouched positions, asses in the air, hands on the ground in front of them, ready to lumber forward. Of all PT exercises, the bear crawl is the most embarrassing.

"Down to the road and back. Go, go, go!"

Bumping into each other, grass hitting them in the face, the guys bear crawled to the road and back as fast as they could. Even at a distance, I could see they were breathing hard when they returned to the starting line. Their chests were out, jaws raised. Some had hands on their hips. But that was just the beginning.

"The flutter kick!"

"The burpee!"

"Low crawl!"

"High crawl!"

"The sit-up!"

"The push-up!"

I looked around at the other girls. They stared at the ground or out over the field, trying to look impassive and failing. Sweat and guilt for being spared this punishment slicked our faces. It violated everything I'd seen so far. We were one unit during the day, no gender distinctions. Did LaMonte want to drive a wedge between us? I almost started walking toward them. I knew the rest of the females would follow. But it was so oppressively hot, and I didn't know how LaMonte or Jennings would react, and the smoking had gone on so long it had to end soon.

"All right, line up," LaMonte shouted below us, evidently unimpressed by the guys' performance. "Two- to three-second rushes. Pretend you have a rifle. Down to the road and back. And I want you yelling, 'I'm up, they see me, I'm down.' Go!"

Two- to three-second rushes are how you're supposed to advance under fire. You start in the prone position, lying down with your rifle, popping a couple shots off. Then you push yourself up, sprint for two to three seconds, and throw yourself down, letting the butt of the rifle help break your fall. To time it out, you're supposed to scream, "I'm up, they see me, I'm down."

Our guys had no rifles to help break their falls. And by then the searing heat had reduced them to putty. Some didn't get up right away after they flung themselves down. Some encouraged each other. Muller's cap fell off and he took his time picking it up. LaMonte was right there in his face, the thick tendon in his neck straining. "What are you doing, private?" Muller slapped his cap back on and took off running. "I'm up, they see me..." Next, LaMonte charged at DuNorde, who was crouched in the trampled grass, a hand pressed against his stomach. "Get up. Who told you to stop? You're pissing me off. You're all shit pissing me off!"

The twelve of us girls snuck angry glances at each other.

"I know it's hard to watch," Jennings said, surprising us. She stood in front, her back to us. "Just be glad you're not down there."

The yells of "I'm up, they see me, I'm down," trailed off. Santos stumbled and barely caught himself. Brown doubled over, dry heaving. LaMonte switched back to flutter kicks, and one last round of the bear crawl.

Back in one formation, we could smell the crushed grass and dirt on the males' uniforms, the sweat soaking their undershirts. Their breathing was loud. Some of them had trouble standing upright. I wanted to reach out and steady Lee in front of me, but I was afraid moving would attract more of LaMonte's wrath.

In the chow hall, the guys picked at their food, staring into space.

"Aren't you starving after all that?" I asked Richards, who sat across from me, head down, even his water untouched.

He raised his head. "I'm too sick to eat."

I set down my fork, ashamed of my perfectly pressed uniform, my immaculately polished boots, my full stomach, my muscles taut with energy.

The guys on either side of Richards nodded.

"Me too."

"I think I'll puke if I swallow anything right now. Anderson already puked."

On my way to return my tray I saw Anderson dumping his lunch in the garbage. A dark patch marred the back of his jacket and I overheard him telling Lee, "He made me roll in it." Whether this was true or not, whether LaMonte actually ordered him to roll in his own bile or Anderson fell in it while trying to do as he was told, didn't matter. A hatred for LaMonte that had been pooling in me for the last hour set like cement.

Everyone else got over the humiliating smoking in a week or two. "I can understand why he did it," they said, or "It was harsh, but I'm not one to hold a grudge." And once they could move without wincing, the guys agreed, "It wasn't that bad anyway."

• • •

While I was nowhere close to forgiving LaMonte, I had better things to think about—mainly, Private Santos, despite my plan to avoid guys after what had happened with Rullen.

"Your last name sounds like a boxer's," Santos told me one day on break. We lived for these short interruptions. Learning about fuel from an Army instructor was akin to watching paint dry. "Put your dukes up, del Duke."

I shook my head.

"C'mon. Give me a little combo." Santos was muscular, but not bulky like Rullen, with ink-black hair and an easy smile that, at its fullest, pulled down the corners of his large, dark eyes. I was a sucker for brown eyes. He held out his palms, one higher than the other, and got low, bracing himself. "Right here. One little pop."

I tucked my thumbs into my fists and gave a jab.

"Whoa, whoa, whoa. That's a good way to break a bone." He rearranged my hands, thumbs out. "Now this time, give me a little shuffle and a nose touch." He skipped back, then forward, fists raised, one hand whipping up for his thumb to brush the side of his nose.

I smiled and shook my head again. He rubbed his hands together, then motioned me forward, thick brows furrowed in mock seriousness. I pulled my BDU cap low and sprung into character, rolling my shoulders, rocking back and shuffling to the side. We circled. The rest of our group stepped back and watched. I sniffed and did the thumb brush, then a bob and a weave, two sharp jabs to his palm with my right, my fist hitting at the end of my reach.

"Holy hell, she's a killer," Santos said, dropping his hands. I felt him looking past the uniform, past the tomboy armor. "Where did that come from?" he asked.

I shrugged, not wanting to admit that what little I knew about boxing came from Robert Lipsyte books I'd read as a kid.

Santos started sitting next to me in class. He took NoDoz so he could nudge me awake when I began to drift off. In a surprising show of emotional maturity for a twenty-year-old Army guy, he slipped me poems and notes. He would find ways to touch me throughout the day, like running a finger over the back of my hand when he passed. When we got a trip to the PX, the Army's version of a general store, he bought walkie-talkies so we could talk after lights out from our opposite sides of the barracks.

"Tell me about your family," he'd say. "Tell me about your home town. What are you like in the civilian world?"

If we had time, we would meet by the gazebo after dinner chow and pretend to polish our boots. This was a popular tactic with anyone nursing a clandestine crush. One particular night I was outside with Hohns, White, Lee, Kirtner, and Santos. Hohns had the hots for Lee, White was being chased by Kirtner, and I'd become smitten with Santos.

We gossiped about platoon politics, our boot-shine kits spread out in front of us in case a drill sergeant walked by. The sun went down. Inch by inch, we started to look more like couples than a scattered group. A few fireflies came out. The warm evening air and the silhouette of the gazebo against the sunset and our puppy-love giddiness tricked us into thinking we weren't entirely bound by the rules of this strange prison.

"Let's go sit against the wall," Santos said, jerking his head toward the barracks. "Anyone inside could look out the window right now and see us."

"Why don't you want anyone to see us?"

"Because I want to kiss you, del Duca."

The wall was awfully far from the other females. But I knew I wouldn't get another shot at my first kiss with Santos for four days, when we were due to get our next off-base pass. And *this* first kiss I craved with overwhelming guilt and trepidation. This was the fling I was meant to have. He stood up and started backing away. I followed.

His lips were soft and full, his mouth warm, his body close, magnetic. He ran his fingers up my forearm, over the inner curve of my elbow, up my long, narrow bicep, under my short PT sleeve to my bare shoulder. I pressed a hand to his chest.

Drill Sergeant LaMonte rounded the corner like a shadow. "What are y'all doing out here, Hohns? It's lights out in five minutes."

Hohns's head jerked up and it took her a second to respond. "Nothing, Drill Sergeant. Just shining boots."

Because we were up against the wall, Santos and I could see LaMonte, but he couldn't see us. Santos scrambled a few feet away from me, and I rushed to grab my boots and shine kit, adrenaline roaring in my ears. I popped to my feet and was inching back toward the other females when LaMonte turned and saw us.

"Aw hell no," he drawled, stalking up to me. "Where's your battle buddy, del Duca?"

I pointed at Hohns.

"No, she's not your battle buddy. She's too far away. You don't *have* one. Y'all thought you'd sneak over here and do a little *face* suckin', huh, Santos?"

Santos stood up and snapped to parade rest. "Drill Sergeant, we were just doing boots, using the light from the windows."

"Bull. Shit. Both of you come with me."

Feeling like a petty criminal, I locked eyes with Santos behind LaMonte's back. Inside, he led us into his office and closed the door. He got up in my face, so close I could see his pores and the deep creases between his eyebrows, and how his front teeth were so square they looked fake. Even though I was five inches taller than him, he seemed to tower over me.

"Del Duca. Why were you so far away from the other females?" His breath smelled like coffee.

"No excuses, Drill Sergeant," I said, looking down at the scratched and chipped tile. Observation and experience had proven that the quicker you acknowledged there was absolutely no excuse for your crime, the sooner you were doled out your punishment and released.

"And you, Santos. Here you've been an example all this time. Why would you throw it away to fraternize? Shit pissing stupid." LaMonte backed off a step and looked at his watch. "Here's what I'm thinking. I get off in an hour. How about I smoke ya until then? Either that, or you forfeit your weekend passes."

We glanced at each other. I thought about the embarrassment of sweating and straining and dropping to the floor in muscle failure in front of Santos. But I really, really wanted that weekend pass.

"How about it?"

"Yes, Drill Sergeant," I said, eager to get it over with.

LaMonte scoffed at me and turned to Santos. "That seem fair to you, Santos?"

Santos gave an enthusiastic "Huah."

That really irked LaMonte. "Changed my mind. I'm gonna smoke ya *and* tell Jennings to take away your passes. *And* slap you both with an Article 15 for fraternizing." LaMonte ran his cutting glare over us.

I concocted sappy scenarios. I imagined that one day Santos and I would tell our children how we'd stood shoulder to shoulder, knowing deep down that our first kiss was worth any punishment—that any penalty was merely a testament to our devotion. We said nothing.

LaMonte stalled, looking back and forth from Santos to me. We were both ready to drop into the push-up position, but he never gave the order. Then the atmosphere in the room changed. I saw the glimmer of a smirk cross LaMonte's face—not a cruel smirk, but a smile of recognition or chagrin. "Go on, get out of here," he barked. "I don't got time for this."

Before parting ways at the bottom of the stairs, I shared a look of incredulous victory with Santos. Jogging down the female hallway, I made a beeline for my wall locker and my walkie-talkie, hidden in a pair of socks. Receiver in hand, I headed into one of the empty bunk rooms that we cleaned furiously every week, but that still looked like it belonged in some building tagged for demolition.

My walkie-talkie crackled alive. "Holy shit, del Duca. That was a close one."

"I can't believe he let us go," I said, nestling into a corner and dumping the contents of my boot shine kit.

"Why'd he do it?" Santos asked.

"Hell if I know. Maybe because he was a troublemaker too when he was a private? But an hour-long smoking would have been worth it. You are quite the kisser."

I heard whoops and exaggerated crooning in the background, then Santos shouted, "Guys! Shut up. I'm trying to have a private conversation." To me he said, "Now I'm in real trouble."

"Sorry! I always forget you're surrounded by people over there." The females barely filled two bunk rooms. I finished rubbing a layer of black polish on one boot and started buffing with the horsehair brush.

"Hold on, hold on." After a long pause he asked in a low voice, "You know what I'm going to do this weekend?"

"Are you alone?"

"Yeah."

"You're going to kiss me again. A lot."

"Yeah. And I'm going to tell my mom about you. She would love you. I wish you could meet her. You ever been to Texas?"

• • •

You would think LaMonte's unexpected generosity would make me see him differently, but I kept on resenting him as much as I resented myself. I hated myself for blindly joining something that felt more and more wrong by the month. Not even Santos could quell the mounting dread. And I hated LaMonte for abusing his power. When it came right down to it, we were all the same rank in this carefully crafted drama. Extras. The chorus. Stagehands. Bound to *the script*.

Our trailer five miles from Fromberg, MT, Summer 1997.

Hiking with Leila and Java about a mile from the trailer, Fall 1997.

From left to right, me, Leila, Alura, Mom, 1987, Phoenixville, PA, my grandparents' house.

The family Spring 1999, after the move into Fromberg due to Mom and "Wayne's" split.

That first picture of me in an Army uniform. Late 1999 or early 2000.

My college roommate, Jill, and Devil Cat, Missoula MT, 2001.

In front of my bunk with my mother the day before boot camp graduation at Ft. Jackson, SC, Summer, 2002.

Me in my Class A's, right after boot camp graduation.

Aaron and me near Morro Bay, CA, 2003.

Surfing with Aaron in Morro Bay, CA, 2003.

A rare moment of down time during AIT at Ft. Lee, VA, Summer 2003.

Polishing boots with "Santos" by the gazebo, Summer 2003.

Part II

End of Innocence

1. Love and Band-Aids

August 2003: Morro Bay, CA

The day after I got back from AIT, my mother called. "How was graduation? How was your trip home?"

"I'm in love," I said.

She took this in stride and, without a shred of dubiousness, encouraged my gushing. Gush I did, not only to my mom, but to my sisters, my roommates, DJ Sasquatch, my hairdresser, and the women at work (I was now the obituary editor at the *San Luis Obispo Tribune*). I even told Aaron, against my better judgment. The plan was to visit Santos in Texas when he finished his post-AIT training, meet his family, and then move south to be together. I pictured us raising a pack of children on the edge of the desert with his huge and warm family nearby, endless summers, and once we both fulfilled our contracts, bliss bliss bliss all around.

It was hard to keep in touch. I had to be home at a time when Santos had access to the pay phones. Hoping to catch his calls, I started rushing home instead of hanging out at KCPR after class. About a month after I got back from AIT, and after about ten days of radio silence from Santos, I picked up the phone and heard his deep voice.

"Del Dukes. What are you up to?"

"Finally! I've been missing you like crazy."

A ruckus burst out behind him—shouts and scuffling. He hollered something back, but the phone was muffled.

He came back on the line laughing. "There are some real psychos here. Nothing like boot camp or AIT. And the females are the worst ones."

"Are you getting my letters?" I asked.

"I got a couple. How many did you send?"

"I send you a letter almost every day. They're not getting through?"

"You know how it is." More shrieks behind him. The line went muddy as he covered the receiver.

I let out a slow sigh he couldn't hear. "Did you at least get the book of stamps I sent you?" The last time we'd spoken he'd complained about not having time to go to the PX.

"I got 'em."

This was apparently all he had to say on the matter. "Well, you should use them," I said, careful to keep my voice light. "I can't wait until you're done with training. Time is moving so slow."

"I sent you a letter."

"That was like two weeks ago."

"What exactly do you expect from me? You know, you're acting pretty needy."

The plastic of the phone creaked and I realized I was squeezing it. "I don't see how me wanting to talk to you is needy." Where was the guy who couldn't get enough of me?

"Dude, every time I hear from you, it's 'I miss you so much and why don't you call me more and why don't you write to me?' Don't you have other stuff to do? It's getting old."

My throat, my chest, felt tight. *Getting old?*

"You're like a different person," he went on. "I don't think things are going to work out with us."

"Wait, slow down. Let's talk about this. How do you think I'm a different person?"

"You've changed. You're a civilian again. This is probably who you naturally are—needy and nagging when I call you. It's just not going to work."

"You're not even going to give me a chance? That's it? You're the one acting completely different all of a sudden." I was too angry to cry.

"I'm the same. You're somebody I thought I knew. Look, it's not the end of the world. We were only together for like two months."

"This is coming out of nowhere! Two weeks ago we were planning for me to come out for your graduation. Can't we talk about it in person then?"

"Don't come. I think we should break up now. Us working was a long shot anyway. Plus I don't want to feel guilty dating girls here."

"Oh, so that's what this is really about."

"It's about both. Look, I gotta go. I'm sorry."

My anger collapsed into devastation and spread like an infection in the following days and weeks. Driving home from school, I would get teary thinking about Santos. Walking in the door, I'd let my book bag drop, do a check of the house to make sure I was alone, and return to the living room, away from sharp objects, to cry for as long as an hour before I cut off the waterworks by retrieving my scissors from my room and adding to the collection of red hash marks on my arms. I felt like my organs had been harvested, like I was missing things vital to function, like I had lost who would have become the great love of my life. And right after I'd told *everyone* about that love.

Santos's transformation and my reaction to heartbreak mortified me. I started to wonder whether I was the most gullible girl on the planet: my recruiter with his seemingly perfect college deal, Rullen, Santos, how I kept forgiving Dad instead of cutting him off like everyone else. I wondered if there was something wrong with me, how I couldn't control my emotions. I wondered how I would bear another three years in the National Guard. And finally, I wondered whether Santos had been some kind of crutch or blindfold, a way to tolerate the organization I felt increasingly at odds with.

In hindsight, this was exactly the case. I wasn't just upset over the loss of Santos. The Band-Aid I'd contrived to cover up my festering angst and unease had been ripped off. Having completed Basic Training and AIT, I was now fully eligible to be called up at any moment. When I returned to drill at Camp Roberts the unit had several new members, including a commanding officer whose goal was to reach capacity as soon as possible. Then in October, thousands of California National Guard troops were called up. I was on borrowed time. Everybody was.

Because I was so engulfed in regretting my contract, so obsessed with my heartbreak, and so committed to wallowing in misery alone, I turned to my trusty friend, physical pain, for help. When I was bleeding, that was all I could think about. Instead of compounding my problems, it actually served a purpose in a warped way. Not only did I snap out of whatever emotional tailspin I was caught in, but afterward, I had to think about things like how to hide my cuts and what to wear that would irritate them the least, how to shower without getting stinging soapy water on them. Every time I winced, the Guard and Santos were pushed down a notch in the pecking order of worries. Plus I had the power to shout "help!" without uttering a word. I knew that if I wore a T-shirt around Aaron or DJ Sasquatch, I could count on them to ask me what was going on—a manipulative trump card that I used sparingly, but to gratifying effect. I needed to hear that yes, I was in a mess, I wasn't a drama queen inventing problems to get attention.

Not that I would have been able to express any of this at the time. In those days, I only knew cutting myself allowed me to act relatively normal when I felt like a hostage forgotten in the next room.

March 2004: San Luis Obispo, CA

Fall and Winter quarter after AIT passed. By the spring quarter, I was the news director at KCPR, making sure Professor Madsen got his daily live news broadcasts, and hosting two music shows a week.

I wasn't exactly in the throes of complacency regarding the war, but I had settled into a comfortable resignation. My Engineering Company at Camp Roberts was struggling to grow. Every time someone wanted to transfer into our unit, they were called up. Things were so desperate that Sergeant Morgan had even bought ad space on KCPR to try to generate interest. I recorded and voiced the thirty-second spot myself, finding construction sound effects for the beginning and fading in one of my favorite Lemonheads tracks at the end.

"Sounds professional," Morgan had said, clapping me on the back when I showed him the final product. "Don't be shy about talking up our unit if anyone calls for more info. We've got a lot of spots to fill."

I politely shined him on. I knew how small KCPR's audience was, and I was also pretty sure our listeners weren't the type to run down to the recruitment office. When we weren't playing the latest experimental stuff, we were broadcasting *Democracy Now!*

At first, half of me dismissed what I heard on *Democracy Now!* as borderline conspiracy theories. But the more I listened, the more I was riveted by a mounting sense of injustice and unease. Amy Goodman was the only journalist calling our presence in Iraq an "occupation" and talking about Iraqi "resistance" to this. She was the only one keeping tabs on how the rest of the world saw the war, the only one suggesting the oil industry, independent contractors, and Wall Street were gaining from the war at the expense of everyone else, and the only one meticulously tracking deaths. On March 19, 2004, the one-year anniversary of the invasion of Iraq, Goodman told us about protests across the globe, how two Iraqi journalists had been gunned down by American soldiers, how the civilian death toll could be as high as 10,000, and how 29,000 US troops had been killed, wounded or injured. She interviewed two "deserters" who had come back from a tour and gone on the run. In that dry, near-monotone of hers, Goodman delivered a stark and very different narrative than the one being told everywhere else. I started to question the way mainstream media outlets were covering the war.

A few days after the one-year anniversary of the start of combat operations in Iraq, I was standing at the counter outside KCPR's on-air room, pawing through a stack of graded playlists to find my own. The music coming out of the speaker above my head faded and DJ Sasquatch started talking in his trademark mumble. "Before I sign off, a plug for Atom and His Package. He's in town next Saturday at SLO Brew. The guy's super keen. And so is his package. Okay, his package is really an accordion-type thing. But still. You have to see it..."

A tall guy in a black T-shirt, black corduroys, and an old-fashioned black hat looked at me expectantly from the studio doorway. "Can't argue with a pitch like that. Are you going to be there?"

I didn't understand what he was asking. "Where?"

"The Atom and His Package show."

"Oh. Not if it's at SLO Brew. I'm not twenty-one yet."

"You're kidding. How old are you?"

"A month shy of twenty-one."

"You don't have a fake ID?"

I raised my shoulders. "Never knew anyone who could make one." And I was way too much of a rule follower to use one.

"What a travesty." He was looking at me like a wolf tracking an injured lamb. I loved it, but I also had no idea how to respond, so I stuffed my playlists into my backpack and looked for an escape route.

He stuck his hand out. "I don't think we've met. I'm Zack, the engineer. I make sure you guys stay on air." He shook my hand too long, gazing in my eyes with a steadiness that made me squirm.

"Are you a student here?" I asked.

"No, I'm a bit older than you kids."

The next time I spoke to Zack, he had traded the top hat for a straw boater and was wearing a collared shirt and old-fashioned vest. He strolled into sun-dappled Mitchell Park with a waifish, adoring brunette on his arm and registered for the KCPR Kissathon, which I had helped organize for my public relations class. The couple that locked lips the longest won a night at a fancy hotel in town, dinner for two, and some other odds and ends my team had managed to get our hands on.

"Nice day for it," Zack said, tipping his hat at me. "Where do I sign this doll up?" He smiled a romantic huckster smile at the waif as I admired his tapered torso, his trimmed beard and Old West mustache, how he seemed remarkably at ease with himself and everything around him.

I spent the next five hours trying not to watch Zack and his "doll" kiss, clown around, and dance to the soundtrack I had devised, starting with Marvin Gaye's "Let's Get It On." They won second place. I didn't stick around to hand out prizes.

A month later I was in San Luis Obispo's news talk station, KVEC, reading over some copy in the prep room, when I heard someone pass in the hall, then stop. Turning around, I realized the *someone* was less than a foot away. My eyes were level with a pair of broad, defined pecs under a black T-shirt. I looked up at Zack, who smiled down at me, his top hat perched perfectly, one thin eyebrow raised.

"You scared me," I said, grateful my gasp hadn't been louder than a sharp intake of breath.

"Did I?" There was a predatory sharpness to his brown eyes.

I blushed and took a step back. This guy was *pursuing* me. The Kissathon waif must be old news.

"I didn't know you worked here," he said.

"I got an internship."

"Why wasn't I notified?" He was suddenly talking like a radio announcer from 1930, or maybe Groucho Marx. "Come upstairs and visit me when you get the chance. I'll give you the extended tour. The tour I'm sure the news dorks didn't give you." He backed into the hallway, digging in his pocket and pulling out a vibrating Blackberry.

I could hear his heavy black boots on the stairs around the corner. Thump, thump, thump, and then a pause.

"Is there anything stopping you from having lunch with me this week?" he called, his voice still in radio affectation. "Or how about dinner?"

I smiled and counted to three slowly, pretending I was weighing the invitation. "I'm up for lunch. What day?"

"I'll have my people consult your people when you arrive for your tour."

Forgetting all about the dangers of infatuation, seeing an exciting distraction from ever-looming war worries, I would soon be hopelessly smitten once again.

2. The Call

August 2004: San Luis Obispo, CA

After our breakup Aaron moved from Morro Bay to San Luis Obispo and tried to avoid me. But I missed him so much that I started inviting myself over every Thursday night, when he and his roommates meandered downtown for four-dollar plates of lo mein at the big farmers market. Eventually, I convinced him to apply to be a DJ at KCPR, even though he wasn't a student. In the summer of 2004, we launched a weekend kids' show together—not because we loved kids necessarily, but out of nostalgia for our own childhoods, I think. Looking back, it makes perfect sense that I would take comfort in the simplicity and innocence of a kids' radio show given what Adult Rosa was dealing with at the time. The songs we put on the air were silly escapes and the stories we played were about underdogs and unlikely heroes.

On a warm, lazy Saturday, two weeks before fall classes began, we were halfway through *The Point*, narrated by Ringo Starr and one of the Brady Bunch boys, when my cell phone rang.

"This is Sergeant Morgan. I got bad news, girl."

A fist grabbed my heart and squeezed. There was no question what "bad news" meant. I wanted to force the words backward, clamp a hand over the phone's receiver, trap them inside.

"I'm real sorry," Morgan said.

I stared at the scribbles on top of the new releases box. *Hello. Burnt dog radio. Class of '86.* I could hear Aaron playing our show's theme song on his ukulele in the next room over, and Ringo telling us that Oblio and his dog Arrow had reached the Pointless Forest.

Morgan cleared his throat. "I suppose I should be more clear, more official. You've been put on a mobilization list. You've been called up in support of Operation Iraqi Freedom. It's an eighteen-month activation."

No, no, no. This isn't supposed to happen this way. We're nowhere near capacity.

"Is the rest of the unit called up?"

"Just you. I guess they're putting you in a unit that needs another fueler."

I didn't even remember how to do any of that fueler stuff. It had been a year since training, and that training had consisted mostly of multiple-choice quizzes. Maybe I could try to find some kind of manual to study. "What do I do? Should I be packing? Should I tell all my professors?"

"It's not immediate, but I'd tell your teachers, your boss, your landlord. Next month you need to report to Soldier Readiness Processing. They call it SRP."

"When am I supposed to leave?" I couldn't control the pitch of my voice.

"All I know is your SRP date. Your mobilization date will be a few weeks after."

He waited for me to respond. I couldn't. I felt like I was trapped at the edge of Earth's atmosphere, watching the pieces of my life tumble into outer space—Zack, the radio station, surfing, all the classes I was looking forward to, my freedom to do and say and feel what I wanted.

"Well, I'll let you go. I'm sure you want to tell your family and whatnot. I'll call you when I know more."

My throat tight and aching, I forced out, "Thank you."

"What just happened?" Aaron was at the studio door, staring at me with a rare intensity, his ukulele cradled, hands frozen mid-strum.

I burst into tears.

Driving home to Morro Bay, a dull roar filled my ears as I time traveled. There I was in the counselor's office, hungry eyes panning the numbers, doing the math. There I was at the kitchen table, signing, signing, signing, and in the ceremony room swearing in, my right hand raised, oaths rolling up my throat, out of my mouth, into the world of consequence. There was the rebel soldier at Ft. Jackson. *Say you refuse to train, and they'll let you go*. There was the sergeant at the beginning of my second boot camp. *You came back?*

I slammed my hand on the steering wheel and then up into the ceiling, *bang bang bang*. I rolled down all the windows and drove in a windstorm, shouting at my reflection in the rearview mirror.

3. Panic

August 2004: San Luis Obispo, CA

I didn't tell my family right away. I spent days raging and pining and imagining myself turning into a completely different person overseas—a shadow, a mannequin. I started a journal and sat on campus benches, filling the pages.

8/27/04

I finally started this journal. The reason why? So I don't go insane thinking about things too much. I am on a mobilization list, but I don't want to talk about it because there is nothing to tell.

I met someone. His name is Zack and I like him even though I feel it's dangerous to do so. He is hard to read and unpredictable and mysterious but I would like to think he's not a jerk, not another Santos. He's certainly more mature. I hope I get to spend time with him and don't get shipped off never knowing what could have happened. I'm so afraid of people leaving me. As much as I push people away I don't like to be alone.

I'm powerless, just sitting here waiting! But there's nothing I can do and as Zack pointed out earlier, I will be pissed later if I waste so much time and energy worrying. Either way I need to make the most of every day.

I need to get my ass in gear and finish my fantasy fiction book. Then I can have Alura and Leila send it around to publishers while I'm gone, if I go. I really do think it's publishable. It's certainly better than some of the trash already out there. It's getting better at least. I'm not an eighth grader anymore.

8/30/04

Going slowly insane. I was pacing the house but my roommate came back and is downstairs. I am "battle rostered" with a unit out of Louisiana. The details are filling in. Freaking out. I almost broke down at work. Zack isn't here and is going to Burning Man soon.

I wonder if who I am will die after full-time war zone Army crap for nearly two years. I don't think I can handle it, seriously. I would do practically anything to get out of this!

I am trying to stay positive but I feel like I'm on a roller coaster and it's mostly on steep drops. I'm a miserable worm! My life is perfect! I swear I would have nothing to complain about the majority of the rest of my life if I could be spared from this. I want to cut myself so bad every night and the only thing stopping me is I don't want my coworkers asking me questions. If it were winter and I could wear long sleeves every day then I would. I need to find a new way to hurt myself that isn't so obvious.

Why do I cry out for God as soon as I'm in a mess? Is there something primal in having faith when normally I believe myself above it? It's convoluted to think God would acknowledge someone who doubts his existence the majority of the time.

I feel like I'm living out some horrid fairy tale where the evil witch tells you it's time to pay dearly for that minute when you asked for something for yourself.

9/07/04

I am officially "activated." I do SRP this weekend and am supposed to leave October 15. The number eighteen is haunting me. Eighteen months. I think I'll go insane. I cannot fight a war. I don't want any connection to what we are doing over there. We end up killing all the wrong people.

I'm doing surprisingly well, I think. I go through phases of depression, despair, confidence, optimism, and then sadness, but I've realized it's not the end of the world. It's just really horrible and it won't last forever. Unless I die. People better be outraged if I die! I keep wanting to say "I'm going to be so pissed if I get killed" before I remember that no I won't. I'll be dead.

A lot of mornings, ever since I was in middle or high school, I wake up and I'm confused as to whether I'm dead or have been dead or I only have a fleeting moment left to live before I go back to an enveloping blackness of nothing. This morning I had to slap myself hard three times in the face before I could get a grip. If I think about it too much I really freak out. It makes everything meaningless and pointless and depressing and sometimes even surreal. I wonder if I could be lying dying somewhere and this is just some odd flashback before I slip away forever. Hmmm. That might make a cool short story. Wait, that already is a story.

My new roommate is more distressed about me leaving than my own mother. When I told Mom, she said, "Oh, I'm sorry. You must be disappointed. I know you were really hoping to finish school." Disappointed?! It's not just school. I'm losing my job at the Tribune, the best job I've ever had. I'm losing my job at KVEC, the field I want to work in. I'm losing my position as News Director at KCPR and my show. When I come back no one will even know me or believe I'm a DJ. And Zack. I want to find out so bad what we could be. We only just met!

Looking back on the journal now, I'm struck by the odd mix of maturity, naivety, ridiculousness, self-awareness, and obliviousness. First, I was overreacting. Yes, I'd lose my *Tribune* job, but I would probably be able to weasel my way back into KVEC and no one would forget I was a DJ at KCPR. A big lapse in school would suck, but it wouldn't be the end of the world. And Zack? He represented freedom and the future, not an epic love story waiting to happen.

What was driving the entries was fear, and not fear of mortality for the most part. I knew there was little chance of me dying or even seeing "action." I wouldn't be patrolling the streets or busting in doors, or flying around in choppers, dodging rocket-propelled grenades. I'd probably be on a convoy or two through the desert, but mostly I'd be on a base, near the fuel, which I would be pumping into trucks and helicopters and generators. A target? Yes. But a protected one.

The main source of the fear was internal and too scary to express in detail. I didn't know if I could keep up the act for eighteen months, not when I was embedded face-to-face with the manifestation of so much wrong, a war that was now an unstoppable colossus. I worried I would snap. I worried I would start cutting more and deeper or stop following orders and get into trouble. Or maybe I would sleep through the war every moment I wasn't literally fueling it and never truly wake up, even long after it was all over.

Behind the fear was anger. I was furious at myself for never thinking seriously about war before signing over six years of my life. I was pissed that Lamson had told me I'd be fighting forest fires, if anything. There were plenty of fires in Montana and California every summer, yet I'd never heard of a unit getting called up to help.

Being a college student compounded matters. On campus it was all laughter and hooking up and complaints about how hard this professor was, how "stressful" this class was. In what universe was it fair for me to spend the next eighteen months fighting a bullshit war for people who didn't even seem to know it existed?

If there had been a clear, imminent danger to mainland America, I would have felt differently. If the UN had been urging us to help stop a large-scale genocide, I would have felt differently. If there had been a devastating natural disaster abroad, I would have gone willingly and happily. Instead, there was a fuzzy war based on suspicions and driven by a campaign of misinformation. There was no link between the September 11 attacks and Saddam Hussein. Yet the US government was fighting tooth and nail to convince the public otherwise. Every single time Bush talked about the war, he brought up 9/11, like if he drew the connection enough we'd suddenly start thinking Saddam, the guy we'd caught hiding in a hole in December, was behind it all, not Osama bin Laden—not with him vanished without a trace for three years now. His strategy worked. Before long, quotes and sound bites from everyday

Americans echoed this revisionist history. Truth was a hot air balloon caught in live wires.

The journal is evidence I was nowhere near this assertive or articulate yet. Because the feelings of wrongness in my gut were complex and multi-faceted, the writing reads like the scattered diary of a worm on a hook. It skirts the core of the problem and indulges distractions. And it omits a big hope I had back then—almost an expectation: that soon, activists or Congress or *someone* would right the wrongs of the Bush administration. Certainly John Kerry would when he won the election in November.

4. The Pitch

September 2004: San Luis Obispo, CA

I was at the *Tribune*, pounding away on a paid obituary, that, as they often did, showed heartbreaking symptoms of the family's inability to paint a meaningful portrait with words: "Ted loved his woodworking and made the best sausage this side of the Rockies, as it was put by Uncle Bob." Answering my cell phone ended the temptation to rearrange the sentence and possibly face the wrath of the family.

Major Bate was on the other end. Bate was a Reserve Officer Training Corps recruiter who'd been eyeing me up at school. I hadn't paid him any mind because I had been determined to lie low in my unit that was nowhere near capacity. I hadn't counted on the Army siphoning me off to another unit.

"I heard you got called up."

His chatty tone irritated me. Had he called to gloat? "That's right. I'll have to leave in the middle of the quarter."

"Have you told your professors yet?"

I glanced back at my boss's desk. I wasn't supposed to take cell phone calls at work, but she wasn't there. "One or two. I'm waiting until I have orders for the rest. Sergeant Morgan says there's still a chance I won't ship out. He knows guys who have gone through Soldier Readiness Processing two, three times and they're still here." I treated these cases as tall tales. Hope was a dangerous thing.

"Huh. Well, I suppose you never know. Just make sure the school refunds your tuition in full. They're required to do that."

I checked my email and found three new death notices. I wished he would end the call already.

"You know." He paused. "If you were in ROTC, they couldn't call you up. You could finish your degree."

"But I'm *not* in ROTC," I said, barely veiling agitation.

"You can still join."

I blinked, body suddenly rigid. "How can I join ROTC when I'm battle rostered to ship out?"

"The Guard has to approve the contract, but they're really hurting for officers right now. They're going to want you in the ROTC program."

Time seemed to both spurt forward and lurch. I replayed his sentences in my head.

"You still there?" Bate asked.

"What would I have to do?"

"Why don't you stop by the department tomorrow and we'll look at the details."

• • •

The new deal was this: if I extended my Army National Guard contract by three years, agreed to minor in Military Science, and forfeited some financial aid, I could finish college and become an officer.

Under the gun, I allowed myself two days to mull over the pros and cons.

If I took the deal, I would be buying time. Time to earn my degree. Time to finish my internship at KVEC, where I was writing real news for air. Time for the wars to calm down, or maybe even end! Time with Zack. And time to find some press corps unit to transfer into. When I went to war, I needed to go as a writer or photographer to keep my sanity.

Then again, even if I did manage to find a press corps job, I'd be pumping out fluff and propaganda. Censored things. Freedom of the press was a civilian concept. And *would* I be buying time in the end? If I left for my tour in October, I would be out of the military completely in two years.

But... the Army was playing dirty these days. Thousands of soldiers were being forced into second or extended tours through something called "stop-loss." John Kerry was calling it a "backdoor draft" in his campaign speeches. The program was created by Congress after Vietnam and gave the president the power to extend soldiers' contracts whether they wanted to reenlist or not. Soldiers at the end of their contracts, more than ready to return to civilian life, were being told *no, you can't leave. Back to war.* Only officers were spared from stop-loss.

On the other hand... going to war now was the fastest way out of this, stop-loss or not. The Army couldn't postpone discharges forever. And maybe I could stay sane through it all by writing about my experiences. I'd come home with the soldier version of *Bridget Jones's Diary*!

Okay, it would be nothing like *Bridget Jones's Diary*. Except for I was a woman. And there'd hopefully be some romance in there to distract from the harsh desert we didn't belong in, the idiocy of the war, homesickness, and the feeling that my hands were tied. Deep down, I suspected I would not do any writing stuck in a war zone, not given how heavy I already felt. I would spend my spare time struggling against sleep or trying to escape through books. I'd notice sharp objects and think about what kind of marks they would leave on my skin. I'd fall in love with the wrong men. I'd fantasize about plotting mutinies. I wouldn't want anyone to leave base, ever. And on guard duty late at night, I'd imagine the tens of thousands of innocent Iraqis killed rising from the dead and walking to America on the ocean floor, overrunning the Capitol, dripping sea water onto the White House lawn, haunting an administration that passed war crimes off as "collateral damage."

I thought about getting in the car and driving for days, disappearing. I thought about getting pregnant. I took frequent trips back in time to our trailer in Fromberg. I'd arrive around 2:00 a.m., strip the covers off seventeen-year-old me, yank her up by her shirt, slam her against the wall.

"You stupid little fuck," I'd snarl. "You go through with that National Guard shit tomorrow, you'll be sorry. You don't even *know* how sorry!" She never knows what I'm talking about, never listens. The twenty-one-year-old me wakes up in the same snare.

• • •

After two days, my back against the wall, I decide ROTC is the answer. A gift from the mysterious powers of the universe. An opportunity. I should be grateful.

5. One of These Cadets Is Not Like the Others

September 2004: San Luis Obispo, CA

"See her form? That's what all these cadets should look like." Major Taulk nudged Major Bate and pointed at me as I ran past. I was a quarter of the way through my two-mile run, imagining I was back on the red dirt track behind Fromberg High School. In reality, it was a cool Friday morning on California's Central Coast and I was in the middle of a physical fitness (PT) test on Cal Poly's perfect Astroturf track. While the other cadets were taking the test for fun, to see how they measured up to Army standards, I needed to pass to join ROTC.

The laps got harder and harder. I still had the slim body of a track star, but my muscles and lungs were woefully out of shape. I puffed past a heavy, red-faced cadet, then a skinny girl, her black ponytail whipping from side to side. A clump of fourth-year cadets scoring the PT test sized me up. Major Bate had told me I was the only cadet who was already a soldier, already part of a unit. That made me an outsider, and from the way the seniors were looking at me, maybe a threat to their right to boss everyone else in the program around.

My last 200 meters I kicked it into high gear, managing to sprint across the finish line. Clocking in at just under sixteen minutes, perhaps my worst two-mile time ever, I hobbled off the track and into the grass, doubled over and coughing. The officers and the fourth-year cadets shot stern looks my way.

A tall, red-haired cadet trudged over to me like he'd drawn the short straw. "You gonna be okay?"

"Just out of shape."

"I thought you were already in the Guard."

"I am."

"Well, don't you take PT tests?"

"Once a year we do," I gasped. I usually trained for a month or two before them. I'd had a whole week's notice for this test.

Red Hair made some marks on his clipboard. "Good job, by the way. You passed."

My eyes narrowed. Of course I *passed*.

As the rest of the cadets finished the run, the third- and fourth-years congregated in a cajoling circle. The first- and second-years had their own little group. I dug through my backpack just to have something to do.

A lanky cadet broke from the older group and trotted over to me. "Welcome to the program. I'm Fleishman."

I shook hands. "Del Duca. Are we done? Do you guys hold final formation or just leave?"

"Formation? We don't do too much of that. Us third-years are headed to the student union for breakfast. Wanna come?"

The idea of wasting money on prepared food while trying to fit in with people who wanted to be in the Army did not appeal. "Thanks, but I have a ton of... stuff to do. At home."

The guys started doing chest bumps with a running start. "Ignore that," Fleishman said, seeing my eyebrows raise. "Come on. We won't embarrass you too much."

I strapped on my backpack and shook my head, smiling.

"See ya Tuesday then," he said.

"Tuesday?"

"Our first day of class? You're a third-year, right?"

"Right. What is that class about, anyway?" I asked. The title Military Science III didn't explain a whole lot.

"Book reports and workbooks and learning how to lead labs. Major White teaches it. He's awesome. Short little guy, but he could probably kick all our asses with one hand tied behind his back," Fleishman said.

"Workbooks?"

"Short answer and multiple-choice stuff. For you it should be real easy. You probably know everything already."

"And lab? What's that again?"

"Every Thursday the whole department meets up for three hours. We do drills and land navigation and stuff like that. Sometimes we run tactical missions."

"Fleishman, New Girl, let's go!"

He quirked his head toward them. "Give us a chance."

Chiding myself for looking this ROTC gift horse in the mouth, for trying to have it both ways, insider and outsider, I gave in. We trouped over to the student union, where the guys headed straight for Chick-fil-A and I got a bowl of oatmeal and fruit. We sat outside, the shade of towering palm trees striping the table tops. I was the only girl in our group of eight.

I learned that the other third-years all lived in San Luis Obispo. That they hit the gym together and partied together on the weekends. None of them appeared to have jobs. None of them seemed worried about how to cover the cost of books this semester. They had credit cards and cell phones and laptops, but no girlfriends. I doubted whether they had a clue what they were really getting into. And as the grateful recipient of a ticket out of deployment, for now, I was in no position to tell them.

• • •

The following Thursday, the ROTC staff and cadets met up at Camp San Luis Obispo for the first lab of the year.

"Okay, del Duca, go for it." Red Hair, who had scored my PT test, was looking at me.

What was he talking about?

"If you need to grab some notes from your backpack, we'll give you a minute, but they're all yours."

"I'm confused," I finally said. Now everyone was looking at me. No, not everyone—the two fourth-year girls, who acted like I had some kind of disease, were looking at the ground, trying to hide smirks.

"You're leading lab today. Drill and ceremony."

Oh. I blinked. "No one told me. Did I miss an email?"

There were sighs, scuffing feet, murmurs. I felt like the butt of a joke in some teen dramedy. They did realize I was new to the program, right? Lucky for me, the officers were too far away to hear what was going on.

"The schedule has been in the main office for a week," Red Hair said. "Do you need someone to take over? Do you want to take a failure for this evaluation?"

I shook my head. "Just give me an idea of what to cover."

"Marching, formation, facing movements."

This would be a piece of cake. I stepped forward and took control, noting that the first- and second-year cadets had probably never stood in formation before, let alone marched in time, and forget calling cadence. I started with the basics—attention, parade rest, right face, left face—before explaining cadence.

"When I sing a line, you listen and shout it back. In unison. The stress of the words goes with your left foot hitting the ground. This is how you keep time, how you stay in step with everybody. Ready?"

Dubious glances were exchanged.

"Riiiiight, *face*," I called. "Forward, *march*! *Left*, left, *left*, right on *left*, right on *left*, right, *left*." I looked over my mini platoon and saw what Drill Sergeant LaMonte would have declared a "shit sack gaggle."

"Platoon, *halt*!" I went over it all again, then led the group around the parking lot, barking my favorite cadences from boot camp. After they got the hang of marching, I tackled the about-face. The first time you execute a proper about-face, you feel like your brain splits in two. You need to pick up your right foot, put your toe in just the right spot behind your left foot, and then spin on that toe as you shift your weight enough to spin on your left heel at the same time. One sucker still couldn't do the turn after I got on my hands and knees to guide his feet.

I was explaining the change step—a sort of skip that gets you back in sync if you ever fall out of step—when I noticed that the fourth-years were paying hard attention instead of gossiping and flirting. It seemed these kids who were a year away from being commissioned as officers in the US Army had never learned the change step. Hell, if they hadn't gone to boot camp they'd missed a mountain more than just marching commands.

Red Hair stopped me after the first try. "That's enough. It's really over their heads."

We broke formation and sat on the curb, sipping water from our canteens and passing around a box of Hot Tamales.

"Nice save," Fleishman said. "That was the best drill and ceremony we've ever had."

I smiled.

Red Hair gave me an "S" on my evaluation. Satisfactory. Nothing special. Substantially flawed. I let the anger bubbling up dissipate. This was all a gift. A goddamn gift. Why did I keep forgetting that?

6. The Secret

September 2004: Camp Roberts, CA

Military paperwork can move at a glacial pace. So even after I was officially accepted into ROTC, I had to report to Camp Roberts for Soldier Readiness Processing or be counted AWOL. Until the Army recognized the new contract and took me off their battle roster, I had to go through the motions to deploy.

I showed up in carefully ironed and starched BDUs, boots gleaming, heart pumping at an accelerated clip, scared they would tell me the ROTC deal was off, and exhausted by the more likely scenario that I was only pushing deployment off by two years at the most. It was strange seeing ghost town Camp Roberts filled with camo. I felt like I was traveling back in time, to when the base had been a big hub in the '50s.

Sitting in a creaky metal folding chair, looking at all the other soldiers being briefed on the importance of bumping up our life insurance payouts, the guilt floodgates opened up. They were headed to Iraq for sure. Some of them certainly believed what I believed: that this war was not their war, shouldn't be anybody's war; that the Bush Administration was unworthy of being trusted with a flea circus, let alone hundreds of thousands of troops. But they were marching into uncertainty and danger without complaint while I, the coward college kid, ran out on them at the last minute.

Makeshift doctors' offices had been set up in one of the original, dilapidated buildings, its windows streaked with years of dirt. The "exam rooms" were created with room dividers on wheels. There was no exam table, just a chair for the "patient" and a chair for the medic. My medic looked bored and irritated, her hair pulled back in a tight bun that I imagined must be giving her a headache. She looked through my medical file, then said in a drone, "Is there anything preventing you from physically carrying out your assigned military occupation?"

I racked my brain, ready to bring up anything and everything that came to mind, unlike my very first Army physical.

Don't give them any opportunity to deny you, 'cause they'll take it, Sergeant Lamson had said. *This kid I signed up last year said his back happened to be hurting that day. They wouldn't let him swear in. He had to get checked out by his doctor and come back in a few weeks. Missed his boot camp date, all 'cause he was too honest.*

Too honest?

Whoa, whoa. Of course, be honest. If you've had surgery, or if you have allergies, be honest. But piddling little stuff? You tried mushrooms once last year? You had a suicidal thought at one point? Leave it off. That's not what they're looking for.

"I do have this thing with my shoulder blade," I told the medic, whose level of irritation kicked up a notch when I didn't answer her question with a simple no. "It keeps grinding and clicking when I move my arm or use my back or shoulders." I shrugged my shoulders up and down and let her hear the thuk-click, thuk-click.

"Does it hurt?" she asked.

"Not really. It gets worse when I carry heavy things though."

"What does your doctor say it is?"

What did she think this was, France? "I don't have a doctor."

"Well, I don't know what it could be." She gave me a blank stare. "Anything else?"

"There's one other thing. My dad is hypoglycemic, and I think I might be too. Sometimes if I don't eat as soon as I get hungry I get these bad stomach aches. Like cramps, but for as long as three or four hours. Sometimes it comes with getting lightheaded and wanting to hyperventilate."

She drummed her fingers on my medical file. "But you don't have hypoglycemia. It's not in your folder."

"That's the thing. I don't know if I have it. I've never been someplace where they test for that."

"So there's no documentation. No proof."

"No."

"Then I can't mark anything down. Take off your BDU jacket."

She took my blood pressure. She had me hold my arms out, palms up, touch my nose, do a duck walk. She fingered one of the scars on my arms, but said nothing. I thought about owning up to this stranger what I hadn't admitted to anyone, including myself. I knew you couldn't have a mental illness and be in the military, that antidepressants were banned. But then I pictured her asking where the proof was with that skeptical little curve to her mouth. Where was the doctor's diagnosis? The documented history of this condition? And I only had puppy depression. I didn't want to kill myself. I didn't have a brutal, insufferable life. "Self-mutilation," a term I'd learned a year or two before and realized applied to me, was a phase I'd grow out of any day now. Maybe the day I finally got out of the Army.

After the physical, the medic gave me a questionnaire to fill out. What vaccinations I'd had. What medications I was taking.

And then there it was.

The Secret.

A little box that asked, "Are you a conscientious objector?"

Thinking it must be some typo, a mistake, I reread the words three times. *Are you a conscientious objector?* The term described exactly what I'd come to feel, but also exactly what I thought the Army didn't tolerate. I thought the term was for Vietnam-era guys who'd burned their draft cards. No one had ever told me I could voice my objection. I'd joined voluntarily after all. But there the words were. *Are you a conscientious objector?*

My pen hovered over the box. If I didn't check it, I would be lying to myself. But if I did check it, the Army would surely assume I was lying to them. I could hear the suspicion and contempt: "Sure, get called up and suddenly you're a conscientious objector." I glanced at the medic.

"Do you have a question?" she asked, the lids of her eyes drooping.

I had a million. This changed everything. My brain felt like a maze flooded with a thousand lab rats. They scurried in all directions, testing the routes, crowding out coherent thought. No, wait, none of this mattered anyway. It was too late. I'd taken my gift from the mysterious powers of the universe: ROTC.

"No questions," I said, leaving the box blank.

The medic resumed picking at her nails.

7. Fifteen Minutes of Fame

September 2004: San Luis Obispo, CA

My joining ROTC became a local scandal. It started on the *Dave Congalton Show*, a news talk program that aired for three hours every afternoon on KVEC. I'd met Dave in passing. My internship hours usually ended before he got in, about the time our programming passed from Rush Limbaugh to Sean Hannity, both of whom I found insufferable. But unlike Limbaugh and Hannity, Dave seemed like a smart, fair, and open-minded host. His show was community-oriented and, when it came to politics, very middle of the road. It was his audience that was significantly more red than blue.

It seemed word had gotten around to Dave that a news intern at his station was getting out of deployment by joining ROTC at the last minute. Who knows, maybe he even found out from Professor Madsen, who did traffic and weather every twenty minutes during Dave's show. At any rate, at the end of SRP weekend, while I was feeling like a rock plunging to the bottom of the ocean, taking too many ibuprofen at a time, hoping it would make me feel calm or at least numb, Dave decided my predicament would make a good topic. An audience spoon-fed conservatism never lacked for an opinion on the military, or Bush, or the war.

I have no idea what was said about me that Monday. But on Tuesday, both the *Tribune* and Dave asked me for interviews. *The Congalton Show* came first.

I walked in to find Major Bate, my ROTC recruiter, already sitting in the studio, wearing Class A's. He stood up to shake my hand, face falling as he took in my outfit. I was wearing BDU pants and a black tank top.

"Where's the rest of your uniform?" he asked.

"I wear just the pants sometimes."

"You can't do that," he said. "It's against regulation. The uniform is meant to be worn properly."

I could feel Dave's eyes on me, and the eyes of Madsen, who'd popped in to tell me not to be nervous. I'd worn the pants on purpose. I'd thought, *What better reflection of a citizen soldier, a girl deciding to extend her contract to finish school?* Besides, this was radio. "I'm sorry, sir. I didn't know."

"How could you not know that? You've been in how long now?"

My blush deepened. "I guess it never came up. I won't do it again."

Bate shook his head and sat back down. I took a chair next to him as Dave handed us headphones and pointed out the mute and on-air buttons in front of us.

"Any questions?" Dave asked.

I still didn't understand what he wanted me to talk about. *A lot of people will be interested in what you're doing*, is what he'd said over the phone. *It's a very relevant topic.*

I figured asking for clarification now would only make me look like more of an idiot, especially after Bate's scolding.

"No," I said.

"Nope," said Bate.

We sat through the news update at the top of the hour. Bate slapped my knee with his yellow legal pad. "You ready?"

I shrugged and gave a wan smile. In reality, I was a ball of distracted nerves, my brain stuck in hyperdrive, taunted by the box I'd left blank. The morning before, I'd driven to campus to research conscientious objection on one of the computers at KCPR. In an alarmingly short amount of time, I'd found an organization called the GI Rights Hotline. I say alarmingly because it was a punch to the gut, seeing how ignorant I'd been this whole time while a world of knowledge sat a Google search away.

Are you in the military or a family member or friend of someone who is? the homepage asked. *Are you confused about your rights? Are you unsure of where to go for reliable answers?* Yes, yes, and yes. They had links for every type of discharge, and a toll-free number staffed with people to answer questions. I'd written down the number and barreled home to use the phone in privacy.

I'd learned that there were two groups of conscientious objectors. The first opposed anything directly related to combat, but were fine working in support roles like supply, paperwork, and food. The other group was opposed to any and all involvement in any and all wars. If you could prove that your beliefs were honest and steadfast, and that they'd developed after you joined the military, then you could be granted a discharge.

Neither of the options seemed to fit me. Fueling was considered a support role—a job unrelated to combat. But the more I thought about it, the more it seemed the very foundation of war. The military couldn't do anything without fuel. Then there were all those people who said this entire war was about oil. On the other hand, I didn't know if every single war was wrong. It hadn't been wrong to enter World War II. And what if, say, North Korea attacked us? How could I categorically label any and all wars as wrong? And proof? I could *explain* my morals, but I didn't know how to *prove* them. And so I fell back into the deep trance of denial.

"I think I'll be okay as long as ROTC becomes official," I told the woman on the other end of the hotline.

"Are you sure?" she asked. "Getting into ROTC isn't going to make what you're feeling go away. It will only put it off for a while."

I would prove her wrong. ROTC had swooped in and saved the day. Now I needed to buck up, grow up, and honor my new contract.

Dave's intro music played and he leaned toward the mic, launching a spiel about the second and third hours of the show. "But first, we have our very own news intern, Rosa del Duca, in the studio today, along with Major Brian Bate from Cal Poly's ROTC department. Rosa, why don't you explain what you've been going through the last month or so? On yesterday's program there was a lot of speculation and I want to get to the facts first thing. So you're in the Army and—" He dramatically spread his arms, inviting me to finish the sentence.

"Army National Guard actually."

"Okay, so you're a Reservist."

"No, that's another branch too. There's the regular Army, the Army National Guard, and the Army Reserves. They're all treated the same in training, but they're separate otherwise."

Dave put his elbows on the table, hands up, gesturing. "So you're in the Army National Guard and you get called up."

"That's right. I was on a mobilization list with a unit out of Louisiana when Major Bate called me and said I could still join ROTC. I really didn't want a huge gap in my education, so that's what I did." Under the table I worked my ring around and around my thumb.

"Did you see that choice as controversial?"

"I can see how people could think I'm trying to get out of something. And I do feel guilty. Because I'm not shipping out, someone else has to take my spot. But I did have to extend my contract to get into ROTC."

"Really? Okay, that clears up a lot."

I pictured all the radios in kitchens and cars and offices. Who were these people, scrutinizing my situation for a full hour yesterday?

"By how much did you have to extend your service?" Dave asked.

"My original contract would have run out in 2006. Now it runs out in 2009."

Bate broke in. "Rosa will still deploy. It's just a matter of when. Instead of going in a month, she'll go in a few years, as an officer, and with a bachelor's degree."

"I see," said Dave. "This isn't a matter of her taking advantage of the system?"

I pried the ring off and shoved it in my pocket.

"Not the way I see it. Not at all," said Bate.

"Is this common, Major Bate?"

"This is extremely *uncommon*. Most of our cadets get interested in the program as freshmen or sophomores. A few were in JROTC during high school. It's much more rare for a soldier to come to us through the Guard or Reserves."

Dave pressed on like a prosecutor. "Did you know Rosa had been called up when you asked her to join ROTC?"

"I know where you're headed." Bate wagged a finger at Dave, who gave a good-ol'-boy smile and shrug of the shoulders. "This was not the first time I encouraged Rosa to join the program. She's known about the opportunity for six months. I told her then what I'll say now. There is a real need for intelligent Army officers coming up the ranks. ROTC programs across the country can't keep up with demand, and she's a perfect candidate. She's a leader, dedicated, has experience, she's already in uniform. It's a win-win."

"Let's bring some callers into this conversation. We've got Sam on the line from Atascadero. Good afternoon, Sam."

"Yes, hello. I wanted to ask the young lady, the young woman, why she joined the military."

Here we go, I thought. *Because I was frothing at the mouth to get out of Fromberg. Because $6,000 sounded like a lot of money. Because I thought I was mature and intelligent. Because I had a dread of debt from how my mother agonized about welfare and student loans and the price of every item we put in our shopping cart. Because I was a tomboy athlete who loved challenges. Because no one tried to talk me out of it. Because September 11 was still a meaningless date.* But I couldn't say any of that, so I settled for the reason everyone swallowed easily.

"I knew I had to find a way to pay for college myself and I thought it would be cool to fight forest fires. I'm from Montana. That's what the National Guard does in the summers. Used to do, anyway."

"You were in it for the college money," Sam said. I pictured him sitting on a deck outside, at a table with an umbrella sticking out of the middle.

"That was the biggest reason, yes."

"It sounds like you're not in this for the right reasons. Sounds like you're out to get college paid for and service to this country comes last."

"Whoa, whoa, Sam," Dave said, meeting my eyes across the table. "She just said she had to extend her contract by three years. Isn't that a little harsh?"

"No, Dave. We've got this all-volunteer army. Kids don't take it serious anymore. To serve in the military is the biggest sacrifice you could make, a tremendous commitment and honor. The decision should not be made lightly. If you want to go to college, go to college. If you want to join the military, join the military. The one shouldn't be a means of reaching the other. That's my point."

"I beg to differ," said Bate. "ROTC's mission is to train college-educated cadets to become officers. The better educated our armed forces, the better our military is."

"ROTC's different," Sam continued. "I'm talking about the Guard and Reserves. You should serve first, go to school later or you've got cases like this. People backing out when the going gets tough. We're in a war on terror here. This is serious. People's lives are at stake. If we don't root out every last terror cell, we're gonna have another 9/11. People are dying and getting blown up and—"

Dave shook his head at the board operator, who slid Sam's audio channel down. "Thank you for your comments, Sam. Let's turn to Derek in Paso Robles."

"What do you study in school?" the new caller asked.

"Journalism." I was still hung up on Sam. He had a point. Despite the war being based on lies, people's lives *were* at stake. That was why, this time, I needed to do what I said I would do, no matter what.

"You couldn't come back and pick up where you left off? The school isn't cooperating?" Derek pressed.

"Cal Poly is required to hold my spot and refund my tuition. But in journalism especially, I feel like I'd lose a lot of ground. The news changes every day. You miss a week and you're…" I faltered. This was sounding extremely selfish. "You're out of the loop. I would—I would feel like I had a lot to catch up on and redo."

"It's not impossible, to come back and get caught up though," he said.

"No, not impossible."

"Mary in Pismo Beach," Dave broke in, "You're on the air, Mary."

"I'm curious what she does in the National Guard." Mary's voice had a tenuous frailty. "I have grandsons in the Army and I can't imagine a woman doing what they do."

Explaining how I'd been helping to build a quarry at Camp Roberts even though I was technically a fueler until I became an official officer took a full five minutes.

"George Ramos is on the line," Dave announced, raising his eyebrows and reading the notes Madsen had put up on the call screening monitor. "For those of you who don't know, Ramos is the head of Cal Poly's journalism department, and a Vietnam veteran. George, welcome and thank you for your service."

Major Bate and Ramos greeted each other like old buddies.

"Rosa's story is much like my own," Ramos said in his animated, almost musical voice. "I joined ROTC at Cal Poly so I could finish my degree before serving in the Army."

"This was during the Vietnam War?" Dave asked.

"Right. I graduated with my journalism degree in 1969 and served as First Lieutenant from March of 1970 to September of '71, mostly in South Vietnam. Rosa's service makes her stand out. She's the only member of the journalism department serving her country while earning her degree. I was surprised when Major Bate told me one of my students had joined his program. Not only that, she's news director of our campus radio station. When I was her age, I was editor in chief of the *Mustang Daily*. She reminds me of myself."

I beamed. Hot damn. George Ramos, three-time Pulitzer Prize winner, knew who I was *and* thought I stood out?

The conversation turned to Vietnam before veering back to an analysis of me and my choice to put school first, the callers a mix of conciliatory and skeptical. An excruciating hour later, Dave took one last caller—Greg in San Luis Obispo.

"I don't see what all the fuss is about. I think you have every right to an education that was promised you in return for your service. As long as you plan on honoring your contract, I say more power to you." There were metallic dings in the background, like he was cooking.

"But I want to hear it from you. Do you plan to honor your contract? Are you going to ship out the next time you're asked? No more training or going on to get a master's or something like that?"

The air in the room had grown hot and stale. I could smell my own breath. I felt like a talking statue, straining to convince the invisible audience I was flesh and blood. "Yes, I plan to honor my contract. I mean, I don't want to go to war. No one does. I really hope the wars are over soon, but I understand the importance of keeping my word." I set the pen I'd been fidgeting with down and sat still. I felt like I was swearing an oath, renewing my vows. In a way that's exactly what I was doing. This was not an act. "I know I have to own my responsibilities. And I'm not special. I'm not better than anyone. The Army gives you this card at boot camp with all the Army values. Loyalty, duty, respect, selfless service, honor, integrity, personal courage. I believe in those values. Those are my values."

Bate was nodding his head. Dave was looking at the clock. The board operator was absently chewing his nails. In the next room, Madsen watched me with his watery eyes, hands clasped on the desk in front of him, a smile on his face. The hundreds, if not thousands of people listening to the radio breathed in and out, their brains transforming the sound of my voice into ideas, images, promises. They all bore witness. The weight felt like a lead flak jacket.

8. Wearing the Lead Flak Jacket

September 2004: Morro Bay, CA

9/17/04

Much has happened in two days. Major Bate called and everything looks like a go for ROTC! I was so happy I cried with relief.

I was on the Dave Congalton Show yesterday. I was nervous and very tired, but it went well and Zack was impressed. He made me feel really good about it when I wasn't sure.

I feel like I've been taken off death row. Then, on the other hand, I'm exhausted just thinking about the upcoming year/years.

9/25/04

I wish I could find some way to hurt myself that isn't as visible as cuts. I can't cut myself until after my ROTC physical anyway. I don't want them asking questions.

I don't know if I can do this. Anything. I don't know. Ahhh! Just thinking about all this has got me worked up and I feel like screaming and raging around breaking things. Maybe I should just go back to sleep.

I think I need to be single again. Any day Zack has off, he's gone, which tells me he doesn't really want to get to know me. When he's stuck in San Luis and wants to kill a couple hours in female company, that's when he shows up. I need more than that. I'm beginning to resent him.

10/2/04

I can tell I will be teetering on the brink of insanity many times this year. Why should I get up in the morning? Because I'm trapped in a cycle of tasks I've deemed obligatory for some idiotic, society-driven reason. Hope and optimism leak out of me slowly, from the time I get up to the time I get home, when there is none left. I should have handled deployment and another year in the Guard because then the pressure would be off and I could see the light at the end of the tunnel. Now it's pitch black again.

Still, I am so lucky and grateful to be born in the United States. In International Communication we watched a film about an Afghan woman trying to reach her sister. It was horrifying. (Prosthetic limbs falling from the sky on little parachutes and men on crutches, missing legs, trying to run for them.) I'll never forget it, just like I'll never forget Forgotten Soldier by Guy Sajer. It is interesting and well-written but very difficult to read because of its nature. He is half French and half German but ends up a Nazi, fighting Russians in World War II. He's not a Nazi though. He's just a teenager trying to survive a horrifying experience.

Zack says he thinks I am looking for someone to latch on to and I think he's right. I need someone with this Army stuff going on. I wish it could be him. But I am waiting for (and dreading) the day when being constantly unsatisfied and neglected becomes too much.

10/18/04

I'm turning into a bad student. I got a B- on my English exam and I just turned in incomplete homework for Spanish! I stupidly forgot I had a test in it today, and I didn't even have a pencil or Scantron. I was so pissed at myself. I hate looking like an idiot. What a great start to the week.

Damn it, why can't Zack be normal? I need someone to understand me so bad and I know that's a lot to ask because I don't even understand myself. I am completely alone.

I am so tired. I listen to the news too much, but how can I not? I'm usually at KCPR when Democracy Now! is on, KVEC is all news all the time, and I need to read the paper for classes. Besides, ignorance about the war is not bliss. It's sloppy avoidance and there's enough of that going around already.

11/21/04

It's been a while but nothing worthwhile has happened save for I realized I hate my life. Curious George Bush won another four years in office. I feel like all the sane people in this country have been in mourning this month. I have no close friends. I hate ROTC. Zack and I were supposed to spend the whole day together yesterday but he never called and didn't answer his phone. I wish I was strong enough to break up with him but I'm not.

Why am I so unhappy deprived of human contact and affection, especially male affection? Is it just because all humans are genetically and socially bred to be that way or is there something wrong with me?

12/10/04

Last day of work at the Tribune. A relief I won't be juggling so much next quarter, or always eating breakfast and lunch in the car, rushing from one thing to the next. Will be nice not to think about death every day too.

2/5/05

I really love my English class. We just read The Death of Ivan Ilych and it was scary but good and even a little life-changing for me. I need to live my life better so when my time on this world is up I'll have no regrets. Or at least a few instead of many. I think it would be a bit drastic to live each day as if it were your last because I would be freaking out if I knew it was my last day and would just want to be surrounded by family and friends. But then does that mean that's how I should live? If so, I'm doing the opposite of that. My biggest regret of my life so far is joining the Guard.

Last week one portion of my brain made an appointment with the rest to take over and cut myself but I was so busy I didn't get a chance and I'm glad I didn't.

3/2/05

I hate the military. I'm going to be so glad when it's over and done with. I don't care what happens but I will not re-enlist. Do you hear that Rosa! Never! Not for a million dollars.

9. Girlfriend Points

March 2005: Morro Bay, CA

Zack and I were killing time at my house in Morro Bay before a KCPR meeting. A dark mood had been festering and all I wanted to do was crawl under a blanket and exist in nothingness until I fell asleep. I knew the meeting would probably keep me out of the quicksand, and if I was around people long enough, the mood might disintegrate altogether. But knowing this offered little motivation.

"I don't want to go." We were lying on my twin-size mattress, which didn't have a bed frame, Zack with a magazine of drum equipment, me with my math book.

"The meeting's only an hour. Let's rally," he said.

I rolled over and stared up at the ceiling, willing Zack to recognize the brewing storm. Of course I hadn't pointed out the warning signs. That would ruin my romantic notion that soon he'd understand my every mood and whim even better than I did.

"I told E.J. to save some time on the agenda for me," he said. "You nuts are slacking off with the legal ID at the top of the hour. That's how you lose your license."

"Why don't you go without me?"

Zack tossed the magazine on the floor and let out an exaggerated groan getting up. I heard him go in and out of the bathroom and grab something from the fridge. I finished my last math problem and closed the book. The front door opened and shut. Zack had probably gone to warm up his truck. Dragging myself out of bed, I found a sweatshirt, then flung myself back onto the mattress. Five minutes passed before I padded out to the driveway in bare feet. Zack was gone.

I made my way back inside, took my scissors out of my pen and pencil mug, bared one dull blade like a knife, sliced at my right arm, and watched crimson lines bloom. A sense of accomplishment grew in my brain. And then, as usual, came the dose of clarity. The heightened, grainy quality of the night broke. The stupidity dawned.

But I wasn't going to waste this. I'd cut myself to show one person. Even though deep down I knew it was screwed up and wildly unfair, I wanted to lay my bloody arm at Zack's feet. *Help me. Love me.*

"Why did you leave? I would have come," I said over the phone.

"You said to go without you."

"I didn't mean it."

"Are you crying?" he asked.

"Not anymore."

"Do you want me to turn around?"

"You weren't even going to say goodbye? Were you going to come back to spend the night?"

"No, I told you I have to stay at my place tonight. I'm going out of town in the morning."

"Then why didn't you say goodbye?"

"Look, do you want me to turn around or not?"

When he walked in, I had a bloody paper towel pressed to my arm. He touched my shoulder like I was a grenade with the pin out. I turned into his chest and he put a stiff hand on my back while I clutched him and cried. The hand was all I could think about, placed there like a mannequin's hand, a cadaver's hand, an obligation. I stepped away from him.

"You want to go for a walk?" he asked.

We wandered down to the foggy marina, silent, not one but two mannequins. He looked like a confused anachronism in his black turn-of-the-century hat and New York firefighter coat. I looked like a boy in my baggy sweatshirt and Army boots, my hair cropped pixie short. With each step I repeated a question silently. The same question. I wanted to ask it so badly. A dozen times I opened my mouth and took that sharp little breath before you say something. Nothing.

"When," I finally forced out. I swallowed and tried again. "When. You." I tried to breathe in, but my lungs were already full. This was ridiculous. "When you left. Did you know I was upset?"

"Yes."

My throat grew tighter, constricting to the size of the eye of a needle, too narrow for even "I," the slimmest word, to slip through. What I really wanted to ask was *why*. Why had he left me when I needed him? And why had I reacted that way? Pop psychology was crowing in my ear: *Because your father abandoned you when you were three, of course! Your inner child is trembling in the corner.* But I didn't think that was true.

Now I wonder if it had something to do with how he could leave any time he wanted. He could leave my house, he could leave town, he could leave the country. He was the very antithesis of a soldier: often late or AWOL, openly contemptuous of rules he didn't agree with, and amused by people who tried to assert their authority. Zack was a free spirit, beholden to no one, outspoken and irreverent. When I talked about the Guard or ROTC, he made dismissive quips. Sometimes I wondered if he was judging me. He was fascinated with American history, often showing me pictures he'd found online of old ships, trucks, cannons, planes, trains, soldiers, and cowboys. He had a somber reverence for first responders and pilots. Firefighters were in a league of their own. His firefighter coat? He'd gotten it off of eBay after 9/11. That was perhaps the most stinging irony. Zack flaunted his no-strings-attached patriotism while I felt like a marionette tangled up in its wires.

Down at the marina, we leaned over the railing and watched the water lapping at the floating walkways, the sailboats and fishing rigs.

"Have you ever thought about seeing a therapist?" he asked.

I rolled my eyes, my speaking problem gone. "I don't need to spend a fortune spilling my guts to someone who's going to tell me crap I already know."

"Have you ever gone to therapy?"

"No."

"Then how would you know?" His Blackberry buzzed in his back pocket and he took it out.

I glared at the phone. I always seemed to be in competition with the thing. "It's in so many books and movies, it's a cliché. Blah blah psychobabble blah. No one can magically change the way you think or feel."

"And you think you're open-minded," he said, punching buttons.

"I am open-minded. And I happen to be opinionated." The skin on my arm was hot and angry, taut like the head of a drum.

"Well, a lot of people think it's a standard part of staying healthy. You go to the dentist, you go to the doctor, and you should go to a psychiatrist. You know, most of my friends have a shrink."

"Good for them."

He tucked the Blackberry away. "I have one."

I stopped scraping zig-zags on the sidewalk with the bit of gravel trapped under my shoe. "You do? Why didn't you tell me?"

"Because it's not a big deal."

I kicked the pebble into the water. "I didn't mean to imply therapy couldn't be helpful. I just don't think it will help me."

"So you're better than everyone else."

"No. I feel like shit because of the Army stuff and a therapist isn't going to help get me out of the Army."

"They could help you deal with it."

I wanted him to put his arms around me or take my hand or kiss my cuts. He leaned on the railing, crossing his ankles in front of him. When we were in bed, Zack drank me in, drowned me in affection, never took his eyes away. Why couldn't he be like that now?

"Besides," I said, "I don't think you're allowed to be in therapy in the military. I know you can't be on antidepressants."

He turned and shot me an exasperated look. "How are they going to find out?"

"I don't feel like lying on more paperwork. And like I said, I don't have any spare cash to waste."

"I bet Cal Poly has something for free. You should check into it."

The wind picked up, rocking the boats. Zack flipped his collar up and hunched his shoulders. I stuffed my hands in my pockets and led the way home.

• • •

Zack was right. Cal Poly students were entitled to free counseling once a week for an entire quarter. That's when he posed the bribe. We were eating dinner at Morro Bay's one great Mexican place.

"If you finish the quarter—if you go to all seven sessions—you'll earn massive girlfriend points. I mean *huge* girlfriend points. I'll be your faithful servant."

Staring into our bowl of salsa, I thought about Zack's capacity to be a faithful servant. On top of work and the Burning Man art project, he'd joined some crazy Bay Area marching band—a gypsy-inspired troupe of drummers and horn players. He played cymbals but had his eye on a snare drum position when one opened up. "What if I go to a few and decide that's enough?"

"Nope. That doesn't count. It's once a week for the rest of the quarter." He leaned across the table and gave me one of his deep, unblinking stares. "Look, I care about you and I really think this is a good idea. What's the worst that could happen?"

10. Surrender

April 2005: Morro Bay, CA

Imagine you are an ant going about your ant business as part of your colony. Imagine the Army is the sun. It's blinding and powerful and you can't look right at it, but it's not always in the sky. You get a reprieve every night—enough to regroup and tolerate the sun long-term. Enter therapy. Therapy is the magnifying glass some cruel kid sticks between you and the sun, to burn off your exoskeleton. Within a few seconds, your shell is destroyed.

Just when I needed to be hard and buck up for ROTC officer training, therapy turned me into an emotional wreck, ready to cry at the drop of a pin. Instead of helping me regain composure, my therapist seemed intent on making matters worse.

"What's so terrible about crying?" Julie asked, her eyes hidden behind glasses, her blank, pale face with its thin lips giving off robot vibes.

I was sitting on the loveseat in her office, a tissue in my fist. She was looking at me from behind her desk, expectant, poised. She always had a notebook in front of her, but she rarely wrote in it.

"It's really embarrassing," I said, incredulous she needed me to explain.

"So it can be embarrassing. What else."

"It's inappropriate. You can't cry at work. You can't cry in class. It makes people uncomfortable. They feel obligated to try and cheer you up."

Julie clasped her hands together on top of her notebook. "Why would that be such a terrible thing? Wouldn't it make you feel better, to have someone reach out to you and show you they care?"

"Not from a stranger. That would be mortifying!"

"Why?"

Was this lady serious? "You look weak and needy and spoiled. One meltdown could get you branded as a wacko crybaby."

"When you see people cry, do you think they're needy and spoiled?"

My eyes darted to the window. I looked out past the enormous ferns and succulents into the sun-soaked California day. How odd that I used to blame most of my "moods" on winter.

"Do you?" Julie pressed.

"I guess not."

"Then why do you assume everyone will see *you* that way?"

I stuffed the tissue in my pants pocket, relieved I didn't need it anymore. "Because I don't have a good reason to be crying. My mom didn't die. My friends didn't get in a car crash. I haven't been raped. There's no huge trauma in my past. There's just the Army."

"You're saying that people need a good enough reason to be upset."

"Yeah."

"So you *do* judge people who get upset in public. You do see them as spoiled crybabies."

"No, I really don't. I—"

Julie leaned forward, comfortable in her scrutiny of me, and waited.

"I don't want pity, especially from strangers. The minute someone's all soft and sympathetic, I lose it even more. They're *my* feelings. Why can't I control them? Like walking in here. Now it's so bad tears start rolling down my face the minute I come in the door, even before I've said anything."

"Why do you think that is?"

"I don't know! That's why I'm asking you. It happens even when I'm not upset." The tears started, on cue. I dug for the tissue. "Look, I'm doing it right now! I can't help it."

Julie frowned. I could see she didn't like deviating from the Socratic Method.

I pointed at my wet cheeks. "This is ridiculous. Why am I crying right now? I just want to know why I don't have any control anymore."

She leaned back in her chair, her still-clasped hands in her lap now. "I think it's a release. You know you won't be judged here. This is a safe, confidential environment. There are no consequences. You don't have to guard yourself in this office. Do you have relationships like that aside from here?"

"Of course," I said automatically. But as soon as I opened my mouth, I realized it wasn't true. I didn't want to worry my mother. With my sisters, I talked about Zack and school, not the Army. Speaking of Zack, I knew better than to let him see me cry again. He could be stoic as a rock about things that mattered. As for my two friends here, Aaron and DJ Sasquatch, I couldn't saddle them with weepy self-pity. Jesus, I still had *some* self-respect.

"Here's what I want you to work on," said Julie, reaching for the notebook and scribbling something. "The next time you feel sad or angry or jealous or anything really, I want you to slow down, acknowledge the feeling, and sit with it. Don't fight it. There are no illegitimate feelings. Give yourself permission to express your emotions in a healthy way. Crying, for instance, is a normal, healthy reaction."

Her little experiment proved poisonous. On therapy days I had to skip afternoon classes rather than endure the looks my red, puffy face attracted. Or I had to wear sunglasses the rest of the day. Math homework brought me to tears. Failed dinner attempts too. I cried when I couldn't paddle out to the lineup when the surf was too strong. I cried at beautiful sunsets. I cried after banging my head on the corner of a kitchen cabinet and I cried after seeing a dead seal on the beach. No matter how horrified I was at my loss of self-control, I couldn't turn off the waterworks. In fact, the more appalled I was, the more I heard Julie. *Give yourself permission to cry. There are no illegitimate emotions.*

That wasn't therapy's only side effect. Julie seemed mildly annoyed when every thread of anxiety and depression and frustration led back to ROTC or the National Guard—a reaction that led me to assume she held conservative views and believed in the war. So coming up with articulate, specific explanations of my feelings became a matter of pride. The scales started to tip. And the more I thought and the more I expressed, the more I realized what I had to do, whether Julie thought it was a bad idea or not. I had to acknowledge my mistake, own my regret, and find a key for the lock on my cage. No one else was going to open the door for me.

• • •

I waited until the ROTC halls were vacant and knocked on Major Bate's door. Bate had been the one to whisk me into ROTC just in time to avoid a tour in Iraq. Of all the officers, he seemed the most open and friendly. He was always checking up on me, asking about school and work and drill. It seemed there was a sixty-forty chance he would hear me out and give me a straight answer.

"Can I talk to you?" I asked.

"Sure, come on in."

I stepped into his office and closed the door behind me.

"Could you leave that half open?" he asked.

"I kind of wanted to speak to you in private."

Bate furrowed his eyebrows. "Let's go outside, sit on the steps." He flipped through his key ring and followed me into the hall, locking his office and fixing a BDU cap over his salt-and-pepper buzz cut.

It was cloudy and gusty outside—one of those spring days that reminds you summer is still a long way off.

"Can this be confidential?" I asked.

"Absolutely."

I unslung my backpack and sat down on the steps overlooking Dexter Lawn, a huge rectangle of lush grass with a clock tower at one end. This was the spot where two years before, students against the war had staged their die-in. I'd seen barely a trace of protest since, on campus or otherwise—only a couple folks with signs from time to time and updates in the *Tribune* when the soldier death toll ticked up another hundred. It was like living in a parallel universe—one where anything that had to do with the War on Terror had been erased from collective memory.

"What's going on, del Duca?" Bate asked.

Fuck. This could be a big mistake. Or it could lead to tangible help. *Here goes nothing.*

I poured out my story—how I never expected to be asked to fight in a war, especially one I was opposed to, how I didn't belong, how I sometimes gave in to the lure of cutting myself. I never used the word depression. I was still leery of that word.

"I don't know what to do. I started seeing a therapist here at school. She says I should consider antidepressants. I don't know if I'm allowed to be in therapy, let alone try drugs. Is there anything I can do to break my contract, legally?"

Major Bate had been listening carefully, quietly. "I feel for you. I really do. I didn't know you were having such doubts when I signed you up. But please, please do not go on antidepressants." He wrung his hands. A blast of wind rippled the grass in front of us. "My son had a terrible time when my ex and I split up. Locked himself in his room, started getting bad grades. My ex wanted to put him on antidepressants. The doctor too. I said whatever they thought would help." He gripped his knees, shaking his head. I realized he was struggling not to cry. "They just... destroyed him. He is not the same person." Bate let out a breath he'd been holding. "I think everyone should try anything they can think of before resorting to antidepressants. I'm telling you, my son is gone. They wiped his personality clean away."

"I'm so sorry. That's terrible," I said, fumbling to fill the silence. "I heard that antidepressants can make some teens even more depressed."

"That's him."

"Is he better now?"

He brightened. "He's off them now. He's not the same, but he's doing okay."

A splinter of suspicion worked its way under my thumbnail. He seemed really upset. But was he exaggerating so I wouldn't leave the program? What if drugs could help *me*? I was willing to try anything at this point. "Antidepressants don't act that way for everyone, though," I said.

Bate shook his head. "No, but even if it's one in a thousand, those drugs should be banned."

The clock tower tolled the hour. The only two people on the lawn took this as a cue to leave. Something stopped me from telling him I was looking into what it took to become a conscientious objector. It was my last card, and one I didn't want to play unless I absolutely had to. When I'd told him about how conflicted I was about the war, he hadn't batted an eye.

"Tell you what I'll do," Bate said. "I will make a few phone calls and see what your options are. I won't use your name, so there's nothing to worry about. This is between you and me."

A week later Bate pulled me into his office and shut the door. "I've got an update for you. There's no way out of your current contracts, but therapy is fine, as long as it's not long-term. What I suggest you do is think about your time left in a manageable way." He pulled a blank piece of paper from his printer tray and lay it on his desk between us, the long way. He drew a line through the middle, then marked the ends. "Here is when you joined in 2000. Here is where you'll end, 2009. And here is where you are." He made an X a little past the middle of the paper. "You're more than halfway there. Here's boot camp and AIT. You soared right past ROTC years one and two because you're in the Guard. All you have left is LDAC, your MS4 year, BOLLOK 2, then your officer basic course and your branch training. After a tour in Iraq, you'll come back and go to captain school. By then you can move on, having fulfilled the requirements."

If this was supposed to be a pep talk, it was having the opposite effect. Staring at the paper, I imaged all those hours dressed up to be someone I wasn't. I'd be twenty-six years old in 2009. And I'd have been in the military all of my adult life. I felt like bursting into tears, but I nodded instead.

"Look, I recruited you into the program because you have potential. You make a good leader. I don't want to lose you." He slid the paper forward. "Take that. Put it on your wall. A little perspective. You're over halfway there."

I held the paper, concentrating on the white between all the labeled X's. All that time *not* in uniform. But I knew I couldn't follow through. Deep down, I'd known it for weeks, maybe months. At some point, the scales had tipped. There was no last straw, no aha moment, just creeping momentum, like a bead of sap working itself out of a pine tree.

The paper did go up on my wall at home. A white flag of surrender. I was ready to admit I was a traitor.

April 2005: Morro Bay, CA

"GI Rights, this is Andy."

Oh God. I wondered whether Andy could trace my call like a 9-1-1 operator if I hung up.

"Hello?"

"Yes, um, hello," I stuttered.

"What can I do for you? Do you have a question for us?"

I left my room and strode toward the living room. "I have a couple questions about discharges."

"Can I ask if you are currently in the military?"

"I'm in the National Guard and ROTC." I strode back toward the stairs.

"You are." He said it like he'd won some prize.

Marching in a loop from the living room's back wall, through the dining room and kitchen, then back to the starting line, I told him my story. "I don't think I can keep this up. I don't think I can... I need to find a way out before I go completely crazy." I was out of breath.

"We can help. What's your name?"

"Rosa."

"There are options, Rosa. For instance, there are conscientious objectors who serve in a non-combat role. They don't carry any weapons. They don't have a direct role in the war. Would you be comfortable doing that?"

"No." There was no hesitation this time. "I don't think we should be over there at all. The Army needs the cooks and fuelers and pencil pushers just as much as everyone else."

"Okay, let's figure out what the basis of your application would be. Are you religious?"

"I'm agnostic."

Andy gave an audible sigh. "That's going to make things harder. Most discharges are given to people whose service is in conflict with their devout faith. Quakers and Orthodox Jews have the best chance."

What did faith have to do with it? "How does that work? Are you saying they won't believe I'm against the war if I don't believe in God?"

"I'm saying it's more difficult to explain your morals and prove their strength if they aren't religious in nature. Now, is there anything medically that would prevent you from serving?"

I dropped onto the couch. I thought about the hypoglycemia possibility, or the shoulder clicking thing, but they were weak arguments at best. There was only one real medical issue with me. "Sometimes I cut myself."

"Are you suicidal?"

"Nothing like that."

"How do you cut yourself? Where?"

"On my arms, mostly. It's self-mutilation I guess."

"How long has that been going on?"

I traced the scars on my arms. They didn't look that bad. I wondered what they needed to look like to be considered legitimate. "Since high school. I mean, it's not serious. It's not very often. I started seeing a therapist at school."

"For depression?"

"Yes," I forced out.

"It sounds like you would fit in both the medical discharge category and the conscientious objector category. We can use one as a fallback. Or combine the two."

A flare of optimism shot out of my chest. "You think I can get a discharge?"

"I think you have a stronger case than most. But I have to warn you, most applications are denied. The Army does not like granting CO discharges. They can make your life pretty difficult during the process too, which takes months, or years. There's a lot of stigma and a lot of backlash, and you'll be getting it from both your Guard unit and ROTC. Are you ready for that?"

I imagined how the guys back in my little engineering unit would react. These were guys who hated Bill Clinton for the sole reason that he'd been behind the biggest downsizing of the US military in decades. They were steadfast Republicans who believed that we were in Iraq because of 9/11. They were so closed-minded—so convinced I was "brainwashed by the liberal media" that I'd insisted on a book swap. I'd read Sean Hannity's *Let Freedom Ring* if they would read something, anything, by a Democrat or Progressive. I held up my end of the bargain. They chickened out. But while they were cowards when it came to political debate, they cared about me, loved me even. One had said he would take a bullet for me and been unflinchingly serious about it. If they knew what I was about to do, they would be disgusted.

Most painful would be Sergeant Morgan's reaction. He'd treated me like a daughter—teaching me how to care for the unit's hulking machinery, helping me rescue three baby rabbits from a freshly tilled field, selling me his old car below Blue Book value when mine crapped out. I imagined watching his face fall and his eyes shut off as I transformed from eager equipment operator to backstabber. He'd feel betrayed. I'd be ashamed. We would never have a real conversation again.

Then there were the ROTC cadets. The cadets could very well make my life hell when they found out I was declaring myself a conscientious objector. I hadn't made an effort to make friends with them despite seeing them all the time—at morning PT, in military science class twice a week, in the food court, and every Thursday evening when we trekked out to Poly Canyon to play war games.

But nothing could overpower the dread and regret that had burrowed deep under my skin. Nothing. "I'm ready," I said.

"Good. I'm going to send you an information packet. It's very important you read all of it. Then give me a call."

"I'll be able to submit everything before I go to ROTC training camp, right? It starts at the end of May." I'd chosen the earliest slot, partly to get it over with, partly to ensure I wouldn't run into anyone I knew. I didn't feel like playing the amiable version of myself I showed the Cal Poly cadets. I felt like playing a shadow.

"There's no way your packet will be ready in a month and a half," Andy said.

"I'm a fast writer. A good writer." I pictured the application as a series of blanks and boxes, a few spaces for long answers.

"It's not about being fast. This will be the most important essay you'll ever write. We'll need to work on it together. Then you'll need to approach people who know you well, who are behind you, to write letters of support. The letters will need revision. *Then* you tell your commanders."

The sunlight was fading fast outside. The fog was rolling in off the ocean and stealing up the streets toward the foothills. I wanted to crawl into bed and hibernate.

"That launches the next phase," Andy went on. "You have to be evaluated by an Army psychologist and a chaplain. Then you're interrogated by an investigating officer before the whole packet goes off for review. All this happens while you keep going to drill, keep doing everything your ROTC program expects of you."

"I can't say I'm a conscientious objector now and refuse to train?" I asked, thinking again of the rebel outside the hospital at Ft. Jackson.

"Sorry. You need to go to officer training camp. How long is it?"

"A month." A month of living lies, a camouflaged imposter.

"Oh, that's not bad at all—in the grand scheme of things."

I got off the phone with Andy and plodded back to my room. I pushed my rucksack into my closet, where I couldn't see it, and crawled into bed. In a minute or two I would be drifting in hibernation—suspended high above the Army tangle. And when I woke up, there might be a whole minute of zen obliviousness before I remembered who I was and who I needed to pretend to be.

On a hike with DJ Sasquatch.

Zack on San Francisco Bay, Oakland in the background, @2005.

The rock quarry at Camp Roberts, CA, 2004.

Sergeant "Morgan" in a new forklift at Camp Roberts, CA, 2004.

PART III

SUMMER CAMP

1. CLAUSTROPHOBIA

May 2005: Ft. Lewis, WA

My Grandma Millie's claustrophobia was so severe she took tranquilizers before boarding a plane. She avoided elevators, walk-in closets, buses, and movie theaters where she couldn't get an aisle seat. If someone on television got stuck in an enclosed space and the music took a menacing turn, she changed the channel. The condition was so foreign to my sisters and me as kids—so dramatic and mysterious—that we developed a curious envy. Every year or so we would take turns shutting each other up in a wooden chest to test whether we had the claustrophobia gene, and if we did, to build up our tolerance. It was training of a sort. Leila and I were all about training.

Alura played along with the claustrophobia test once. Three and a half years older than me and six years older than Leila, I remember her assuming a haughty air in the face of our antics most of our childhood. In any case, Alura wanted out of the chest immediately, declared the experiment a success, she'd been "very uncomfortable," and never agreed to go in again. Leila wanted to be left inside for long periods of time to *really* give it a chance. But no matter how long I sat on the lid with her trapped inside, she emerged unimpressed.

Maybe it was the lack of drama from my sisters that made me strain for a reaction when it was my turn. How cool would it be to have claustrophobia? So in the darkness, breathing in the chest's wood-wool scent, I'd imagine the walls closing in, compressing until I couldn't breathe. I'd start to gasp and pant. I'd push against the lid, trying to tip Leila off. And after a calculated time, I'd ramp up my manufactured panic and yell, "Let me out, let me out!" Leila would fling open the lid and I'd clamber out, chest heaving, eyes wide. "I think I felt it."

As my plane touched down in Seattle, I stared out the window at the tarmac, my mind racing—searching for a crack, a keyhole, a fissure, something I'd overlooked that would release me from *the contract, the contract, the nine-year contract*. We taxied to the gate with a brisk urgency that squeezed at my throat. The air was smothering and full of static and my seat belt was too tight and the seats too close together and I couldn't move my legs—but I didn't want to trade this small claustrophobia for the large Army claustrophobia lurking outside. As everyone filed off, I waited, thinking how if I slouched down far enough the flight attendants would start boarding the next flight and soon I would be Elsewhere—off the grid.

But no. I'd merely be AWOL from Leadership Development Advanced Camp (LDAC), which was required of all ROTC cadets heading into their senior year. I stood up and wrestled my backpack down from the overhead compartment.

The tincture of defeat and apprehension running through my veins thickened when I spotted the first eggheads in the airport corridors. They weren't true eggheads, like boot camp guys with their hair shaved down to the skull. These were half-eggheads, with high and tight military cuts, ramrod posture, and eyes trained straight ahead. Some wore black combat boots with their jeans, and I was sure some were itching to break out CamelBaks and start sucking down water like they were already in the desert. The women were harder to spot, but not impossible—young, little to no makeup, sports bras instead of normal bras, jeans instead of shorts, hair up in braids or buns.

I turned into an empty gate area to make a goodbye call to Zack.

"Well, well. If it isn't del Ducathon," he said. "Miss me already?"

"Like crazy." Despite how unavailable he was and my unease at knowing I liked him more than he liked me, we hadn't broken up. Every time I reached the end of my rope he'd pull some irresistible move and I'd turn into a deer caught in the headlights. Sometimes it was little gifts or dinners out. But most of the time all he needed to do was corner me and growl as he kissed my neck from ear to collar bone, sliding his hands into my back pockets. I'd never been so physically attracted to someone. And that chemistry, for the foreseeable future at least, was far more powerful than rational thought.

"Do you have time to talk before they cart me off?" I asked.

"Can you call back in ten minutes, beautiful?"

"I don't think I'll have ten minutes."

"Sure you will. I need to put out this fire real quick."

In the spirit of living lies—that Zack would love me as much as I loved him if we moved in together, that I was a highly motivated cadet, that my emotions were not dust devils spinning out of control—I said, "Okay. I'll call you back in a while."

I took a shuttle to a far corner of the airport, bright and airy with sunlight flooding through tall windows. The check-in station was clearly flagged—not with signs, but hordes of eggheads sporting ROTC shirts and, just as I'd suspected, CamelBaks. I thought about calling my mom or Leila or Alura, but I couldn't weather another conversation that would reinforce the sensation that I was caught in the steel jaws of a bear trap while everyone else enjoyed a normal summer. I thought about calling Andy from the GI Rights Hotline for moral support, but quickly remembered I'd left the number at home. I didn't want to be caught with it when they combed through our things. I checked in and dumped my bags on a nearby chair.

"Are you ready for *LDAC*?" a husky guy asked me, grinning.

I gave him a blank stare, pausing, pausing, pausing. "Oh yeah."

He waited, perhaps hoping I was trying to make some kind of joke, then shrugged. "Well somebody's grumpy."

We tramped out into glaring sunlight and lined up on the sidewalk to wait for our bus to Ft. Lewis. I assessed packing jobs with clandestine glances. Everyone else looked ready to move overseas for the summer while I had brought the bare essentials. I didn't expect our entrance to LDAC to be any more dignified than boot camp, and I didn't have the energy to carry anything extra, not even a journal.

The ride to Ft. Lewis was over all too soon and I spent the rest of the day bracing for lockdown—a paranoid little turtle. I barely noticed where I was. But after hours of waiting in the shade of oaks and Douglas firs as we went through a series of in-processing stations, it dawned on me that we were on the prettiest base I'd ever seen. Where the parade grounds ended, prairie spotted with wildflowers began. Beyond the prairie rose a tall, dense, green-soaked forest. The treetops pierced a blue sky almost as vast as the sky in Montana, and in the distance were purple-hued mountains. The mountains would have been impressive on their own if they weren't dwarfed by Mount Rainier, looming like some colossus, mist shrouding its snowcapped peak. It was all very striking, especially compared to the ugliness the Army had inflicted on the landscape. Rows of whitewashed barracks looked like transplants from another era, and like a storm might reduce them to piles of plywood. The parade grounds outside the barracks used to be asphalt but were now mostly gravel. Instead of sidewalks there were gray, dusty trails.

Around 6:00 p.m., we filed across the parade ground to the Third Platoon barracks for "shakedown." The time and place seemed perfect for them to shatter our complacency, so when I fell into formation next to the overenthusiastic cadet from the airport who'd declared me grumpy and who now gave me a carefree smile of recognition, I thought, *Great, this chump is going to make our lives hell.* Sure enough, while the rest of us held formation, Chump moseyed up to the sergeant, who was paging through a sheaf of papers, and asked, "You in charge of Third Platoon?"

The sergeant studied him with wild blue eyes and a tiger's smile. "Why yes I am, *Cadet.*"

"I wanted to introduce myself," Chump said, extending his right hand.

I realized I was holding my breath and cringing.

"The name's Nissenger," he said, still holding out his hand, "but everyone calls me Nis."

"Is that right." The sergeant looked like Baloo from *The Jungle Book*—paunchy build, relaxed demeanor, quick smile—but unhinged somehow too, like he was fresh out of an insane asylum. He took his time looking Nissenger up and down with those crazy eyes of his, then shifted the stack of papers to his left hand and shook. "Where you from, Nissenger?"

"University of San Diego." Nissenger puffed out his chest.

"You prior service?"

His posture fell slack. "Yeah. I'm an SMP now."

My eyes widened. Same as me. SMP stood for Simultaneous Membership Program, meaning you were both an ROTC cadet and enrolled in a National Guard unit. How could he be prior service and act like this?

"Why don't you fall in, Cadet," the sergeant told Nissenger, walking to the front of formation. He didn't call us to attention or put us in parade rest. He didn't even introduce himself. But by now I could read his name tag: DENSEY. "All right, here's how this'll work," he said. "I'll call off an item, you hold it up, and I'll check you off. Huah?"

"Huah," we echoed.

"Six pairs white PT socks."

We held them up. Densey glanced at each of us and made a mark on his paper. This wasn't like any shakedown I'd seen before. Usually you upended all your stuff, scrambled to arrange it in piles, and rabid drill sergeants pawed through everything in the hopes of finding something embarrassing, like scented tampons or contraband, which included virtually everything: phones, food, gum, Tic Tacs, multivitamins, over-the-counter drugs, headphones, makeup, nail polish, perfume, diaries, hair dryers, sports bras in colors other than black, white or gray, colored hair bands, books (except the Bible), magazines, porn, matches, jewelry, playing cards, condoms, computers, cameras, civilian clothes, and the kitchen sink.

"Underwear, hold 'em up." Sergeant Densey called.

"Is it okay if I only brought two tighty-whities?" Nissenger asked, hands on hips. "I know the packing list said ten, but I usually go commando."

A round of snickers went up. Sergeant Densey shot me his tiger grin. *Why me?* I snapped to parade rest.

"You're funny," Densey told Nis. "And you're on my list."

"Your list," Nissenger beamed. "I'm honored, Sergeant, absolutely honored."

Half an hour later we were repacked, no sign of lockdown. As everyone else milled or flopped down on duffle bags to talk, I kept tabs on the cadre walking past, tracking them until they were out of sight, ready to snap to attention and salute if I saw officer insignia. Jesus, they were really fucking with us. Either that or we had landed somewhere over the rainbow.

After dinner chow we were siphoned into the rickety barracks to unpack. Our acting platoon leader directed me up a flight of dirty brown linoleum steps. At the top of the stairs was a long room lined with bunk beds and wall lockers on either side, camo gear strewn everywhere. About a dozen guys attended to their lockers or read manuals or stood around talking. We were going to sleep in the same room as them? *That* was new. But when I checked behind me, I saw a battered door marked "Female Only."

The room should have been condemned. A layer of filth coated the walls and ceiling. The warped floor was pocked with rust spots. The windows leaned out of the slots they were supposed to fit in, their tattered screens rippling in the breeze. The two bunks had spindly metal frames, stained mattresses, and springs that sagged like hammocks.

"There's an empty locker over here," said a pale, freckled girl with glasses. "I'm Hall. Fourth squad."

"Del Duca," I said, lugging my bags through the door. "Third squad."

A tiny, compact girl finished dumping her duffle onto a bottom bunk and waved. "I'm Gill, fourth squad. An' before y'all ask, I might as well tell you the accent's from Texas."

A girl that could have passed for thirteen came clomping in behind me, a bag slung over one shoulder and a dazed look on her face. "Who's the other female in third squad?" she asked.

"Guilty." I said, raising my hand. I took in her stubby arms and legs, her crooked glasses, her looped ponytail likely to slip loose at any moment.

"Jessie Ayma." She extended her hand.

"Del Duca. I guess we're going to be battle buddies."

"I know; I'm so excited!"

The declaration took me by surprise. It was something you'd say if you had been imagining some glorious friendship, some intimate bond of warrior sisterhood.

Like she'd envisioned us sharing pilfered food from the chow hall and swapping secrets on guard duty late at night. Like she expected this friendship to tie tight like a knot, and in a few years, we'd be bridesmaids at each other's weddings and send each other long letters at Christmas. I couldn't help but smile back. The crocodile smile of a mole. An imposter. I retreated to my corner and tried to shove down the dry-socket, sandpapery, coiled-spring, locked-in-the-trunk-as-the-car-sinks-underwater feeling. *Claustrophobia.*

2. OH LORD, I WANNA GO

May 2005: Ft. Lewis, WA

When we fell into formation at 4:45 the next morning, the sun was already rising.

"It's all downhill from here!" someone shouted.

I wanted to roll my eyes but closed them instead.

"How about that shower last night?" came a voice from first squad. "Nothin' like standing around naked in front of a bunch of guys in a cement room."

"How about your *mom* last night?" came a voice from the back.

The platoon let out a loud, collective "ohhhh."

"Already with the mom jokes?"

"Taxi?" someone called.

Our temporary platoon leader (PL) shouted, "At ease!" At ease isn't just a position. It can also be an order to shut up, or an order to stand at attention because an officer is approaching. In this case it meant shut up. "Now what do y'all think about comin' up with our platoon motto?" the PL said in a southern drawl.

"Already done," someone announced.

"It better not be lame," the cadet next to me said.

The banter ramped up. "Don't you guys have anything better to do with your time?"

"Overachiever."

"You're just jealous."

"How about 'kill'?"

"How about 'LDAC rules!'"

"'It's all downhill from here!'"

"At ease. Now let 'em tell us what the idea is," the PL broke in.

Nissenger stepped out of first squad and turned to the platoon, ruddy-faced and pleased with himself. "Ready for it?"

"Huah."

"'Always hard, always ready.'"

A round of snickers went up from the guys, and I felt a smile threatening to surface on my own face. There were no objections. So we started practicing.

"Platoon," the PL called. "Atten-*huh*."

We snapped to attention and belted out, "Always hard, always ready!"

"Parade, *rest*. That sounded sloppy. Let's try it again."

Sergeant Densey rounded the corner from the direction of the chow hall. The PL had his back to him, but everybody else saw Densey fold his arms across his chest and stare at us like an alligator might stare at a potbellied pig.

"Atten-*huh*!"

"Always hard, always ready," we thundered.

"That was a good one, y'all. One more time."

"Hold up," said Densey.

The PL whirled. We remained frozen at attention.

"That your motto?" Densey asked, enunciating the two syllables of motto.

"Yes, Sergeant."

"What is it? I don't know if I heard right."

"Always hard, always ready, Sergeant."

Densey ran his crazy-stare over the first rank. "And who thought of that?"

Nis raised his hand. Densey threw his head back and studied the sky. "Cadet Nissenger, what does that motto mean to you?"

"That a warrior should keep in top physical shape and be prepared for anything, Sergeant."

"Oh, really?" Densey stalked the length of first squad, but kept on walking into the barracks, calling over his shoulder, "Go on and get some chow."

The feeling of impending doom in my gut heightened. Surely we wouldn't get away with this. Surely they were giving us free reign only to yank on the choke collar when we were least expecting. Then misery would descend and I could serve my time in misanthropic peace without these idiots trying to make things fun, trying to enjoy themselves. They could still go back to their colleges and say, "No, I'd rather be a civilian," and walk away, no consequences. They'd joined ROTC like it was some club, some extracurricular activity or frat project, hence all the joking and bravado. I hated them for this. No matter how goddamn likeable they were.

"Right, *face*. Forward, *march*."

And we were off in ragamuffin style, because the jokers couldn't keep time, or formation, to save their lives. Instead of opting for practicality, they'd apparently devoted themselves to learning the Army's most ironic cadences of all time.

"They say that in the Army, the coffee's mighty fine," the PL shouted, completely out of sync. The cadets around me echoed the line back, maybe thinking there was actually coffee waiting for them in the chow hall.

"It looks like muddy water and tastes like turpentine."

"Oh lord, I wanna go."

"But they won't let me go."
"Home, hey!"

3. SUMMER CAMP

May 2005: Ft. Lewis, WA

"I heard that you're required to touch your chest to the ground for them to count a push-up," Tinning was saying when I joined formation the next morning. Tinning had a rich, robotic voice that sounded like he'd been groomed to work at NPR from birth. "And if you lift a finger off the ground, merely one finger, you have to start all over."

I tried to remember the names of my squad members as they traded horror stories about the PT test, which was the day's first activity. It was hard without their BDU name tags. There was NPR Tinning, Hunt, who looked like a tall, gangly scarecrow in his black PT shorts and gray shirt, and Stinson, who was the baby of the platoon at eighteen.

"Our fourth-year cadets told us they won't count the first five push-ups, guaranteed," said Kassano, who'd explained to us that he was a "little sore" that he wasn't allowed to wear his combat patch at LDAC. He'd already done a tour in Afghanistan. As for his cracked glasses, he hadn't had time to fix them before coming.

"No, they count every other one," Ayma said. She'd used one of those thick black ties to put her hair up, but I could tell it would slide out before we were through the first event.

"Just do one push-up a second," said Kilgore, who cracked jokes with the ease of a professional comedian. He looked like an elf next to McGreer, who was the biggest cadet in the platoon, as well as the best looking: well over six foot, a cut two hundred pounds, green eyes, dark hair, and a dusting of freckles. McGreer had told us he went to a military school in Oregon where he was an art major, a cage fighter, and played the bagpipes. Beyond that, he hadn't uttered a word.

"Fall in!" the PL yelled.

We marched over to the PT test grounds—a dirt track surrounded by rubber-top. The whole company was there, over two hundred cadets.

"Take a knee," one of several fresh-faced lieutenants ordered.

We arranged ourselves on wobbly knees. I found a tuft of grass so mine wouldn't be ground up by the gravel.

"You are about to take the Army Physical Fitness Test, a test that will measure your muscular endurance and cardiorespiratory fitness. Listen closely to the test instructions…"

I tuned out the lieutenant (LT) and admired his PA system. He was using a wireless microphone, his voice amplified through two speakers. Fancy. Suddenly a phone ringtone blasted through the speakers. The female lieutenant demonstrating how to do correct push-ups dug in her shorts and pulled out a cell phone.

"Hello? Oh really? Well, I'm a little busy right now. I'll have to call you back." She flipped the phone closed and shoved it back in her pocket.

My eyebrows shot up. They were making this a *skit*?

The LT shook his head in mock disapproval. "You may reposition your hands and/or feet during the event as long as they remain in contact with the ground at all times," he read from the regulations.

I looked around at the rest of my platoon. It was like glancing sideways in a dark movie theater, seeing their glassy eyes fixed on the entertainment. Some smiled or laughed as another cell phone blast washed over us. Cage fighter McGreer was the only person who looked impassive, but I had a feeling that was standard for him.

"What do you want?" the female LT whined into her prop phone. "I'm in the middle of something important."

"Your performance has been terminated," the male LT said.

It finally dawned on me that the crackdown was never coming. They were going to treat us like kids, not inmates—not even soldiers. Half-soldiers. This was how LDAC had earned the nickname "camp." Nissenger had known it all along, the bastard. Sure, there were rules and challenges and punishments here, but they didn't come close to what enlisted soldiers had to endure upon their "welcome" into the Army. The question was *why*?

I tuned out the rest of the demonstrations, turning over the *why*. It was clear the majority of cadets at LDAC had no idea how the real Army worked—how tough boot camp was, how dysfunctional monthly drills could be, how rank often made no sense. Maybe ROTC leaders wanted to keep it that way. They didn't want to make LDAC as long or hard as boot camp and AIT. Not with us fighting two wars. Not with recruitment down. Not until next year's commissioning cemented the deal, roping them into a binding contract. Maybe camp was part of a carefully concocted façade—a bubble separate from the real Army, where cadets believed they were part of some big fun family that understood *they* were too smart for the training enlisted soldiers had to go through. What a waste of time *that* would be. They were college-educated, after all. They were natural leaders.

Instead of being relieved, I was angry. It burned, this realization we were off the hook. Yet another double standard. I sucked in the anger like a fire sucking air, obliterating the nagging leak of traitorous guilt that had pooled in my shoes that morning. I wasn't gaming the system by being a conscientious objector. The system had played me, was playing us all in some way or another.

In the chow hall I dropped my tray next to my blonde beanpole roommate, Hall, across from Kilgore. Ayma, whose PT shirt had somehow acquired a large grass stain, squeezed in next to me. Hostage to the ever-encroaching worry that I'd end up ravenous before our next meal, I ripped the foil off my yogurt and gulped it down in three spoonfuls before moving on to the hash browns.

"How did you do, Ayma?" Hall asked. We'd both passed her early in the two-mile run, her hair halfway out of her ponytail, one shoe untied.

"I passed. That's all that counts," Ayma said, forking a lump of powdered egg into her mouth. "One step closer to commission."

Hall and I shared a look.

When no one took her bait, Ayma asked Kilgore, "Do you know who the other end-of-camp commissionee is? I heard our company had two."

"I don't." Kilgore squinted at Ayma. "Are you saying you're getting butter bars at the end of camp?"

"That's why this summer is so important. I'm fast-tracked. If I don't pass everything I won't get commissioned, and then I can't start law school in the fall. I'm going into JAG Corps." She fumbled with her milk carton.

The guys around us perked up. Everyone else needed another year of ROTC and yet another "summer camp" before being commissioned. Congratulations ensued. McGreer, the Scottish giant, removed the milk carton from Ayma's clumsy hands, opened the spout, and plunked it in front of her.

Ayma gave a little sigh. "You guys are the best."

The girl we'd have to salute in four weeks needed help opening her milk. Summer camp.

4. REEVALUATION

May 2005: Ft. Lewis, WA

Finn shook out his legs. "Why am I so tired when all we've been doing is standing?"

It was 1:30 p.m. and the sun had been blazing down on us for two hours. I was being evaluated as platoon leader for the day, and he'd been assigned platoon sergeant (responsible for making the PL's orders happen). As leaders, we were stuck at the pre-rehearsal of our Regimental Activation Ceremony. The rest of the platoon was under the shade of trees a few hundred yards away studying for the written land navigation test.

"It's the heat," I said, beads of sweat working their way down my back.

"They should have done this in the shade. I wonder if this is a test. If one of us should challenge the location of the ceremony."

I furrowed my eyebrows, wondering if Finn thought this worked like some kind of reality TV show. "We should at least have everyone unblouse their boots," I said. "It's hot enough someone should have given the order hours ago."

"Good idea," he agreed.

We watched the platoons snake their way toward us. As usual, Third Platoon resembled a drunken caterpillar.

"Everybody, we're unblousing boots," Finn shouted once the platoon reached us. Half the cadets bent down immediately. The other half watched from the corners of their eyes, curious what unblousing meant, before yanking their pant legs out and rolling up the cuffs.

"Are we unblousing?" the Second Platoon leader called to me. He was a short redhead, freckles like paint splatters.

"My platoon is."

"Who said you could?"

"Me." I frowned. "Can't we do stuff like that when we're leadership?"

He shrugged and turned to his platoon sergeant. Second Platoon's cadets started to unblouse.

The cadets of Fourth Platoon started gossiping with our cadets.

"Are we supposed to do that?"

"I don't know."

"Are we rolling up our sleeves too?"

"I hope not. Mine always come out uneven."

The beefy cadet who was being evaluated as company commander trotted up to Finn. "I know it's hot, but everyone needs to be dress right dress for the ceremony. We can't have one or two platoons unbloused."

As Finn started apologizing I joined the huddle. "Doesn't it make the most sense to have everyone unblouse then? It must be at least CAT 4 out here."

The cadet squinted down at me, face slick with sweat.

"You know, heat categories?" I said. "Even at CAT 3 you're supposed to unblouse your boots."

"We're not going to be out here for that long," he said.

"We probably have another hour of practice before the actual ceremony. People might start passing out," I said.

"Tell your cadets not to lock their knees then. You need to conform with the rest of the regiment."

I could see Beefcake was being an ass because he was the ranking leader here. He was in charge. He must assert his authority, or risk getting a bad score on his precious evaluation. (At the end of camp, our "Blue Card" evaluation scores were added to other test scores for an overall ranking. That ranking was a big deal, and could mean getting into the branch you wanted, or falling short.)

"Did the cadre tell you we can't unblouse?" I asked.

"*I* told you."

Christ, it was going to be a long month. "Would you mind if I checked with the cadre? We're all going to bake on this asphalt."

"I'm company commander. I'm giving you an order."

I gave up. An hour later, practice ended and the ceremony began. My heartbeat pounding in my head, my heels heavy enough to bore holes in the ground, we went through a jumble of calls to attention back to parade rest. We listened to creeds and saluted the flag, sweat dripping off our chins. The loudspeakers blasted the history of the Sixth Infantry Regiment for the umpteenth time, and for the umpteenth time we heard how the Sixth Regiment had been a main force, for fifty years, in the Indian Wars. I glanced to my left, my right, hoping to catch flared nostrils, a glare, a sneer. Nothing but blank eyes, bored faces, cadets discretely shifting their weight.

I thought about the word *evaluation*. It was a charged word here at LDAC. Yet year after year, this ceremony had taken place and no one had stopped to think: *gee, I don't know if we should expect cadets to be honored to carry on the name of a group that was a "main force" in the genocide of Native Americans for half a century*.

Maybe that was the problem in Washington too. The more the media uncovered about the Iraq war, the more it proved that a faulty evaluation from one source had led to a war against an abstract idea: terror. And now that the wars were freight trains, no one was reevaluating the necessity, the principle, the myriad costs.

Reevaluation was my way out of the Army. A group of my "superiors" would judge whether I fit the category, whether I was worthy. I let the line of officers across the parade ground come into focus. Unlike the cadets around me, they were not shifting their weight. They stood still and heavy as statues, faces shadowed under their caps. I imagined trying to explain myself to any one of them. We might as well have been standing on opposite sides of the Grand Canyon.

5. NAVIGATION

June 2005: Ft. Lewis, WA

The whole battalion met up for land navigation, which began with the night course. Packed into bleachers bordering a warm, green meadow, we waited for the sun to set, the atmosphere strangely like a party—hundreds of college kids scoping each other out, a loud buzz rising as we realized no one was going to stop us from socializing.

"I'm so nervous," Ayma said, pawing through her plastic bag of extra supplies, which included a granola bar, two mini flashlights, socks, protractors, pencils, and a whistle. "I only got two out of five when my school did night land nav."

I hadn't found shit on Cal Poly's night land navigation course. Not one point. But I wasn't about to admit that to anyone.

Kassano fell into his role of reassuring Ayma as I watched Hunt initiate a pebble-throwing fight with a girl from Fourth Platoon. Finn started showing Nissenger martial arts moves as NPR Tinning and Kilgore the Elf worked on a secret squad handshake. Maybe the atmosphere was more like a Boy Scouts Jamboree than a party.

As if cued by that thought, Second Platoon erupted in one of their "Whose house, our house!" rants. Stinson exchanged a smirk and nod with Nissenger. Soon the whole platoon was discretely elbowing each other. I'd almost forgotten about our little plan to embarrass Second Platoon. Two full minutes passed.

"Whose house?" roared Second Platoon's leader a final time, hoarse as a donkey.

"Our house!" the platoon screamed back.

Silence.

"In the middle of our street," we sang.

The bleachers erupted in guffaws. I found myself giggling, then stopped. What was I doing, goofing off with the rest of them, acting like this was a joke, like we weren't all headed for a war zone in a year or two? I pulled the brim of my BDU cap low and slouched against the bleacher behind me, arms crossed.

Hall leaned to peer under my cap. "What's going on under there?"

I uncrossed my arms, remembering I was undercover. The Pretender. "Just enjoying the show," I said, forcing a smile.

Dusk settled onto the treetops like an illusion—light one minute, dim the next. A group of second lieutenants emerged from the tree line to warn us of past disasters:

"We had one cadet last cycle, dropped his map and supplies down a Porta-Potty. Had to fish 'em out of the shitter and keep going."

"We caught one particularly bright crayon using a cell phone to call OnStar for the grid coordinates of his points. All y'alls cell phones better be locked up back at the barrack storage containers."

"Do not leave the course, cadets. We are on the edge of the base. Cross the course boundary, and you will be tackled by a security team."

"Do not fall asleep on the course. Last time we spent the whole night on search party detail."

"Do not let us catch you speaking to anyone, including yourself."

"Do not come back without your map, your protractor, your compass, and your pencil, or you will fail."

Their spiel over, the lieutenants released us. The tension dripped out of my body as I stood in line for my test supplies, knowing I'd be on my own for the next three hours, in the dark, with no need to police what came across my face. Invisible. Kneeling on the dirt road, I plotted and triple checked my points before joining the swarm of cadets striding off into the night, so many ants.

• • •

Eight hundred and forty steps later, I turned to face a dark tangle of forest. If I'd done my math right, my first point was straight ahead, one hundred meters. Peering into the woods, I tried to make out a tree to aim for in the brush, but all I saw was a bulk of black. With my dimmed flashlight clipped to the front of my Load Bearing Equipment (LBE), I crashed through the undergrowth, my pants growing wet. Almost immediately, a post with a green glow stick emerged. This would be a piece of cake. I wrote down the post's code, punched my card with the "clicker" hanging from the post—evidence I had physically been there—and strode back toward the road, humming a little victory song.

I'd gone at least two hundred meters and still hadn't hit gravel when I started to get worried. All I saw were cadet trails of flattened grass. How could I have gotten off track when I'd just come this way? Bringing out my compass, I calculated the azimuth back to the road from my map. It seemed like with every step I either slid off a mossy log or stumbled over some stump or rock. Branches clung to my gear and reached for my face. And instead of the road, I hit another land nav point. The four cadets clustered around the post glanced at me. I let my compass dangle from my belt and pretended to write down the post code on my card. The number was the same as the point I had just left. I'd walked in a big circle.

Tears sprang to my eyes. God, I was stupid. Charging off blind, thinking I was all badass when I couldn't even walk straight. And now I wanted to cry like a baby because I'd been lost for ten minutes. This whole thing was a disaster. Not declaring myself a conscientious objector the second I'd realized I was one. Starting therapy sessions—sabotage sessions was more like it—right before coming to "camp." I wasn't a soldier. I wasn't even human. I was a blubbering puddle of emotion.

Give yourself permission to cry, I could hear Julie saying, her voice all smooth like some laundry detergent commercial. She did that sometimes, popped into my head like my very own shrink peanut gallery.

"Shut up," I muttered, kicking and lashing and stumbling my way back to the road, my compass clutched in my palm. *Shut up, shut up, shut up!*

I clicked my card at my second post and returned to the road to get my bearings. Post three was three hundred and fifty meters from an intersection half a mile away. If I was going to pass this goddamn test I couldn't afford to plunge further down the mine shaft. I set off, replaying scenes that would drub up rage.

• • •

"Five more years really isn't that long," Julie had said one day.

My eyes narrowed. "Five more years is a very long time."

"What would happen, realistically, if you spent another five years in the Army?" she pressed in her maddening, velvety voice.

I stewed a long time, feeling like a witness led by a prosecuting attorney. "I'd go through officer school and get called up. I'd probably do two tours in Iraq, hopefully helping with supply and admin. I'd somehow keep from going crazy. I'd survive."

She nodded a slow, contented nod.

• • •

Fury ignited like a matchstick. Who was Julie to tell me five years wasn't that long? I'd like to see her—anybody—stuck in something they hated year after year and not try to do something about it. *Surviving* wasn't the point. Being able to endure a shitty situation was not a reason to shut up and put up. I fed the flame.

• • •

"Hey Fleishman, do you have your yarmulke on underneath that cap?"

I was in a group of eight or so ROTC cadets marching out to Poly Canyon to help set up some activity. Earlier that week, soft-spoken Fleishman had told our instructor that ordering him to take off his yarmulke while we were all in civilian clothes was like ordering a Christian soldier to take off his cross necklace. Since the yarmulke was considered "headgear" he had lost the challenge.

"What if I do have it on?" asked Fleishman.

"Nothing," said Jones. "I was just curious."

"Say Fleishman," Rusk said. "Are you going to have a problem on gas chamber day?"

"What do you mean?"

"You know. Are you going to have a problem, going in the gas chamber?"

Jones punched Rusk, laughing. "You mean cause he's Jewish?"

• • •

The fire flared. These were the future leaders of our military. Jerks who thought it was okay to joke about the most sickening mass murder in recent history. I piled on fuel: Dad abandoning us and then having the audacity to be judgy about the military debacle. Aaron's friends telling me I was brainwashed coming back from boot camp. The DJs who sneered at my uniform and asked, "Are you into the military or something?" All the people going about their happy little lives, oblivious to the dirty war their country was waging.

With volcanic anger established and the danger of a breakdown gone, I scribbled the code of my third post onto my card, punched it with the clicker, and stormed off into the night. Two more points and I'd never have to do night land navigation again, unless it was my idea. I slipped my hand in my cargo pocket, rechecking the test supplies I'd been issued. Only this time, the stiff feel of plastic was gone.

Stopping in the middle of the road, I rifled through my pockets, my ammo pouches, my canteen holders. The protractor I'd had for the last two and a half hours had vanished. I double-checked everything—even my back pockets, where I never put anything—then hunched to check the road. Retracing my steps, I waited for my weak, red light to catch the gleam of plastic. Nothing but pebbles and puddles. Back at my last post, I scoured the brush and the trampled grass. No, it had to be in one of my pockets. It couldn't have fallen out. I tore through the contents again, then stopped to strategize.

If I found Ayma, I could borrow one of her extras. Or I could try to run to our bivouac site and get my own extra protractor from my ruck. *No, no, no.* How the hell would I randomly run into Ayma? And how would I happen to find the right bivouac site when the whole regiment was out here? And was it worth the gamble of being caught leaving the course? If I failed this test I'd have to retake it later, which would make me miss something else, and could bump me back to a later graduation date.

A cadet emerged from the darkness and made his way toward the point. I whipped my hands out of my pockets and pretended to study my map. The cadet wrote down the point code and turned to leave.

I decided to break the primary rule of the test. "You wouldn't happen to have an extra protractor, would you?" I whispered.

The cadet turned back.

"I lost mine," I said.

He flipped off his cap, but didn't move. I wondered if he was an officer, waiting for me to dig a deeper hole before he kicked me off the course, or if he was ignoring me. Then I realized he was holding his BDU cap *out*. I took a step forward and saw a protractor inside. "Oh my God, thank you."

"No problem," he said. "I already lost my pencil, but luckily I had a spare one of those too."

My anger evaporated, replaced by the easy camaraderie I'd felt on the bleachers. If I was honest, I'd felt that camaraderie the first morning, upon adoption of "always hard, always ready" as our platoon motto. How was I supposed to navigate LDAC when no one was playing their part right? They were supposed to be moronic, characterless, closed-minded, immature Army zombies. I was supposed to be the older, wiser underdog—floating on a sea of indignation until I could come home and stick it to The Man. *This is your war, not my war.*

But embedded face-to-face, all the ammunition I'd stored up sounded weak. Let me go because I'm emotionally screwy. I'm conflicted. Let me go because I don't believe in the war. *Let me go because I'm different.* Bullshit. In many ways we were exactly the same.

6. THIS IS MY RIFLE

June 2005: Ft. Lewis, WA

When Leila and I were in grade school, we loved pretending we were secret agents, treasure hunters, runaway orphans, or survivors of some natural catastrophe. We'd race from playground to playground on our bikes, composing our own theme music—full orchestra, heavy on the strings and brass. One summer we decided we needed to arm ourselves with water guns. We bought the cheapest we could find with our dollar-a-week allowance money—two pistol-shaped pieces of plastic. When our mother saw us filling the guns in the kitchen sink, her face tightened.

"Where did you get those?"

"At the dollar store."

"When?"

"Yesterday."

"On your own?"

I rolled my eyes. "Mom, you said we can go wherever we want as long as we keep off the busy streets."

"Fair enough. What are you going to do with those guns?"

"They're water guns," Leila said. "You fill them with water and shoot 'em."

"I don't like that."

Leila and I shared a look of exasperation.

"Are you saying we can't play with them?" I asked. "Because these cost us two dollars."

Mom shook her head and let out her angry sigh, more like a hiss. "No, I just wish you would have asked me. I want you to keep them out of my sight. They're too realistic."

We looked down at the toys. They were ridiculously unrealistic: neon yellow and orange.

"She just doesn't get it," Leila said as Mom stomped away.

I joined in the grumbling. "It's not like we're going to pretend to kill people. We're just going to shoot water. What's the harm in that?"

"Yeah, they're supposed to be fun."

We plugged the leaky guns and went outside. "Let's stand in a line and see whose goes farther," Leila said. "Or we could set up a target."

"Hold on, I'm thirsty," I said, pointing the gun in my mouth and shooting out a stream of water. I liked the gushing sound it made, the tickling on my gums and tongue. I gargled, cracking Leila up, until I spit the water onto her shirt, declaring war.

• • •

The Marines have this creed they memorize, dedicated to the rifle. How it's their best friend and how they're useless without it. "My rifle is human, even as I, because it is my life. Thus, I will learn it as a brother. We will become part of each other." The Army isn't that fanatic about the M16, but there is a sense of reverence and ritual attached to the rifle. You must carry it a certain way, stack it a certain way, check it in and out of the armory a certain way. You must memorize its serial number. You must call it a "rifle" or a "weapon," and never, ever a "gun." It must be with you at all times, even when you're sleeping. If a drill sergeant sees you drop it, they'll make you lay the rifle over the backs of your hands and do push-ups until their rage fades.

Waiting in line to be issued my M16, I thought about how, as a conscientious objector, I shouldn't like the idea of going out to the range. I tried to work up a superior attitude. Take the number of bullets we wasted, the land we destroyed. Atrocious. And the disturbing sensuality of being in a firing lane? Creeptown. There's nothing in the foxhole but you and your weapon—a weapon you cradle in your hands while you lay your cheek along its smooth, warm side. As you line up the front sight post with the shape of a human torso, you wait for your body to fall still at the end of a breath. This moment of frozen attunement is when you coax the trigger back with the soft pad of your index finger and feel the gun jolt alive. If you've done everything right, the half-person down the lane falls backward and lies flat on the ground. You can count how many people you would have killed had the targets been flesh, blood, and bone. My mother would be horrified by the whole thing.

But as I stepped forward and was handed a rifle, I was looking forward to getting in a foxhole and seeing if I could shoot expert this time. I trotted out of the armory and back to formation, slipping in next to the Scottish hunk, McGreer. For once he didn't ignore me, but raised his eyebrows.

"What?" I asked.

"How old is that thing?"

I turned the rifle over in my hands, noting its nicks and scrapes, how it was more gray than black. "It's beat up, that's for sure. And the handguards are different."

Kassano rejoined formation on my left. "Whoa, let me see that."

I traded weapons with him. He and McGreer exclaimed over the serial number. Then the entire squad had to pass it around while I shoved down unease at being empty-handed, at letting my rifle stray so far from me.

"What's the big deal?" I asked Tinning.

"It's an A1," he explained in his measured, public radio drone. "They made them back in the 1960s."

"Good luck qualifying on that dinosaur," Kilgore crowed, handing it to Hunt.

"I bet this thing's seen some action," Hunt said.

"It's probably killed people," Babyface Stinson said, passing it off to Nissenger.

"I'll trade you weapons, del Duca," Nissenger said. "This is so badass. It should be in a museum."

"She can't trade," Kassano said, pushing his cracked glasses higher up his nose. "They write down the serial numbers and you have to turn in the rifles in that exact order or there'll be hell to pay."

Nissenger rubbed the rifle's side with his chubby hands and gave it a pat goodbye before thrusting it at me. I hesitated, assumptions I'd made the past four years falling like dominos. I'd never thought about the possibility that the weapons I'd held could have been in combat. I'd never pictured someone looking down their barrels, squeezing the trigger, and seeing someone die. I'd assumed they were extras. I'd assumed they'd always been used for training. The assumptions of a child.

I reached out and reluctantly took the rifle. Already, it felt heavier. I pictured it locked up in the dark armory at night, reliving nightmares of dense jungles and smoke and death, remembering the hands of its wartime owner—some kid from Ohio or Texas or Alabama. I couldn't wait to turn it back in.

7. The Budding Saboteurs

June 2005, Ft. Lewis, WA

The night before our first day on the firing range I was trying to fall asleep, one arm slung over my eyes, my palm resting on my ear, muffling Hall and Gill's fourth-squad political argument: whether Morgenson was a better leader than Lemon. I heard Ayma clump through the door.

"That girl from second platoon was in there again, plucking her eyebrows at the sinks, *nude*."

Gill snorted. "Ayma, it's a shower room. People are gonna get naked," she said in her Texas drawl.

"Fine, but be naked in the *shower*. I don't want to be subjected to that."

Ayma's own shower routine went a little like this: Scamper in door, eyes down. Lug sack inside bathroom stall and lock door. Emerge in largest towel ever manufactured, bra and underwear still on. Dash to shower stall. Spend five minutes securing shower curtain and removing bra and underwear. Shower for 20 minutes. Scurry back to bathroom stall to dry and dress.

"Subjected to what?" Hall asked.

"Their junk all hanging out."

"Girls don't have junk."

"You know what I mean, Hall."

"Some people are comfortable with their bodies."

"Right! That doesn't mean they should assume everyone else is. Ooo, more tootsie rolls." The bunk rocked as Ayma dropped onto the bottom mattress.

Now that we were eating MREs more often, Ayma's posse of admirers would come by and drop off tootsie rolls whenever they had the chance. Ayma would trade any entree for two tootsie rolls. She was also a fan of the pound cake and life savers. Boys would leave the candy on her bed as a surprise or give it to her in person to hear her reaction: *Oh my goodness. Oh my goodness! You don't have to do that. Let me get you something. Do you like meatloaf? Chicken tetrazzini?*

The tootsie roll thing irked me because I knew that underneath Ayma's innocent little exterior lived a denizen of Dante's ninth circle of hell. Ayma kept us awake doing lord knows what until midnight every night, dragging things across the floor, dumping out her foot locker and tossing things back in, "polishing" her boots and leaving black streaks on the floor, changing the batteries in her flashlight because she always fell asleep with the damn thing on. In the mornings it was my job to make sure she got out of bed and to formation on time. It was like giving a cat a bath.

"This makes twenty-eight tootsie rolls in all," Ayma announced. "I won't have to eat any entrees."

"Girl, you gonna have to eat more'n tootsie rolls out in the field," said Gill.

"I don't like MREs. I just *can't* eat them."

"You better start," said Hall. "Or you'll starve."

"No, really, I'll be fine. I don't need that much food."

"Ayma. You're gonna be walkin' all day with a thirty-five pound ruck." I could picture the look Gill was shooting Ayma. Her annoyed Xena warrior princess look.

"I know, but I'm still not going to eat them. One thing that does worry me is I don't like water either."

I bolted upright and leaned over the side of the bunk. "*What?*"

Ayma was folding a pile of wrinkled brown shirts, smoothing them out with her doll-sized hands. "Water tastes nasty to me. That's why I don't really drink anything during the day and fill up on juice in the chow hall. Remember when we went to the PX? The reason I got as many Gatorades as I could is because I don't like water."

"That is *insane.*" I threw myself back on the mattress, setting the bunk frame creaking. "Drinking water is the most important thing in the field." I told the ceiling. "What happens when you're in the desert?"

Ayma laughed. "I won't be in the desert. I'll be in an office, remember? I'm JAG Corps. I'm never going to have to do any of this infantry stuff."

"Fine, forget about the desert. What happens when you have to drop out of field training and be treated for dehydration or heat exhaustion?"

"Butt out, del Duca. I've gotten this far fine on my own."

I rolled over to face the wall and flung my arm back over my ear and eyes.

• • •

"Thanks a lot, del Duca," Ayma said the next morning. Without my help, she'd been so late to formation the platoon leader had sent a team to extract her from our room.

"I thought you were just fine on your own," I said sweetly.

"Platoon, atten-*tion*!" Kirchov cut our conversation short and drove us through a whirlwind of pushups, sit-ups, and sprints before launching a platoon run.

"Two old ladies lyin' in bed," he belted out. We repeated the line.

"One rolled over to the other and said:

"I wanna be an airborne ranger

"Live a life of guts and danger…"

• • •

After a bone-jarring cattle car ride out to the range, we were stuffed into heavy flak jackets. As the temperature climbed to 95%, we sweltered. I'd never shot in a flak jacket, but it made sense given all this was practice for shooting in combat. Feeling like a snail in an ill-fitting shell, it took me an hour to zero. (It's important to zero before you go to the real range. You keep adjusting the sight posts until you can shoot a cluster of two shot groups within four centimeters of each other.)

My jacket not only kept me from putting the butt of my A1 in my shoulder pocket, but it knocked the back of my Kevlar up, which meant the front went down over my eyes. I couldn't see shit. Was this what everyone in Iraq was dealing with?

Wet with sweat, fantasizing about ripping off all my gear, all my clothes, I waited in line for twenty-round magazines at the qualification range.

"Foxhole number ten, cadet. Range walk, range walk!"

I hurried to my foxhole and found four other cadets sitting on a bench. I recognized Lemon from my platoon. He was holding a pen and a piece of paper.

"What's that for?" I shouted. We all had in earplugs.

"Oh, this?" he said in his Minnesota accent. "I'm gonna write down the order of when the targets pop up. For anyone who wants to memorize it for qualification day."

I frowned. "Isn't that cheating?"

"Cheating? It's being prepared. You still have to hit all the targets."

I nodded instead of pointing out that insurgents didn't pop up in pre-arranged patterns. We watched the girl in the foxhole miss all but four targets. The vest she wore looked like it was swallowing her whole.

Lemon jutted his chin toward the foxhole. "You see how her rifle kept slipping?"

"Yeah. Mine does that too," I admitted. "There's no good place to put it with the vest on."

"When you get up there, open the top of your flak jacket and slip the butt inside."

"We're allowed to do that?"

"I've been doing it the whole time," Lemon said.

I wanted to yell at him. *It's a bulletproof vest! You're going to want every inch of protection when people are shooting at you so get in your practice while you have the chance!* The command came from the tower for the next shooter in line to "take up a good foxhole position." The guys motioned me ahead.

I crunched through the sand, set my rifle in the v-stake next to the foxhole, lay my two magazines next to my weapon, and jumped down. Standing on a wooden box, I adjusted my sandbags, then grabbed my A1 and slid the butt inside my flak jacket, a hypocrite. Nothing felt right, but I didn't have time to fuss around.

"Lock and load one twenty-round magazine," came the thunderous command from the tower. "Scan your lane and fire when ready."

I slid in a magazine, felt the *thunk* of the bolt and bullet locking into place. With the tip of my nose squashed against the charging handle and the front of my Kevlar propped up on the carrying handle, I lined up the front and rear sights. My left hand cradled the handguards, ready to pivot. My right wrapped around the pistol grip. The 200 popped up to the left and I swiveled, focusing just above the front sight post as I breathed out, froze, and squeezed. The green head and torso fell back down behind the berm. I breathed in traces of gunpowder. One down, 39 to go. The targets came up and down, up and down, strange dolls on invisible strings. More and more pop-ups stared back at me after I'd taken a shot. I imagined the A1 working against me out of spite, out of shared animosity. The longer a pop-up remains standing, the more you imagine a face.

"How'd you do?" Ayma asked later. The platoon was scattered around the base of a huge tree eating MREs.

"Bad. Twenty-four."

"I only got eighteen."

"Don't worry, Ayma," Nissenger said. "It's just the first day. You'll get there."

I dumped my MRE guts out on the ground and pawed around for the drink mix. Orange. I knew if I offered it to Ayma she might actually drink some water.

"It's so frustrating," she said, shoulders slumped. "I'm never going to fire a weapon again after this summer. What does it matter if I qualify or not? What's the point?"

I gritted my teeth, watching Ayma noisily chew a tootsie roll. "Waste of my time," she mumbled.

I ripped open the orange packet and poured the powder into my own canteen.

8. Disorientation

June 2005, Ft. Lewis, WA

We hit Branch Orientation on the way back from our last day on the shooting range, as the sky slid from blue to grey and as the wind picked up, driving a light rain. Orientation was like a job fair in that each branch of the Army had a tent set up, staffed with ambassadors who tried to woo you into listening to their presentation.

We were ordered to listen to five presentations. Shoulders hunched, I wandered from tent to tent, hovering on the periphery, pretending to be excited about all these possibilities. I'd listed Adjutant General Corps on my paperwork solely because it had the shortest school. I had no intention of attending *any* branch training.

When it came time for the last presentation, I spotted Hall heading to the aviation tent, virtually deserted, and followed her. Under the awning, a tall, dark, dashing man in a flight jumper stood in front of glossy pictures of helicopters and planes. "You two look like a couple of pilots," he said, flashing a smile. "Why'd you wait this long to come on over?"

Hall blushed. "I failed my eye exam, so I figured I better look into alternatives."

"What about you?" He leaned toward me, his elbows on a high counter. Up close, I saw the countertop was actually a collage of pictures of helicopters and grinning soldiers under a layer of clear plastic.

"I'm just here with my battle buddy, I said."

"All right, no pressure. I'm warning you though, you're gonna want in."

I gave a quiet scoff disguised as a laugh as he turned his attention to Hall. "Did you put aviation as your number one choice?"

"Of course. Even though I don't have a shot at it anymore because of my eyes."

He waved a hand. "Don't be discouraged. What you do is you go home, and you get corrective eye surgery."

Hall perked up like a puppet on a string. "Really?"

"Yeah, a lot of people do that. If you really want it, and I can see that you do, we want you. That's why we don't even consider cadets who don't list aviation as their number one choice."

Hall punched my shoulder and grinned up at the pilot. "Why didn't anyone tell me this before?"

A few other cadets wandered up and the pilot turned the charm up to boiling. Aviation wasn't a job, he explained—it was a thrill, a hobby, an extreme sport, a rush, a privilege reserved for the cream of the athletic and mental crop.

"I wouldn't trade this job for anything in the world," he said. He was beaming, glowing. "Nothing compares to flying. Nothing. I can still remember trying to hover a training chopper for the first time. For weeks, I couldn't do it. Grabbed that stick and wobbled and tipped all over the place. Then one day I got in, took the controls, and hovered like a pro. Something in me *switched*." He snapped his fingers. "I could feel it turn on like a light bulb. That's when you know you're meant to fly."

Meant to fly. We stared at the posters of Black Hawks and Apaches and Chinooks, imagining ourselves at the controls, failing and failing and then lifting off, weightless.

"Then there's the money. You won't know what to do with it all. And get this. If you fall behind on flight time, they pay you extra to get in a bird and fly around for a few hours."

It sounded glamorous, exhilarating. The helicopters weren't choppers, they were *birds*, the epitome of freedom. You could escape the constraints of terrestrial life, work in the sky, control something beautiful and powerful, be paid to spike your adrenaline. My imagination flickered alive like a firefly at dusk.

Back in our cattle car I imagined the electrification of breaking the sound barrier, what the coastline would look like from the windshield of a Huey, the beautiful precision of the Blue Angles when they flew in formation, and how pilots could have a career with commercial airlines after they got out. Maybe *I* could get paid to travel the world. Skip the quicksand of trying to get out as a conscientious objector.

The driver hit the gas and I lurched into Stinson as Gill fell into me. The recruiter hadn't mentioned that. Actually, he hadn't mentioned the wars at all. A pothole sent us up into the air. The landing came with incredulity. For fuck's sake! Pilots probably dropped bombs and shot missiles and picked up the dead and wounded in Iraq. They didn't get paid to take joyrides in *birds*. They were undertakers. Killers. Targets. But the smooth talker had known better than to mention any of that.

I listened in on some of the conversations around me. Nissenger was raving about Transportation Corps. Chuang was intent on the contents of his Signal Corps folder. Kirchov and Dexter were arguing about whether Field Artillery or Air Defense Artillery was better.

"Dude, Field Artillery's slogan is King of Battle. There's no contest," Dexter said.

"The fact that they need a slogan should tell you something," Kirchov countered.

The driver hit the brakes and I struggled not to fall into Stinson again. "Do you still want to branch infantry?" I asked him.

"Of course. McGreer and Finn too."

I thought about the three of them clearing buildings in Baghdad, riding in Humvees with makeshift armor, zip tying prisoners who would end up in black sites. I thought about everyone around me playing his or her part in the huge war machine.

We hit a curve and my helmet clunked into the wall behind me. I choked on my follow-up questions.

9. HOW DO YOU FEEL NOW, CADET?

June 2005: Ft. Lewis, WA

I was squad leader the day we were scheduled to go through the Confidence Course. We emerged from our cave-like cattle car into a bright, warm Washington day. Shaded by a huge tin roof, pale woodchips under our boots giving off a rich, fresh smell, we learned how to tie Swiss seats for rappelling. I liked rappelling and I focused on this impending fun because after lunch we were headed to my least favorite place: the gas chamber.

An instructor helped me with my rope seat, yanking it tight around my hips before sending me on to the checker. The checker cranked the rope tighter, making me wince, but I kept my mouth shut. I was going to enjoy this once I reached the walls.

Standing in line for the "short wall," my legs grew numb.

"They put this thing on too tight," said Hall, in front of me.

"I know," I agreed. "It's like they lashed the rope around my bones and then squeezed. It's better if you bend over."

We waited for our turn with our hands on our thighs, then hobbled backward down the short wall, gritting our teeth as the rope took our full weight.

On our way to the medium wall, another checker waved Hall through but flagged me. My harness was cranked tighter still.

"Can I loosen this? It's really uncomfortable."

The sergeant waved me off, already tugging on the next cadet's rope. "It needs to be uncomfortable or it won't protect you, cadet."

I walked gingerly to the medium wall, climbed a series of platforms, and got in line behind McGreer.

"Del Duca," he rumbled. "You okay?"

"This rope's digging into my sides so bad I have cramps," I said, aware too late that I was acting like a whiny girl in front of the toughest guy in the platoon. My throat tightened in that pinch that lets you know tears are on their way. *Not again!* I scrabbled to replace the pain and embarrassment with anger at Julie, the instructors, the Army, McGreer's heavyweight-wrestler-nothing-ever-fazes-me back.

On the top of the wall, crouched at the edge, an instructor asked, "Are you afraid of heights?"

I shook my head. Backing over the edge, I bit back tears as the rope dug in. I couldn't help but lean forward when I knew I needed to lean back.

"You're fine, you're fine," said the instructor. "Make a T and then bound down."

I held my breath and tried to lean back, knowing my body couldn't cooperate. Making a T meant I was supposed to form a right angle with the wall. My boots slipped slipped and I slammed into the wood face-first, dangling twenty feet off the ground. McGreer watched me from his post on belay, his neck craned, his feet wide, clutching the rope that kept me from falling. In fact, everyone was watching now.

I fell twice more before finally reaching the ground. I backed off the line, blinking, blinking, trying to ignore the *motherfuckingcrowdofeveryone* watching me lose it.

"What's wrong, soldier?" asked a hard-faced major.

"My seat's too tight, sir," I choked out. Head down, I concentrated on getting the infernal rope off. I knew what my face looked like when I was upset: beet red, puffy eyes and lips. I didn't even have my cap to hide under.

"Here, let Specialist Syth take you to get that retied."

Damn Julie's mind games! Here she was again, leaning back in her chair, hands in her lap, voice all syrupy. *You have a right to feel. Soak in those feelings. Express them.*

The specialist coiled the rope. "This is a really hard rope. I can see why it hurt," he said.

My jaw trembled. Anything but sympathy. Anything. *Give in, let it out,* Julie said.

"Do you need help?" Ayma was at my elbow. I was sure the guys had sent her over, some kind of wuss ambassador. She was a girl. She was sensitive. She would know how to handle the blubbering squad leader. *Are you ever going to forgive yourself for joining the National Guard?* Julie asked.

"No." I turned my back on Ayma and tied another harness, two instructors watching and messing with my rope. If I was alone I'd be able to punch my legs or slap my face or stomp on my foot and get rid of the tears. But I was surrounded.

"I'm not going away," Ayma said.

She followed me as I walked to the tall tower. I counted my steps up to ten and then started over at one, two, three, four. It was obvious the cadre had been warned about me. The four of them at the top flashed smiles and moved slow, like I was some skittish colt.

"Come right on up."

"Nothing to be afraid of."

"We'll walk you through every step of the way."

A young, handsome sergeant motioned me to the carabiner in front of him. I concentrated on his instructions, backing over the edge of the enormous wall, forming a T, the rope digging in again.

"Wave at me with your left hand."

He wanted me to *let go?* "I'm going to fall."

"You're not going to fall. Hold the rope with your right. Wave at me with your left."

I forced myself to let go and raised my left hand.

"See? You're in control. Now walk down a few steps."

I felt like a listing boat, ready to tip over at any moment. "I'll fall."

"No you won't."

"Keep going, cadet! Conquer that fear," came a shout from below.

I fumed and took a step back. Miraculously, just as I thought my face would meet wooden planks again, the rope eased through the carabiner. I bunny-hopped the rest of the way down, where the instructor on belay clapped me on the back. I concentrated on taking off the rope, ignoring the group of officers who had gathered to watch my performance.

"How do you feel now, cadet?" one of them asked, grinning.

"Good, sir," I lied, ducking my head, tears squeezing out the corners of my eyes. "Really good."

"That's why it's called 'confidence training.' I bet you could go back up there and come down in three bounds."

I strangled a scream and forced out a laugh.

Rejoining the platoon, I slapped my BDU cap on and pulled the brim down to my nose. I saw a pair of large boots step in front of me.

"I fell too." I recognized Nis's voice. "Finn was on belay and probably saved my life."

I didn't say anything.

"Plus I was all the way upside down. It took me forever to work around. Can you imagine Finn waiting for my fat ass to get down the rope?" Nissenger tried to peer under my cap.

"I don't want to talk about it." Why did everyone here have to be so goddamn nice?

• • •

After a six-kilometer road march to the gas chamber, I finally had a grip on my emotions, but I could tell my face didn't reflect it.

"Maybe you'll be immune," Ayma said, eyebrows raised. "Remember Sergeant Densey saying every cycle there's at least one person who finds out they're immune?"

"Ayma, I've done this before. I know I'm not immune to CS." That wasn't all I knew this time around, thanks to Google. This time, I knew CS was also known as "tear gas." It was the same thing police used to disperse rowdy crowds. I knew studies had linked the chemical to pulmonary, heart, and liver damage, and an increased risk of miscarriage. I knew the US Army Center for Health Promotion and Preventive Medicine advised anyone exposed to its "very toxic fumes" to seek medical attention immediately. What still baffled me was why the Army insisted on making it a routine part of training. Why not just order us to suck on a tailpipe or huff some glue?

I led the squad up a hill and into a clearing of trees and immediately brightened. There was a pile of Mission Oriented Protective Posture (MOPP) gear waiting for us—thick trousers and jackets with hoods and rubber gloves and boot covers. As an enlisted soldier I'd never been offered MOPP gear going into the gas chamber. Maybe this wouldn't be so bad after all.

Three instructors met us and went over MOPP protocols. Two of them were identical, red-headed twin sergeants. The other was a pimple-faced spec-four.

"When you get in there and they tell you to take your mask off, breathe in right away," Twin #1 said.

"That's right. Get it over with as quick as you can. You'll be glad you did," said the specialist.

Hah. I refused to be a gagging, slobbering mess on top of everything else today. I'd do what I did in Boot Camp #2: hold my breath, speedily clear and seal, and waltz out upright.

Twin #2's walkie-talkie crackled. "Ready in ten."

"Okay, go ahead and put on your MOPP gear."

When we got down to the gloves I discovered I only had one instead of a pair. Twin #1 frowned at me. "We can't have you going in all Michael Jackson. Put that glove in your pocket, cadet."

The spec-four shot me a sympathetic look. "Don't be nervous. It's not as bad as you think."

"I'm not nervous."

"The glove wouldn't have made much of a difference. You can't really feel it on your skin," he said.

"I've been gassed four times already."

He straightened up on his stump and furrowed his eyebrows. "Four?"

"Twice in the chamber, twice in the field in boot camp."

"You're prior service?"

"So is Kassano. He's already been over to Afghanistan." I loved telling him this, watching his face morph. I wanted to add that McGreer was from a military academy and probably knew more about the Army than he did. I wanted to lecture that we weren't the naïve, inexperienced babies he'd been picturing all morning. Well, except Ayma.

But a thunderclap of apprehension stopped me. What was I doing, thinking in *we*, in *us*? It came so naturally. And it highlighted a fear that had been low-crawling forward from the back of my mind all week. All this rah-rah camaraderie could make me chicken out on declaring myself a conscientious objector. I had backed down before.

"Lead 'em on down, squad leader," Twin #1 said.

I made a last-minute check of the squad, fixing Ayma's collar and her overcoat's drawstring. And then we were up against the back wall of the cement room at the bottom of the hill, looking like strange workmen with alien heads. I put a hand over my canister and breathed in, feeling the mask suction harder onto my face. The edges started to prickle. Even though we'd cleaned the masks with alcohol pads, there was still some CS residue on the rubber.

The door next to me clanged open. A large man in a mask motioned us inside his dark lair, the ceiling low, chemical lights putting off a glow from the corners. Three more instructors watched us file in. They carried themselves like gladiators—calculated, balanced, larger than their actual frames. One of them broke open several CS tablets, which started spurting clouds of neon yellow. This was much, much more CS than they'd used in boot camp. The gladiators sprung alive, pacing and yelling. *"The side-straddle hop!"*

"The side-straddle hop," we echoed, the words muffled by our masks. We stood ready to spring into jumping jacks on his command.

"One, two, three," the lead instructor sang.

"One!" we shouted back.

"One, two, three."

"Two!"

After jumping jacks we moved on to overhead arm clappers, flutter kicks, and finally push-ups, fumbling in our gear, sweating and fogging up our masks as we yelled, never loud enough for the gladiators. My sweat loosened my mask's grip, intensifying the burning there, as if tiny fire ants had burrowed into my skin and stung.

"Now that we're warmed up, the fun begins," an instructor shouted through his mask, rubbing his hands together. "You." He pointed at me.

I walked through the thick, yellow air, stopping directly in front of him, my chest heaving as I gulped in as much clean air as my lungs would hold.

"Take off your mask."

I flipped the hood over my head and started yanking the straps over.

"Get it off!" he screamed.

I pulled the mask away from my face and held it in one bare hand. Before my eyes started to water I met the sergeant's stare, startled at how green his eyes were, and how they had the same rabid-dog quality as Sergeant Densey's. But I had something he didn't know about. Lungs full of sweet, filtered air.

"What's your name, Cadet?"

"Rosa del Duca, Sergeant."

"Social Security number."

I told him.

"Open your eyes! What platoon?"

"Third, Sergeant."

"What school are you from? Open your eyes."

"Cal Poly, Sergeant," I shouted, thinking this *had* to be the last question. I was running out of air. Water poured from my eyes, leaving hot streaks on my cheeks. He paused, staring through the smoke at me with those uncanny eyes. I pretended to take a tiny breath in, raising my shoulders, twisting my face in mock misery.

Four years before I'd taken this punishment willingly, maybe even eagerly. To prove something, to feel closer to my battle buddies, to earn that money for school, to tell stories to people back home, to feel a shred of what people who'd actually been gassed felt and remind myself that *this* was why we needed an army. Now, everything was in question. Maybe the sergeant sensed it this time around. The fact that I was pretending.

He shifted his weight and crossed his arms. "And where's that?"

"California, Sergeant." I was out of air.

He paused a few seconds more and I panicked, drawing in a small breath, tipping the first domino. I coughed and gasped for air, but the more gas in my lungs, the harder I coughed, gagging and miserable, my mask useless in my hands.

"There we go. Out the door, Cadet."

I turned around and almost ran into the wall, hysteria building in my gut, and then someone was guiding me, and I had enough sense to stretch my hands out so I didn't ram into anything else. I moved through a corridor, and then out the door, where I stood doubled-over, retching and gulping. I tried to force my eyes open, but they stayed clamped shut.

"Open your eyes," someone called.

"Flap your arms, Cadet."

"Say you love your mask."

I recognized the voice of Sergeant Densey somewhere in there.

"Cadet, say you love your mask."

What were they talking about?

"Sound off! Say 'I love my mask.'"

I choked, then mumbled, "I love my mask."

Someone scoffed. "Where you going, Cadet? Go around the circle, don't come over here."

What circle? All I saw was a blur of green and tan. I stumbled away and after a few more seconds of furious blinking, saw the outline of a dirt track in a field. Behind me, the rest of my squad trickled out, hacking and screaming, "I love my mask!"

We came together in the middle of the field. Kilgore whooped and waved his mask in the air. "It's all downhill from here!"

"You are a badass, del Duca," said Kassano, his face wet.

"Yeah, how did you do that?" asked Stinson. "I got halfway through one answer and that was it. Couldn't say anything else."

I forced a smile and fished my BDU cap out of my cargo pocket, bending the bill to have something to do with my hands.

"As soon as I got the mask off, I took a breath and then I was like, shiiiiiiit," said McGreer, giddy as a Ranger after his first jump, grinning back toward the chamber. Of course McGreer, the man's man, the soldier's soldier, would have enjoyed that.

"I did exactly what they said," Ayma said, fixing her long brown hair into a sloppy knot at the back of her head. "I took a breath right away and they let me go."

They chattered on, but I wasn't listening anymore. *Yes, Ayma, be a good little automaton*, I thought, slapping my cap on, stomach still queasy. Doing what you were told was easy. Thinking for yourself was hard.

• • •

When we got back to the barracks that night I waited in the pay phone line for a chance to talk to Zack. Miraculously, he picked up.

"Well hello, gorgeous."

"You wouldn't say that if you could see me right now." I had BDU cap hair. My uniform hadn't been washed in three days and I was sure my feet reeked of sweaty leather and wool. I pictured Zack going about his business back in San Luis Obispo, where the girls would be wearing skimpy jean shorts, lacy tank tops, sandals, and perfume.

"Nonsense, my dear." He was in his Cheshire Cat mood. The one where his voice sounded like a radio announcer from the '30s, crossed with a mustache-twisting villain from a black-and-white Western. The mood where he backed me into corners, pinned me, and kissed me. "Pray tell, what have you been up to?"

"Getting gassed. Shooting things. Marching around. Eating greaseball food. Getting blindfolded and shoved off the high dive with a rubber rifle. Thinking about you for hours on end."

"Should I drive up and rescue you?"

"Do you really have to ask?"

"We'll be on the lam. We'll live forever or die trying."

I smiled. "Have you been getting my letters?"

"Ah, your letters. They're adorable. I keep meaning to write back but I've been tied up."

I bit my tongue before I could point out that he probably had a bit more free time than I did. Instead, I said, "Will you please, please send me a picture of you?"

"Oh, right. I'll do that. And there's something I want to let you know about." His voice finally sounded serious. "I decided to go on tour with the band after all. I'll be in Europe when you get home. And afterwards, New York."

I hadn't been to an Extra Action Marching Band show yet, but I'd seen pictures—Zack hefting huge cymbals, shirtless, a cigar sticking out of his mouth, his black top hat askew, sexy as all hell. And I'd heard stories. The band's flag team of risqué, gender-fluid dancers often ended up topless at the end of the night.

Possessiveness flooded me. Then fatigue. I thought about the pair of scissors back in my wall locker.

"You should come overseas and visit," he said.

He made it sound so easy. No, what I needed to do was make some money when I got back. That and work on declaring myself a traitor. Plus, there was still drill every month.

"I can't," I said.

"Well, I'll be back before you know it. At which time I plan on removing all your clothes with my teeth."

Unlike usual, this wasn't enough to distract me. After the trip, he'd be in the Bay Area working on his Burning Man project, and then at Burning Man, and then I'd be back in school. And then I'd be engulfed in my war against the war. "Pictures. Don't forget."

"An elephant never forgets. One morning I shot an elephant in my pajamas. How he got into my pajamas I don't know."

"You've been watching Marx Brothers movies without me."

"Never. Hang in there, kid."

I hung up and plodded to the barracks for my shower bag. Pointedly ignoring the drawer my scissors were in, I could feel the contents of my brain shifting and spinning like the needle of a compass at the North Pole.

In the latrine, I discovered a thick line of bruising and raw skin across my back, around my hips, and curving down my inner thighs, thanks to the ropes back at the confidence course. This was the type of harm I didn't like. No one would see it. I couldn't even bring it up as proof I wasn't a total wimp unless I wanted to look like a drama queen. I padded to the showers, wondering if my tolerance for pain had changed. If types of tolerance were connected—emotional pain getting mixed up with physical pain. One thing was certain: the tough tomboy was gone and I missed her like hell. Who was I now?

As the warm water hit my head, I imagined Zack pushing aside the shower curtain and slipping inside the stall, a mischievous smile under his mustache, his hands following my curves. I held him tight, drawing strength for the next day like a leech. He was right. I was looking for someone to latch on to, like a drowning girl spotting a buoy. I hadn't chosen very well, but there was no way in hell I could let go now.

10. FIGHTING THE CURRENT

June 2005: Ft. Lewis, WA

The jokers kept joking, kept drawing me closer to them with their charming little flaws and quirks. On a particularly crammed cattle car ride Kilgore and Nissenger burst out in, "You've lost that lovin' feelin', whoa that lovin' feeling. . ." and the whole platoon joined in, like it'd been planned. "Baby baby, I'd get down on my knees for you!" We tore through "Pretty Woman," "Sweet Home Alabama," "Friends in Low Places," "In the Middle of the Night," "Shoop," and even the entirety of "99 Bottles of Beer on the Wall."

When they weren't being silly, they talked about what they were studying in school, what they wanted to do in life. Kassano wanted to plan an epic proposal to his girlfriend, get married, have kids, and become an engineer. McGreer wanted to be an artist as well as an infantryman. Tinning, the Future Voice of NPR, was a chemistry major and wanted to work in labs, running experiments. Kilgore the Comedian, to my surprise, belonged to an agricultural fraternity back in Wisconsin and was majoring in business and political science. Finn wanted to take over his dad's ranch after his service. Just when we'd concluded he was gay, he suddenly started mentioning a girlfriend back home, as though he thought he needed a cover. While the Army was still under Don't Ask, Don't Tell, we didn't care. This was the next generation. We were beyond petty prejudices. At least, that's what we'd decided one day, sitting in a circle, seeing who could toss the most pebbles into an upside-down Kevlar helmet.

We marched and ran and trained and sweat and got very little sleep. We learned how to turn our uniforms into flotation devices. We rode a frighteningly high zip line over a lake, hoping our grip on tiny handlebars would hold. We learned our new favorite word, "cockswain," and raced rubber boats around buoys. We followed stupid orders and tried not to give stupid orders. We swatted fire ants off each other and kicked each other awake and shared smuggled food from the chow hall. We loaded and fired a Howitzer and threw live grenades.

Through it all, Sergeant Densey was there to give us tiny signals he was proud when we did well, and to accuse us of eating "dumbass toast for breakfast" when we screwed up. And through it all, I rode a seesaw of guilt, trepidation, disgust, and empathy. There were moments I looked at the platoon and wondered how I could possibly abandon them when I got home. There were moments I wanted to shake them. There were times I wondered what they would look like in five years. Would they have all of their limbs? Would they be remotely as happy and well-adjusted? I noticed how they took even the most glaring of warning signs in stride.

"Are you religious?" Nissenger asked Sergeant Densey one day. We were cleaning our rifles outside the barracks. It was Sunday, and a few cadets had gone to church.

Densey looked like he was holding something sour in his mouth, wondering if he should spit it out or swallow. "Not anymore."

"What were you, Catholic?"

Densey crossed his arms and raised his eyebrows at Nissenger, an unspoken reprimand for prying. But then he said, "When you've seen what I've seen, it's pretty clear God doesn't exist. Last time I stepped foot in a church was in Baghdad. Never been back since."

We stopped scrubbing at our rifles.

"What happened?" Nis asked.

He shrugged. "Lost my faith. And not just in God. The whole shebang. All of it."

We waited for him to go on. He was about to tell us a war story. "Now how about you quit your yackin' and clean your weapon. You got the attention span of a bunch of preschool kids."

We bent our heads and got back to work. I took apart my bolt, incredulous that Densey had just admitted he didn't have faith in the Army or the war. That had to be what he meant by "the whole shebang." It flooded me with determination. But on its heels came confusion.

Here Densey was, helping send the next round of leaders off to lose *their* faith. I would be part of the next generation of faithless nihilists if I lost my nerve about the CO application. I would drift along without a heart, faking it because it was easier than fighting the current.

I thought back to the ethics class I took as a freshman. Kant would not approve. The entire situation was full of failed categorical imperatives. If Densey didn't believe the war was legitimate, necessary, or doing good, it was imperative he end his involvement. And it was imperative he warn us. Kant would have said that if it was wrong for one person to fight in a fabricated war, it was wrong for all. Then again, Kant had warned that you couldn't change a choice based on what happened afterward. We were in this screwy war as a result of a series of bad moves. Maybe now it was our duty to end it as peacefully and quickly as possible. Yet how could we do that if the Deciders couldn't be trusted to make the right decisions? How could anything change if we all walked away from the mess instead of fixing it? I turned the choices over and over in my mind, wishing my hands held pen and paper instead of a rifle.

11. COVER ME WHILE I LIE TO YOU

June 2005: Ft. Lewis, WA

We marched out to the Individual Tactical Training site and crammed into rickety bleachers. I didn't know what we were supposed to look at. There was a narrow road cutting through the forest in front of us, but not much else. My knees jammed into Hall's back while someone else's knees wedged into my back. I eyed the infantry and ranger patches on the Training, Advising, and Counseling (TAC) officers, who looked mildly up the road. Soon, a dull roar filled the air. The loudspeakers blared mock communications as two armored vehicles called Strykers charged toward us. A simulated bomb blast made me jump. Beside me, Ayma yipped and slapped a hand over her mouth. Another simulated bomb disabled one of the Strykers. Gunfire erupted from the bunker. Rangers came dashing out of the second Stryker and cleared the bunker, then picked up their casualties, masking their movements with smoke grenades. It was like a scene out of a movie.

When it was over, the guys to my left and right nudged each other, nodding and grinning, like they were in on some big secret. I was growing increasingly annoyed with demonstrations like these. It was propaganda. Glorification of something that in reality would be horrifying. And of course the demonstration looked nothing like what we would be doing.

We split into squads to practice moving under fire with a buddy. A posse of infantry soldiers watched us with downturned mouths and crossed arms. "I can't wait to paint these guys up," I heard one say to another.

Tinning, my partner for moving under fire, waited until we were back at the bottom of the hill, then asked, "Did you hear that?"

I was winded from the run because of a chest cold. What I really wanted to do was hock up some phlegm, but Tinning was so proper I knew he'd tease me. "The paint-us-up comment?" I asked.

"Yeah, they mean paintball. They're going to shoot us with paintballs while we go through the Audie Murphy course."

"No," I scoffed. "They're just trying to intimidate us. Paintballs leave welts." This was summer camp after all.

The infantrymen showed us how to navigate concertina wire. Then we practiced setting up in a "fan," all four team members in the prone position, boots together, each scanning a different triangle of forest. We checked for mock booby traps, passed through trenches while expecting fire, cleared rooms, and took bunkers.

I tried to keep my panting quiet as a particularly ripped infantryman frowned at the squad. "Y'all are ate-up. You go over to Iraq like that, you're gonna get yourself killed." He spat and walked over to the rest of his wolf pack.

Hunt let out a frustrated sigh. "They could teach us what we're doing wrong. We've never done any of this before. That's what today is for: training."

No one had time to answer, because the full wolf pack was approaching.

"We're sending you on to the Audie Murphy course. Y'all know who Audie Murphy is, don't you?"

McGreer nodded.

"One of you? One?" barked the ripped soldier. "Well, enlighten us, McGreer."

"He's the most decorated combat veteran in all of US history."

"That's right. Hero doesn't begin to cover it. It's a disgrace you don't know who he is. This guy jumped on a burning tank and held back an entire Nazi platoon. Completely on his own. Killed fifty Germans that day. There's about a dozen stories just like that one. When Audie Murphy got home he starred as himself in war movies. *To Hell and Back* was filmed right here. I can't believe this bullshit, cadets coming to Ft. Lewis and you don't even know—"

A shorter infantryman stepped forward to cut off his buddy. "You'll be going through the course in teams of four. We'll be timing you and judging your performance. Use the skills you learned here. Do it by the book. Now go on down to the course and meet up with your TAC officer."

I was siphoned into a team with Finn, Gill, and Kassano.

"Del Duca. You're team leader," a tall lieutenant announced. He led me to a terrain model of the course. Looking down at the tiny, intricate model, I was surprised at how close together the lanes appeared to be. We'd probably be able to hear cadets in the lanes next to us. And while the terrain started pretty flat, we'd be charging uphill for most of the run.

"You're in enemy territory. Take that into consideration. Your mission is to clear insurgents from the top of this hill." The LT pointed at a tiny building set on a tiny hilltop. "Another thing you should know is there are big ant piles near a lot of the trees. We won't paintball you if you're short of using a tree for cover because of a nest. But any other time you don't take good cover, you'll get hit. Believe me—you don't want to walk around with paint on your uniform the rest of the day."

He fished in a cargo pocket and pulled out four pairs of yellow foam earplugs. "Wear these." He picked up a stack of face shields from the table beside him. "And these. Make sure the visors are down all the way at all times." Holding the masks out to me, he looked stern and annoyed, like he expected me to complain.

I sneezed. "Yes, sir."

"Bless you. Brief your team. You've got ten minutes."

I blew my nose in my wet handkerchief and motioned the team to come over.

"What's the plan, del Dukes?" asked Kassano.

"We basically go up this lane, navigate any obstacles we come to, and clear a building at the top," I said. "Oh, and they'll shoot us with paintballs if we're not behind cover."

Gill, my roommate with the southern drawl, looked up from fixing her knee pads. "Are you kiddin' me? They really gonna be running around with paintballs?"

I shrugged. Finn rubbed his hands together, exchanging a grin with Kassano.

"Take good cover and they should leave us alone. The LT said if an ant pile is in our way they won't shoot."

"What else?" Kassano asked.

I looked at the head of the trail. The lane curved almost immediately behind thick shrubs and ferns. "We'll take everything as it comes."

We put in the earplugs and strapped on the masks. The plastic shields were scratched to hell, but I was grateful there was no chance I'd get a paintball to the face. I turned to the lieutenant nervously.

"That's it? You guys ready to go?" he asked, shooting me a disapproving look.

"Yes, sir."

He handed us two magazines of blanks each, then pointed at Kassano. "You. Give me your glasses."

"Sir, I really need them to see, especially with the mask."

"No glasses. People get hurt or break them or lose them."

Kassano handed his glasses over. We stood shifting our weight, our breath fogging up our face shields.

A call came over the officer's radio and he signaled us to begin. I took off for the path at a trot. Hemmed in by a mess of green tangle, the world muffled by the ear plugs, my vision blurred by the mask, I felt outside of myself, like I might be in the middle of an anxiety dream. Suddenly the LT was by my side.

"How safe do you think it is to go running into enemy territory?"

I slowed to a walk. He was probably breaking the rules, giving me this hint. I'd assumed speed was the goal, what with the run being timed. "Probably not very safe." I said. "Should we buddy rush?" That would take forever.

He hesitated. "Just slow down."

A huge boom shook the air. I knew it was only simulated artillery, but damn did it sound real. Gunfire opened up ahead and we threw ourselves to the ground.

"Cover me while I move!" shouted Kassano. I could barely make out the words over the rumbling and popping.

"Gotcha covered!" I yelled back, fogging up my mask even more. I gritted my teeth, wondering how we were going to get through this half-deaf and half-blind. Looking back at Gill and Finn I saw two infantry guys step onto the path behind us, casually holding paintball guns.

"Del Duca!" a muted voice punched its way past the background noise. I whipped my head around and saw Kassano set to cover me. The next tree stood too far away to get there in a three-second rush. I pushed up and counted, *I'm up, he sees me, I'm down*, before diving to the ground and high crawling to the trunk. A bed of ants met me and I scrambled back, shaking them out of my sleeves, before remembering to throw myself flat.

"Buddy set!" I screamed. A panic was overtaking me. I had to do this right. What happened if the Army didn't let me out? Or if a war broke out that I *did* believe in? I would need to know I could survive for more than five minutes in a real assault.

Finn and Gill buddy rushed. Kassano and I leapfrogged. The team moved forward, a disjointed sea monster. I couldn't see shit, could barely hear the shouts of "cover me while I move." My pant legs had come out of the tops of my boots. My knee and elbow pads were crooked, and bark, dirt, and pine needles worked up my sleeves. I threw myself behind another tree. I could hear the LT shouting something in the background, but he was drowned out by a thunder of artillery, and then a burning sting hit my leg.

I'd been shot. Whipping my head, I saw a splatter of birdshit-white marring my BDU pant leg. Luckily, the top of my boot had shielded my skin from the full sting. I imagined my leg bloody, shattered bone sticking through my muscle.

The lieutenant crouched by me. "You're going to get hit again if you don't find better cover."

I nodded, drawing my legs up and getting as close to the tree trunk as I could. Tilting my head back to see out the bottom of my mask, I spotted a spiral roll of concertina wire ahead—our first obstacle.

"Fan! Fan!" I screamed. Gill didn't look toward me but I couldn't wait for her. Kassano, Finn and I lay in formation, our boots nearly touching. We waited for Gill to join us and cover our rear. I wondered if the paintball guys would take this opportunity to shoot us up. There was no cover here. Not a shred. They spared us, for the moment.

After the concertina wire, it was trenches and traps. The obstacles blurred together under the booming blanket of gunfire and artillery. I threw myself into another mass of ferns at the bottom of a redwood, hoping there weren't too many ants. A sneeze sent a chill and a flash of heat through my body. Ahead of me, Finn jumped up and beat at his BDU jacket.

Both infantry guys were ready to pop him in the back at close range.

"Get down, soldier!"

"What the fuck do you think you're doing?"

"I landed in a fucking ant pile," he said.

"Watch your mouth and deal with it."

I wondered how much longer this could go on. We must have been over a mile into the course. We'd been going uphill forever.

"Gotcha covered," Kassano yelled, motioning me ahead.

I trotted to an arbitrary tree and flopped down on the ground, no energy left for high crawling, even under threat of more paintballs. God, I made a terrible infantryman.

"Keep it up, del Duca," Finn yelled.

"Stay strong," Gill called from behind.

Great, I thought, coughing up gunk. Everyone could see I was dragging ass when I was supposed to be leading. Where the hell was this building? I rose to my elbows, tilting my mask up to see what lay ahead. A zing of blue streaked past and splattered in the dirt a foot from my face. I jerked back as an excruciating pinch slammed into the small of my back. My upper body went rigid in a strange muscle cramp.

I was dead, a bullet in my leg and another in my spine. My throat tightened, the first sign of impending tears. *Jesus fucking Christ, not now!* I got into the prone position and screamed, "Buddy set."

"Cover me while I move," Kassano shouted back.

"Gotcha covered!" My ammo pouches were empty of blanks so I put my cheek along the butt of my rifle and pretended to sight into the woods above. A man with a black PT cap, his face obscured by camo, slid out from behind a thick, red tree trunk and disappeared behind another. I had a strange premonition that my weapon wanted bullets. Real bullets. It was designed to kill. It wanted to be with someone who could kill.

"Del Duca! Buddy set!" Kassano's voice burrowed through my earplugs. The booming ramped up to a monstrous roar. Finn was gesturing and yelling but I couldn't hear. I lifted my face mask to find where Kassano had landed, then slapped it closed as two smoke grenades arced through the air and landed in the bushes to my left. It was my turn to scream for Kassano to cover me, but I couldn't catch my breath, paintballs were stinging the ground to my right, ants were in my sleeves biting my arms, and the LT was hovering over me.

"You're dead, Cadet! You're dead. Find some better cover."

Pushing myself up to all fours, a low, guttural, inhuman sound came up my throat and fell out my mouth. Part croak, part groan, part animal cry.

"Jesus, move, Cadet!"

A wave of shame burned through my body. A sob was chasing the animal sound up my throat, rolling like a slick ball of oil—unstoppable. I wanted to clap my hands over my mouth, but instead, heaved myself straight and charged uphill to a fallen log.

Smoke from the grenades was clearing and I spotted Kassano, pointing and shouting. My heartbeat thudded in my ears, competing with the artillery. I tried to make out what Kassano was saying, but shook my head and pointed at my ear. He darted to a tree a few feet away from me.

"That's the house!" he shouted, jutting his chin ahead. "The room!"

I pulled my mask up but couldn't see anything in the mess of green and brown. I shoved the sob back down enough to scream, "Where?"

"It's right there. Straight ahead."

I squinted. Finn and Gill slid in behind us.

"I don't see it," I said. "Kassano, you lead the way."

Kassano dashed up the hill. I stumbled after him, and then the four of us were lined up outside a door. Gill tapped Finn. Finn tapped my shoulder. I tapped Kassano and then we were filing in, rifles raised, each focused on a certain dark corner or doorway. The place was empty. Gill marked the door with chalk.

"Time," called the LT.

I ripped off the mask and bent to gulp in fresh air, hiding my dirty, wet face.

We followed the lieutenant to log benches and sat, trying to brush ourselves off. Covered in wood chips and dirt, our camo smeared away, our BDU bottoms untucked, our boot laces dangling, we took long guzzles from our canteens. Kassano shook leaves out of his sleeves. Gill threw her head back and poured the rest of her water over her face.

Finn clutched at his collar and looked down his shirt. "I think I lost my dog tags back there." The infantry goons picked up their paintball guns and left, leaving an unspoken understanding they would try to find the tags.

"Now none of you thought that was so hard, did you?" the lieutenant asked. He was looking right at me, but I kept looking at the ground. All I could think about was the strange sound I had made—how I couldn't describe it and would never be able to replicate it. Yet it had come out of my mouth like instinct. Like animals made sounds.

I thought about how war reminded us we were animals. How I couldn't even save face in a fake battle. How I'd like to see all the members of Congress who'd voted for Bush's war go through that course every day they sent more troops to Iraq and Afghanistan.

• • •

"You got shot," Kilgore laughed as we rejoined the rest of the company.

I stared at the ground. "Twice."

"Don't worry. Some other people did too. Besides, it's over now. Another thing checked off our list. All downhill from here, baby."

I looked around and found a few white splatters on uniforms. None were as conspicuous as mine though, right in the middle of my back. Densey was glaring at me and I knew he'd seen.

We settled down to wait for some colonel who wanted to address us. Tilting my patrol cap low over my face, I leaned back against my ruck and closed my eyes. I could hear Ayma jabbering a few spots over.

"I was so worried I wouldn't make it, but I just made up my mind that I couldn't quit. They had to help me, but I didn't stop. They almost gave me a positive spot report for it."

I opened my eyes a slit.

"Yeah, you guys should have seen little Ayma," said Nissenger. "Her face was so determined and she was charging up the path like Rambo. Her hair was all over the place, covered in mud, but she was great."

Ayma let out a coo. "Oh, Nis. I didn't want to let you guys down. That was the hardest thing I've done in my whole life. Ever."

"Tell us the whole story, Ayma," someone said.

Ayma took a deep breath. I rolled my eyes. But before she could launch into the whole thing, the cadre told us to stand up and be quiet so we didn't look like ragamuffins when the colonel arrived.

The colonel showed up forty-five minutes later, in a caravan of white SUVs, and delivered the classic stump speech, a series of one-liners:

"You are the next leadership of the United States Army."

"I'm proud of your commitment and dedication to the armed forces."

"The training you went through today is just the beginning."

"Listen closely to your cadre. Make the most of your experiences here."

"The young men and women to your left and right will be your friends for life."

The colonel's speech made me think about all the sterile sound bites politicians gave when they talked about war. How Americans liked to think we were civilized and sophisticated. When we talked about "taking up arms" it was with reason and lofty ideals and patriotism and the lament that war is a terrible thing, but necessary.

I thought about the Green Machine and all the kids going through boot camp in South Carolina, Georgia, and Missouri. About the money from all the taxpayers fueling the planes and tanks and feeding the men and women stuck in the desert. I thought about the insurgents blowing up hundreds of their own people at weekend markets, when it seemed they really wanted to blow up

Kassano, Finn, Gill, and everybody around me. And I thought about the CO application waiting at home and how ridiculous it might sound to some that I thought the war was wrong.

That sound I'd made. It was like everything I'd been feeling the last four years had manifested in that one cry, to remind myself that I couldn't keep bottling things up. It was a demand for me to find my voice, and soon.

12. BODY DOUBLE

June 2005: Ft. Lewis, WA

The day before our ten-day trip into the field, we packed our A-bags, got handed a new Standard Operating Procedure (SOP), repacked, got handed yet another SOP, packed again, and finally dragged our duffels outside to be checked and rechecked by squad leaders.

"Are we ever going to see this stuff again?" Hunt asked, staring at our duffels, fat with sleeping bags, field jackets, boots, and extra uniforms.

"Not likely," said Kilgore. "When they said they'd *try* to get us our A-bags at *some point*, that meant 'what you pack in your ruck better be all you need.' Don't you speak cadre, Hunt? Good thing you have me to translate."

Sergeant Densey came out of the barracks. "Ayma." He jerked his head. Ayma pushed her glasses up her nose and trotted after the sergeant.

"Where's she going?" Hunt asked.

"To get a haircut," I said.

The guys raised eyebrows.

"She's been begging Sergeant Densey for days."

"That girl has a way of getting what she wants," Stinson said, looking after them.

"Hey!" Finn shouted, pointing to the cattle car that had pulled up. "Grab those A-bags and throw them in the truck."

We loaded the truck and then sprawled outside the barracks, making last-minute plans.

"I've got extra TA-50 cord," said Kassano. "Nobody else needs to bring that."

"And I have sunscreen to share," Tinning said.

"You might want to leave it," I said. "Ayma has a big bottle."

"Well tell her not to bring it."

I shook my head. I'd already tried this reasoning. "Ayma will insist on bringing her own. She's also bringing foot powder, extra baby wipes, a hairbrush, shampoo, conditioner, soap, face wash, a huge tube of toothpaste, hand warmers, and a box of letter-writing supplies."

Kassano pointed at Ayma's ruck, next to mine. "Are you saying she's not done packing?"

"Nope. She'll probably pack all night and then fall asleep with her huge flashlight on, which she also plans on taking, along with extra batteries."

"She's not going to be able to fit all that crap, let alone carry it," Hunt said.

I nibbled a blade of grass. "She knows she doesn't have to. I'm already carrying her baby wipes and foot powder so I don't have to hear her wail about it. And when she sees she can't fit in the rest she'll come knocking on y'all's door."

"I am not carrying any bullshit we don't need," Stinson said.

"But it's Ayma's birthday present to you," Kilgore blubbered, feigning distress. Stinson would be turning nineteen while we were in the field.

"Del Duca, give me your ruck," McGreer said.

I heaved my ruck into his meat-hook hands and watched him push the crossjoint of the metal frame back an inch.

"Try that on."

I blushed, remembering how I'd been complaining about my ruck, how I'd been planning to tie some kind of cushion onto the joint so it didn't dig into my back. I flipped the ruck over my head and onto my shoulders. "You fixed it!" I exclaimed. "This is perfect."

He shrugged.

Stinson shook his head. "Guys, seriously, what are we going to do about Ayma? She needs a reality check. Someone needs to tell her it's not okay to make us her packhorses."

The guys looked at me.

I held up my hands. "Oh no you don't. First of all, she doesn't listen to me. And second, you can't argue with a spoiled brat."

Kassano cleared his throat theatrically and tilted his head to one direction. We all turned and saw Ayma walking toward us, her head down, trying to hide a red and puffy face.

"What happened?" I asked.

She gulped, shifting from foot to foot. "We got to the hair place, which I *had* an appointment at—" Her voice went into a squeak. "And this woman says she doesn't have time for me. I tell her I have to get my hair cut no matter what. She says she doesn't have time and then Sergeant Densey asks if she can give me a quick fix. She says yeah, she has time for a quick fix, and leads me over to the counter, picks up a pair of scissors, yanks my ponytail back, and cuts it off!" She lifted her cap and let what was left of her hair fall down. It hung crooked and jagged, too short to fit in a ponytail, but too long and loose to meet regulation.

I knew it had taken Ayma years to grow her hair out to the middle of her back. That she'd hated the idea of cutting it but had become convinced long hair would be a pain in the field.

"Can you go back?" asked Kilgore.

"No! I'll try to fix it myself, I guess." She was about to cry again.

I nudged Hunt, who was trying not to laugh. "You've got a pair of those little sharp scissors, don't you?" I asked.

"In my locker."

"Let me borrow them."

In the bathroom after dinner chow I evened out the haircut, crouching low and soothing Ayma. "She should have just left it alone if she didn't have time to cut it," I said.

"I know! And she thought it was funny afterward. I'm about to cry and she's about to laugh."

I snipped at a clump of hair. "That's terrible."

"I hope someone does that to her someday. See how she feels."

"Okay, take a look at the back. What do you think?"

Ayma turned around and held up her hand mirror. Her face bloomed into a smile. "Oh my goodness. This looks even better than if a real hairdresser did it."

I doubted that.

"I mean it. You're really good at cutting hair. Thank you, thank you, thank you."

It was a brief respite from our usual skirmishes, which weren't only caused by Ayma's incompetence and my impatience with her. We operated on different wavelengths. Summer camp was teaching Ayma to be a gear in the machine at the same time I was becoming a wrench. And because it was clear Ayma couldn't pass LDAC without a lot of help, I sometimes felt a unique guilt around her, like I was feeding her to the Army in some kind of sacrifice, a body to replace my body.

13. VORTEX TIME

June 2005: Ft. Lewis, WA

"You have entered a war zone," TAC officers told us at the end of a long road march. "The country is called Zarabar. It's a large nation, some desert, some forest, some mountains. There are two main religions in Zarabar and one main language but different dialects. We are in Southern Zarabar, where there have been increasing reports of insurgents. These insurgents are incredibly adept at blending in with the locals. *But,* do not assume everyone wandering around on your missions is the enemy. And do not piss off the locals. We have several friendlies in country…"

"Why make up a fake country exactly like Iraq and Afghanistan?" I muttered to Hall when the briefing was over. "Why not treat this like the real thing?"

She shrugged. "I guess they didn't want to make it political?"

If not now, when?

We pulled security as the mist turned to rain, as our uniforms got soaked, and as the biggest mosquitoes I'd ever seen descended and feasted, biting right through our clothes. I gave up trying to get comfortable in the bramble patch Ayma and I were assigned to and surrendered to Vortex Time.

You know how moments from your past can stretch forward with a long finger and tap you on the shoulder years later? How certain time capsules lie curled in the back of your mind, waiting for the opportunity to unfold? That's Vortex Time. It's like going through a wormhole in space. For instance, there is a vortex leading straight to Charlie Company at Ft. Jackson, South Carolina. I can run up and down the steps to the female barracks any time, day or night. In the third-floor bay, the kill floor perpetually gleams and the bunks stand like soldiers, green wool blankets tight enough to bounce a quarter, laundry bags cinched in front with no actual laundry in them because it would look sloppy. I know what the inside of every wall locker looks like and can smell the musk of sweat and bleached sheets and floor wax. Sometimes the bay is empty, like a set. Sometimes it's full of activity. The chow hall is the same way. The barracks at Ft. Lee are in suspended animation too, right down to the ceiling panel above my old bunk that lifts up, a perfect hiding spot for contraband.

Being in training, and the field especially, is like navigating a minefield of Vortex Time wormholes. There is nothing to do but silently wait and think, so it's no surprise your mind wanders.

I'd managed to keep my wormholes mostly positive and strictly civilian throughout camp. I'd visit my grandparents' house in Pennsylvania, eat toast with my grandfather in the breakfast nook, sit with my grandmother on the front porch swing, and compose epic duets on the mini-grand piano with Leila. I roamed my favorite childhood hiking and camping spots and roasted cheese over candles with my sisters in the old horse trailer behind our first house in Missoula. Certain playgrounds were rooted in place, certain elementary school classrooms... Perhaps it was all the focus on childhood haunts that first night in Zarabar that led me to remember a long-buried knot.

• • •

I was eleven years old. We were living in a trailer in Missoula across from a burned-down lumber yard. I'd come home from school to find the trailer strewn with half-packed boxes. My mother was in the kitchen, slamming cabinets.

"There's lunch meat and cheese for sandwiches. You girls are on your own for dinner. I have to go to campus." She was halfway through her bachelor's degree in education.

"What are all these boxes for?" I asked.

"Wayne's moving out."

She had been crying. "Do you want him to?"

The fridge door was open and she was bent over, leaning inside with that glaze to her eyes people often get while standing in front of an open fridge. Except hers was different. She didn't see the leftover spaghetti or the crinkly bags of deli meat and cheese or the heads of broccoli. "He said he wants to leave. I'm not going to stop him."

She let the door swing closed with a clink of condiment jars, shoved an apple into her beat-up canvas backpack, and bent down to kiss the top of my head, petting my hair. I hated it when she plastered my hair down like that. I ducked out from under her hand.

After she drove away I found paper and markers. I made signs and left them on top of the boxes.

Don't go.
Stop.
I love you.

I felt a crushing need to leave the house before Wayne got back. How would I explain what I'd done? What if he kept packing or grew angry or...? Without finding shoes, I ran out of the trailer and walked the mile to Franklin Park. The August afternoon was so warm they had the stone turtles spraying water high into the air. Little kids were screeching and running and splashing. I walked past the pool and the playground to a huge tree near the basketball court. The rough bark dug into the bottoms of my dirty feet. I climbed to a height where no one would notice me and straddled a thick branch. I waited a long time, spying on the people below. A few adults saw me and I swung my legs and smiled, pretending everything was fine. As the sun sank behind the mountains, I clambered down and walked home to find Wayne and my mother standing in the living room like wary, wild animals. Attuned. Suspicious.

"Did you write these?" Wayne held up the stack of my signs.

"Yes." I curled my toes into the carpet. I wanted my mother to ask where I'd been, why I'd left without shoes.

"Why would you do that?" My mother was exasperated. "He thinks *I* wrote them."

"I thought you didn't want him to go."

Wayne shook his head, muttering "sorry" to my mother. He looked at me, his ridiculous trucker hat high on his head. "I'd be gone right now if I didn't think your mom wanted to talk."

"Well, this doesn't really change things on my end," my mother said.

"Linda..."

I slunk back to the room I shared with Leila and Alura. Leila was drawing dinosaurs. Alura was reading on the top bunk. We pretended to occupy ourselves, but really we were listening through the thin walls.

Inside the vortex, I went back to my mother slamming things in the kitchen. I explored the trailer, examining Wayne's resolve. He would have done it. He would have left. And we would have stayed in Missoula, where my mom had a community and support, where I might have had a high school guidance counselor who actually guided me, where someone could have helped correct my distorted understanding of debt. When you grow up on welfare, when you remember wanting to hold your mother's hand, but she thinks you're asking her for money, when you're warned over and over by American culture, by adults you respect, about how expensive college is, you are bound to fear, hate, revere, and misunderstand money.

• • •

The rain kept coming down. We were finally given permission to wear our ponchos and eat our MREs (meals ready to eat). I forked in clammy pasta and canned peaches. It grew dark. The order came down that we were not building hooches. We were sleeping out in the elements. And then I was pulling security again, alone in our bramble patch, trying to escape my wet, cold body, wondering why the hell I'd written those signs in the first place. It was impulsive and the opposite of what I had wanted. I didn't love Wayne. I'd relished the weeks when he was gone trucking, when it was back to the real family. And by then I knew Wayne was a creep, one of those people they warned you about in school. Or had it happened in the reverse order? Had I stood up for him only to be taken advantage of?

• • •

Wayne had this chair. A recliner covered in worn, fuzzy, mustard-colored material.

"Come on up here," he'd say when the TV was on. He preferred what my mother called "shoot-em-up-bang-bang" movies. If it was a John Wayne movie, I was allowed to watch, so I'd catapult myself onto the chair, straddling him, and use his chest like a pillow. He'd turn the chair sideways so we could both watch. I'd done this for years during Wayne's golden era, which had been peppered with family camping trips and punctuated by Christmases where we'd unwrap beautiful doll furniture he'd made in his wood shop.

I didn't like to be tickled, but when he started tickling me I put up with it because I didn't want to hurt his feelings. Maybe he was just trying to fit in. My mother and Leila had tickle fights that sometimes lasted thirty minutes.

It started innocently. Arms and neck and knees. But then he discovered the insides of my thighs were very ticklish. Little by little he'd work his fingers higher. And higher. Until he was tickling my crotch, which was not ticklish, but which he seemed to think *would* be ticklish if he found just the right spot.

"Are you ticklish here?"

"No."

"What about here?"

"Not really."

He was not deterred by my lack of reaction, his fingers moving slower and slower.

"Does it tickle here?" he'd press. "I bet it does. You're only pretending."

After a few movies ended in non-tickling, I was stumped. I kept telling Wayne I wasn't ticklish where he wanted to tickle me. It made me angry and uncomfortable. Was this what they called "inappropriate touching?" I went through the checklist. Someone touching your privates. When you didn't want them to. Yep. My mother would probably want to know. I went into the kitchen one day when Wayne wasn't home.

"Can you tell Wayne I don't like him tickling me?" I asked my mother.

She was rolling out crust for chicken pot pie. I knew she hated making pie crust because of the way she ranted when she tried to get it in the pan and it broke.

"Why don't you like it?" she asked, wiping at her forehead with the back of a flour-white hand.

"Because he tickles me here," I said, pointing.

The rolling pin rattled and spun. "You should tell him to stop."

"Can't you?"

"If something bothers you, you need to tell that person yourself."

"I don't want to talk to him about it."

"Then it sounds like it's not that big of a problem."

I didn't talk to Wayne. I stopped sitting on his lap. I pretended I had no interest in shoot-em-up-bang-bang movies.

"Why don't you sit with me anymore?" he asked a few months later.

My eyes wandered to John Wayne, giving his steely squint from the TV. "I'm getting too big," I lied. "I won't fit."

"Oh." He looked crestfallen. Pathetic. I decided to give him one more chance—which he failed. So that was that.

No matter how much time I spent in the vortex I couldn't understand why my mother had reacted the way she had. The warning signs couldn't have been more obvious. Your daughter tells you your boyfriend is touching her privates. Conclusion: your boyfriend is a creep.

Maybe she'd assumed I was exaggerating or maybe she hadn't understood what I was trying to tell her. Maybe she had a million things on her mind. Maybe she didn't want to make the connection. Or maybe she thought I'd resolved a situation that wasn't really a situation to begin with. After all, I'd told her *one time*. I didn't keep bringing it up. And Wayne's other misdeeds in this department would remain secret for years and years, even to me.

My mother always describes the Wayne years as dim and fuzzy. She argues she was brainwashed, she wasn't fully in control, she didn't feel like herself, she did things and thought things out of character. Stuck in Army contortions, I could relate. And I could easily forgive. Not because I didn't think she should have investigated further that day I came to her, not because I didn't think she should have stood up for me, but because she'd been through so much and has always harbored an ocean of sadness under the surface.

Imagine growing up honestly expecting your life to end when one day all those hide-under-your-desk Cold

War drills turn into the real thing. When the world miraculously doesn't end, imagine going to college, falling in love with a fellow penniless hippie, and having two children and a bun in the oven when the love of your life leaves you for one of your best friends. Imagine moving in with your helpful but judgmental and controlling parents. Picture packing up your three children and the barest essentials into your aging car and moving to a state you've never seen. Alone. A few hundred bucks in your bank account. Imagine getting there and knowing one childhood friend—a friend who is happily married with two children, a secure and respected job, a house with a big yard, and a pantry full of food. Surrender to the fact you need food stamps to survive. Turn your living room into a daycare. Dream about going back to college. Go on a date with a man you don't find particularly attractive, but who is into you, tries to impress you, tries to relate to your children. Ask your kids if it's okay he moves in. Think you are starting over, building your own ideal family. It's only a matter of time before you kick welfare, get married, go back to school, watch your silly, sensitive tomboys turn into vibrant young women, and live happily ever after.

Yes, I could easily forgive. That wasn't the problem.

Some things from your childhood infect you for the rest of your life. Some moments seep droplets of poison deep into the bedrock of a relationship, even one you want to be perfect. I don't have a lot of these dark moments with my mother. I can count them all on one hand. And yet they spawned instincts to keep her at a distance—instincts I sucked at fighting. She kept trying to move closer. I kept sidestepping away—whole states away, where I had the power to answer phone calls or ignore them; the power to come home, or not.

• • •

I didn't bother taking off my wet BDUs or even my boots before squirming into my bivy sack. I found my field flashlight, spread my poncho over my bivy, and pulled the top over my head. I was carrying a letter in my cargo pocket. My favorite note from my mother. She'd written it while I was in Boot Camp #2. I pulled the letter out, safe and dry in its plastic baggie.

Dear Army Warrior Chick,

Guess what! Aunt Bev is coming to your graduation also! It was real good to get your letter. Sounds like you were <u>really</u> worried about passing your rifle qualification. I'm glad that you are able to find the strength to do amazing things and that you think I have something to do with it. You are <u>very</u> important to me, as are your sisters. I think you each are wonderful people, and so different, which makes our family even more interesting. You are my tough warrior, because you have great discipline and determination to accomplish your goals—and your goals are high ones. Yet, you are also a sensitive young lady.

Well, hang in there, kiddo. It's been a long haul, but <u>you're almost through</u>!

Love you very much!!!
—Mom

I folded the letter, put it back in its bag, back in my pocket, and settled in for what I hoped would be two hours of sleep, using the butt of my M16 as a pillow.

Shivering, my socks squishing in my boots, I listened to the splatter of rain outside my cocoon and the whine of mosquitoes hovering outside my breathing hole.

I thought about how every moment since the beginning of the universe had led up to this moment, right now, with me personifying the expression "drowned rat" in the Washington woods. How my ancestors had been in the right times and places to survive and have babies and survive and have babies, all the way back to primates. What would they think if they could spy on me? Could I spy on my children's children's children? I closed my eyes and tried to break into a vortex that shot ahead, not back. I was tired of looking back.

14. PATRIOTS

June 2005: Ft. Lewis, WA

The rest of our time in the field passed in a semi-monotonous, slow-motion blur. Instead of setting up patrol bases with the whole platoon, we split off into squads and ran endless Situational Training Exercises (STX). We camped against hillsides, in bramble patches, on the edges of fields so beautiful I didn't want to leave in the morning. We ran missions and more missions and acquired bruises and heat rashes and mosquito bites and strange tan lines.

I grew closer to the guys—Tinning, who always reminded me to put sunscreen on my neck, and Hunt, who woke me up for guard duty with whispers and adorably polite taps on the shoulder, and Kassano, who always tossed me the drink mixes out of his MREs.

We honored an unspoken pact to make each mission stand out, no matter who was getting scored. We horsed around. We grudgingly put up with Ayma, the guys playing rock, paper, scissors each exercise to see who had to carry her ruck. We joked about how much dirt and sweat our uniforms could hold. On days it didn't rain, we took to coating the insides of our BDUs with deodorant.

Unwittingly, I kept growing closer to the guys—McGreer, who helped me clean up Ayma's disaster zone every morning; Stinson, who made me a team leader on one of his missions, no hesitation.

We checked each other's heads for ticks and literally got ants stuck in our pants. We survived on five hours of sleep a night, sometimes less. We froze in the mornings and sweltered in the afternoons. We ate MREs for breakfast, lunch, and dinner. I hoarded the napkins for my runny nose. The guys bit the ends off the matches because they'd heard the sulfur kept mosquitoes away. We pulled hours and hours of security. And even though conversation was rare, I felt more than ever that this was the closest I would come to having brothers.

On our last day of individual STX, we were treated to a ride to another area of the base in a chopper—a Black Hawk, with both doors open. The scenery was even more spectacular from the air. Tall pines massed on the outskirts of green and golden fields. Brilliant flashes of light shone on the surface of marshes as we swooped low. A vulture paralleled our flight for a moment before wheeling away. I glanced over the top of my rucksack to share a grin with someone, but the only face visible was Hunt's, and his eyes were closed, his head leaned back against the wall.

A stream up ahead sparkled and rippled with tiny currents. Two fishermen stood in the water, lines cast, flannel shirts rolled up to their elbows. I leaned forward, imagining myself in their place, cold water gushing around my boots, a sandwich and an apple in the cooler for lunch. We left the fishermen behind and passed over a highway. Even though we'd only been in training a month, it was strange seeing the crawling line of colorful cars and trucks. Soon I would be back down there. A civilian.

A strap from the empty seat next to me whipped in the wind and slapped my nose. I drew back, the sting spreading from my nose to my cheeks and eyes. The universe was at it again. Reminding me how every day for the last week I had made a firm decision. I would not apply to be a conscientious objector. I would suck it up, serve my time. I would not abandon these people. They were smart and strong and funny and kind. They were altruistic. They were patriots. They were better than me. But every night I made the opposite decision. These guys were delusional, misguided, and about to be sorely taken advantage of. Guilt was a stupid reason to keep doing the wrong thing.

The chopper was going faster now and the extra seat belts writhed like cobras poised to strike. I drew back behind my ruck and watched the civilian world slide away, replaced by barracks, motor pools, dirt roads, and a field dotted with hundreds of cadets. Our landing pad.

• • •

That last day in the field felt like a reunion. The squads ran toward each other, shouting, ignoring tactical rules, meeting in chest bumps and bear hugs that grew into group hugs that ended in dogpiles, howls of "it's all downhill from here" rising. Chow was a hot meal served cafeteria-style instead of yet another MRE. Standing in line, we traded stories. Nissenger had accidently ambushed a Humvee of officers instead of his real target and gotten reamed for it. Gill had to go to the hospital because she'd gotten stung by a bee for the first time in her life and found out she was allergic. Givozzi had thrown his tennis shoes into a ravine because he didn't want to carry them anymore and when the cadre found out, he got stuck carrying the whole squad's shoes. He'd looked like some cartoon character with nine pairs of tennis shoes hanging off his ruck.

Sergeant Densey came through with mail. He handed me two envelopes, one from Zack, one from Alura. I stuffed them in my pocket for later and piled my tray high with mashed potatoes, green beans, chicken-fried steak, bread and butter, a brownie, and an apple. I picked my way back to our platoon area, careful not to tip anything off my plate.

"It's like a big picnic," I said to Hall, unslinging my rifle and sitting down.

"All our best meals have been in the field," she said through a mouthful. "It's glorious."

"Hey, Finn, what's in your care package?" someone called.

Finn was sitting next to a box.

"Yeah, who's it from?" Kilgore asked.

"My parents," Finn mumbled. He picked up the box and we all watched him open it. He held up a fistful of paper. "Blank sheets of paper, pens, envelopes, and a note that says, 'Nice of you to write.'"

We erupted in groans and laughter. Tinning sat down next to Hall and me.

"Mind if I join you ladies?"

"Not at all," Hall said. "I've been meaning to ask you, what did you say in that platoon meeting way back when that set everybody off?"

"What platoon meeting?" Tinning asked with his typical robotic inflection.

"The one right before going to the field." Hall looked at me, her eyebrows raised. I shrugged. I guess I'd missed it too.

Tinning scratched his head with tight, deliberate movements, then held up one finger. "I remember. You know that cadence that goes: A yellow bird. With a yellow bill. Was perched upon. Da, da, da da?" He bobbed his head from side to side, half singing.

"Yep."

"Okay. So, you know how it has a part about squashing the little bird? And also the part about the moral of the story being to get some head you need some bread?"

Hall put her fingers in a steeple under her chin, smirking. "Uh-huh?"

"I asked what exactly the offensive portion of the cadence was. The line about killing a small animal, or the line about getting head."

"And you were completely serious?" Hall asked.

"I guess I was the only one wondering." He let out a laugh that belonged to a Transylvanian vampire. *Ah ah ah ah.*

As the rest of the squad trickled in around us, I opened my letters, Zack's first. The Extra Action Marching Band had played with David Byrne and he'd cut out a newspaper review about the performance. But I went straight to the pictures. There was one of him intently digging into a box of Lucky Charms at my house in Morro Bay—one of the only times he'd ditched his trademark black shirt and black corduroys in favor of another oddball outfit. There was a black-and-white picture of him by his drum kit, holding a pair of mallets. And there was a close-up of his face, smiling under his mustache, the Bay and Port of Oakland in the background.

"That's your boyfriend?" Nissenger asked.

I passed him the headshot.

"Does he gun people down for a living?"

I cocked my head, glancing at the rifles by all of our sides. "Why do you ask?"

"The mustache. It screams vigilante."

"Let me see," Kassano said. Nissenger passed him the picture. "Damn. The mustache is fierce."

The whole squad passed it around. It felt good, sharing a slice of my real life. I pictured them in civilian clothes, going to class, hanging out with friends. A part of me wished we could all stay friends. Stinson handed the picture back.

"What's the attraction?" I asked him. "Guys are always commenting on his mustache. I don't get it."

"It's... just cool," said Stinson.

Kilgore chucked Stinson on the shoulder. "Don't worry. You'll become more verbally expressive as you get older. Happy birthday, by the way. We didn't forget."

Stinson blushed. Kassano cupped his hands around his mouth. "Hey everybody! It's Stinson's birthday. He's a whopping nineteen years old. One, two, three..."

The platoon sang "Happy Birthday" to Stinson. As we finished, Finn jumped to his feet and ran to the guidon. "Mine friends," he shouted in his Arnold Schwarzenegger voice. "Vee haven't counted our spoils of war in many moons." He held up the streamer we'd won for land navigation.

"One streamer," we thundered.

He held up our basic rifle marksmanship streamer. "Two streamers!" The heads of the other platoons turned. They all knew Third Platoon had taken the most streamers. We were top dog.

Finn held up our first aid streamer. "Three streamers!" He hefted the guidon. We shouted together, "We'll find you *and* we'll shoot you. Then we'll effing heal you!"

Densey watched from the trees, arms crossed, a big smile on his face. The smile on my own face slipped. This wasn't supposed to end this way—me feeling like I belonged, like I was back in the Army family fold.

Or maybe this was exactly how it was supposed to end. I'd come here wanting to hate them because of what they believed, what they were doing. That was impossible now. I knew them. It must work the opposite way too. They knew me... I was suddenly dying of curiosity. Could they, would they, accept the real me? Or what if I wasn't really alone? What if someone else was waiting to hear their own misgivings voiced? Surely someone felt a hint of what I did—Kassano or Hall. Surely Kilgore. He was skeptical of everything.

Don't ask, I told myself. *Don't ask, don't ask, don't ask.*

"Can I ask you guys what you think of the wars?" I said.

"What do you mean?" Stinson took a noisy bite of apple.

"Like, do you believe in them?"

"What, like believing in fairies?" Hunt guffawed.

"I'm serious. Do you think we should be over there?"

"That's not for me to decide," Hunt said, frowning. "My job is to become an officer and go from there. If they send me to Iraq or Afghanistan then the last thing on my mind is questioning whether we should be there. We *are* there, and we all have jobs to do."

Kassano stared at me. "I wouldn't be here if I didn't think we were making a difference," he said. "When I was in Afghanistan, we did a lot of good. We built schools and relationships. We changed how the locals thought about us. They would come to us for help. I completely believe in what we're doing over there."

"What about Iraq?" I asked.

"They're virtually the same mission."

Stinson wiped his hands on his napkin. "I told you guys this before. I joined to kill terrorists and they're coming out of the woodwork in Iraq. The faster I can get over there the better."

"Same here," McGreer rumbled. "Until we wipe out al-Qaeda, we'll always be watching our backs."

"What about you?" Kassano asked.

The curiosity burned like a cigarette tip on skin. "I don't think we should be over there. I think the occupation is breeding more insurgents. And I don't respect Bush as a leader."

All chewing stopped. I had their full attention.

"You *have* to respect him. He's commander in chief," Kilgore said, gaping at me. "What you just said is, like, illegal."

Hall looked from Kilgore to me, clearly uncomfortable. "Hey, I voted for Kerry too, but we live in a democracy. Majority rule. And Bush doesn't act alone. He has a ton of military advisers."

"Let me get this straight," Stinson said. "You think we should just let the terrorists do whatever the hell they want over there?"

I swallowed and plunged ahead, even though I knew I was digging myself a deeper hole. Acceptance had been a pipe dream. "Do you guys remember how the war in Iraq started? I'm a journalism major so I was paying attention. There was intelligence that Saddam Hussein was hiding weapons of mass destruction. Supposedly. So they sent in weapons inspectors. The inspectors never found anything. But the next thing you know they're told to get out of there, and then we take out Saddam, and then there's chaos. And *then* we find out there never were any WMDs. No one ever proved Saddam gave any money to the 9/11 terrorists either. The only thing that's clear now is we started a civil war between Iraq's two main religious groups."

"Saddam was horrible!" Hunt said. "He gassed his own people. He needed to be taken out."

"I agree, he was horrible," I rushed. "I just don't think Iraq is better off today. All those reports about us being seen as saviors? That's not true either. And any Iraqi against the occupation immediately got branded a terrorist, not a resister or protester or activist."

"It's a little late to be having doubts, del Duca," Tinning said.

I stared at the ground, my throat aching. "I'm not like you. I didn't join last year. I joined in 2000. No one had any idea what was about to happen."

"You still didn't answer my question," Stinson said. "You would have us pull out entirely and let the terrorists do whatever they want? If we don't go over there and stop them, who will?"

"Sounds like private security contractors like Blackwater will," I said. "Aren't you guys pissed that the government is spending hundreds of millions of dollars on guys who do the same work you'll be doing but get paid double or triple? And they aren't bound to any kind of moral code? And they can peace out whenever they want?"

"Blackwater guys are mostly ex-military. They know what they're doing," McGreer rumbled.

"That's not the point," I said.

"What the fuck is?" Stinson asked.

I wished I could shrink and disappear into the grass. I didn't have a simple answer for him. That was the whole problem. War wasn't black and white. It was all gray. But the military was a black-and-white organization that injected recruits with the same disease. *Yes, no, shoot, hold your fire, forward march, move move move, huah?*

"Here's how I think of it," Hunt said. "You know how people say it's a different world now? Or they call it the 'post-9/11 world?' We have to accept that wars are completely different than in the past. I for one feel a whole lot safer knowing we're over there, taking care of business. If more people joined the US military there'd be no need for companies like Blackwater."

"When we wipe the terrorists out, we'll all get to come home and enjoy peace," Stinson said.

I shook my head, wanting to plunge forward, to point out that our very presence was creating more depravity. That you couldn't force democracy on a country that wasn't ready, whose people saw you as invaders. That while the number of US troops killed in the war on terror was over two thousand, there were so many tens of thousands of civilian deaths no one could even agree on a number. Terror cells were popping up everywhere:

Pakistan, Saudi Arabia, Yemen. Did that mean we'd soon be at war in those places? Who knew with Bush at the helm. And if soldiers were writing home begging for body armor and vehicle armor, the Department of Defense had no business raining down money on private contractors like Blackwater. But it was time to backpedal. "I wish I could see it that clear-cut, that uncomplicated." I wondered whether my face was red or whether that tingling I felt was all the blood draining from my face, leaving me pale. Then I remembered I was wearing a thick layer of camouflage.

"Hey, takes all kinds," Hunt said, clearly uncomfortable. "We're all entitled to our opinion. As long as we can still do what's expected of us."

"Yeah, you better come to terms before you get commissioned," Kassano said.

"I've come to terms," I said, feeling my weak kitten of a secret swelling into a lithe jaguar.

The silence stretched. Hunt opened his packaged brownie, the crinkly plastic loud as a bulldozer. I left to dump my tray, knowing they were all waiting until I was out of earshot to ridicule, knowing that this was probably all they would remember about me from camp, and in a year or two, they probably wouldn't remember me at all. I would remember them forever. They'd live in that fenced-off part of my brain where I put things I couldn't resolve. The complicated pen. The guilt-trip holding cell. The angst tank. I kept people who were perpetually angry, disappointed, heartbroken, or disgusted with me in there. These people could be resurrected at any time for a fight, a rehashing. Maybe I'd argue with my squad for the rest of my life because the more I thought about it, the more I saw myself as just as patriotic.

While they wanted to defend and honor Status Quo America, I wanted to reject it. I wanted us to grow and change. I couldn't help but hope that decades from now it would be a matter of American pride to deal with threats through smarter, more effective means than packing up all our weapons of war and invading. And I couldn't help but hope that future college-educated soldiers could deviate from the Army's party line. It was childish to believe America could be rescued like a damsel in distress—slay the dragon of terrorism and we'd all live happily ever after. It screamed of escapism to ignore all the sins that came along with war—special interests, dirty money, exploitation, collateral damage, environmental destruction. I guess while I respected Kassano and Hunt and Kilgore and all the rest, I didn't respect the way they thought. Not about this.

15. THE PERPETUAL PERIPHERY

June 2005: Ft. Lewis, WA

There was a hugging, laughing, buzzing crowd after graduation. I hung at the periphery, watching Hunt lift his mother in a bear hug. Stinson cajoled with three buddies, probably friends from ROTC judging from their posture and haircuts. But mainly, I was surrounded by strangers. Celebrating. I wondered whether they'd look back on this day with nostalgia and pride or with regret and resignation. I heard my name being called and spotted Ayma worming through the crowd.

"Del Duca, you have to meet my parents." She grabbed my wrist and pulled me past clots of people. She stopped in front of a short, round woman and a short, thin man who looked nothing like Ayma and who were dressed in clothes that resembled something from a '50s TV show—not old or strange necessarily, but a different style than anything I'd seen.

"Mama, Papa, this is my friend, del Duca."

The man held out his hand. "Nice to meet you," he said in a thick accent. The woman clasped my other hand between both of hers and smiled up at me. "Thank you," she said. "For..." she leaned forward, searching for the words. Ayma thrust a disposable camera at her mother before she could falter further. "Get a picture of us!"

I put an arm around Ayma's shoulders and smiled. Bricks were tumbling in my head, the image I'd had of Ayma collapsing and stacking back up in a different shape. I was surprised she'd called me her friend, surprised she wanted a picture of us after so much animosity. Early on, I was forced to take on the role of babysitter with Ayma, which she hated, and yet relied on at the same time. She couldn't even get to morning formation without me reminding, coaxing, and then outright goading her. But now here were her parents. Clearly immigrants. Which meant she was first-generation American. She was one of those kids who'd had to translate parts of the world for her mother and father—school, TV, doctors' visits. She'd hidden it well, going on and on about Providence College, no hint of an accent. What else had she been through? Behind the camera, her mother beamed and her father's eyes sparkled. They were so proud of her, joining the Army to become a lawyer. Had she done it because she'd felt the same pressure I had? To make something bigger of herself? To distance herself from how she'd grown up? Maybe I had a lot more in common with Ayma than I thought.

Ayma's mother handed the camera back and rattled off something I didn't understand.

"She says thanks for helping me. She knows you cut my hair. And she says you're very tall." Ayma darted into the crowd and came back with Hunt, Kilgore, Tinning, Stinson, McGreer, and Kassano in tow. "Picture time!"

We posed, smiling big-fat-lie smiles for posterity, the month of hard feelings against our impossible weak link suspended for the moment.

"Should we start saluting you now?" Tinning asked, looking at Ayma's collar, where in another hour she'd be wearing butter bars.

She blushed. "I'm not commissioned yet."

"Practically," Kilgore said. "The big question is, are you going to make us salute you when you get back to the barracks?"

"You guys don't have to do that."

"You earned it," Kassano said, drawing looks from Stinson and Kilgore. "Come on, let's practice." He snapped to attention and held a salute. Ayma touched the brim of her beret, satisfaction written across her face.

The platoon handicap now had the most power. And I had taken the lead in helping that handicap pass LDAC, knowing full well she was headed for JAG Corps, an agency that might come after me in the very near future. I could have been flooded with spite, but it was so ridiculous, so ironic, that I found myself giggling.

Ayma shot me a glare, and just like that we were back to normal. Thinly veiled enemies.

Me across from our barracks at Ft. Lewis, WA, 2005

Leila and I on the steps to our Missoula trailer, about the age we bought those water guns.

The platoon on a cattle car ride, Ft. Lewis, WA, 2005

Some of 3rd platoon outside our barracks very near LDAC graduation, 2005.

Zack eating Lucky Charms at my house in Morro Bay, CA

PART IV

WAR AGAINST THE WAR

1. DIRECTIVE

July 2005: Morro Bay, CA

I'd found an apartment of my own in Morro Bay before shipping out to LDAC. It was half a block from my old room, and wasn't really an apartment, but a run-down suite at the Morro Hilltop Motel—a bedroom, bathroom, and tiny kitchen. I'd daydreamed about it all through summer camp—my own place on the second floor, with a big window framing the harbor and Morro Rock, no nosy or messy or infuriating roommates. Lugging my bags up the motel's stairs, breathing in the familiar musk of saltwater and sand, I grinned. I would be doing this every time I came home. Treading this neon-blue carpet, trailing my fingers over the railing, and taking in the ocean. Home.

Turning the key in the lock and opening the door, I discovered that not only had Zack moved all my boxes over, but he'd set up my bed and shelves and left me chocolate in the kitchen. Not bad for an escape artist. I threw my Army stuff in a closet and got to unpacking. As soon as I had my apartment in order, I could deal with the other looming mess: my conscientious objector application.

Of course I didn't deal with it right away. Under the excuse of needing a vacation from pressure, I shoved it to the back of my mind and achieved a great deal of success in forgetting about it, ignoring it, patting it on the head and saying *maybe tomorrow, maybe next week*. I went surfing and hiking. I dinked around on my acoustic guitar. I cooked and baked. I visited my Cal Poly doctor and started taking antidepressants.

I also threw myself into work at KVEC. The morning news anchor, Paul Kelly, had died a few months before in a gruesome car crash—something I was still getting over. Paul had taken the time to coach my newswriting. He'd taught me how to use the equipment in the booth and found a way to get me on-air, voicing news updates that played throughout the day. Noticing that I never bought anything from the "roach coach" and that my standard lunch was either a peanut butter and jelly sandwich or a cheese sandwich, Paul had often overbought on his trips to the vending machine, offering me crackers, trail mix, juice. The pain of him getting himself killed by driving drunk, when any number of people would have gladly given him a ride home, went beyond losing a mentor and budding friend. Besides my grandfather, no one I knew personally had ever died. It was stunning to think that one day he was telling me to have a good weekend and the next he was gone. Forever.

Paul's death left KVEC's managers so off-balance they let the business of reporting the news fall into the hands of amateurs: three Cal Poly students, only two of whom were journalism majors. We hit the air at 5:00 a.m. and read the news round-robin, rotating every story. We took turns voicing the news updates that played throughout the morning. We stood a little taller walking in and out of the station, striving to fill very big shoes. Professor Madsen couldn't have been more proud. At home, I followed his suggestion and spent half an hour a day reading aloud to train my voice—the newspaper, the back of the cereal box, old textbooks.

But I was not training myself to write the most convincing conscientious objector application I could. Or preparing to deal with months of being ostracized. Instead, when Zack's band returned from Europe and hit New York, I decided, on a whim, to splurge for a ticket and meet him.

August 2005: New York City, NY

"Hey beautiful," Zack said, bear-hugging me outside JFK airport.

It was 6:00 a.m. and I'd been on three different planes to get there. But as soon as he grabbed me I was electric awake. I pressed against him and rose to my toes to kiss him. He let out an adorable half-sigh, half-growl, and tugged me closer.

"What now?" I asked, finally pulling away.

He jerked a thumb to a cab behind him. "Take a load off, doll."

I sat in the middle seat, leaning against him. He was wearing his firefighter's coat and his black top hat. I wondered how the coat felt, being back in New York.

"I have rehearsal in Central Park at 10:00 a.m. Let's drop your stuff at the hotel, grab some breakfast and head over."

"Are we going to ride the subway?" I asked, excited.

"Why do you want to take the subway?"

"I've never been on one before." In fact, I was curious why we weren't on the subway now. Weren't long cab rides expensive?

"Fret not. We'll ride the subway. Although I'd prefer not to." Zack knocked a knuckle on the window. "See those skyscrapers across the water? That's where the Twin Towers used to be."

I sat up straight to see where he was pointing, and the fatigue of the journey hit like a swinging door. This is where it had all begun—the mass murder that launched two fucked up wars. The eye of enormous devastation that had spiderwebbed out to twist, taint, and change so many lives. My mind automatically played the news footage of the towers collapsing, the bodies falling. I tried to imagine what the towers had looked like as part of the New York skyline, their windows gleaming in the sun—tried to conjure the disorientation New Yorkers felt when they looked toward Manhattan. All I felt was frustration at trying to penetrate the abstract. The same frustration I felt at the thought of trying to explain my "situation" to the Army or even to the average citizen. I'd tried to start my application on the plane and given up, a page full of crossed-out first sentences.

I do not belong in the military because

I cannot continue to wear the uniform. I am suffocating under

Once I thought I shared the same values as the US Army: honesty, integrity, duty, respect. But in war

The cab left the highway and entered neighborhood streets. Soon people on the sidewalks were wearing black coats and black hats a little like Zack's. The men had beards and long curls of hair in the front. Some of the women wore scarves over their hair.

"Are these people Hasidic Jews?" I asked, staring. They looked so sophisticated, so anachronistic.

"You really grew up in a black hole, didn't you?" Zack said.

The cab stopped in front of what looked like a large, old house.

Zack caught my eyebrows rising. "It's a little unusual, but this was the cheapest place I could find. And it's near the subway, my dear."

In the lobby, a small young man who looked like he was about to attend a funeral in 1890 greeted us. I felt self-conscious about my tank top, but the desk clerk didn't even glance at me.

"May I ask how you heard about us, sir?"

Zack smiled his wolf smile—mischievous, pointy incisors showing. "You've got a gorgeous place. Word gets around, man."

The man furrowed his eyebrows, then picked up a pen and opened a ledger. "Are you married?"

"Nope."

The clerk frowned. "I'll give you number nineteen. Come with me." He ushered us into a teeny elevator that had an ornate metal gate instead of a door. "Are you a fireman?" he asked, looking at Zack's coat. Zack shook his head.

"Then why are you wearing that coat?"

"I like it," Zack said.

The clerk finally cracked a smile. "It's fashion? You're making a fashion statement?"

"You could say so."

He took us to a room with two tiny beds pressed against opposite walls, a large dresser between them. Once he left we looked from the beds to each other, laughed, and rearranged the furniture.

That afternoon the band played to a small crowd of confused and curious onlookers at a Central Park bandstand. The drums and horns sounded small outside. Zack played the cymbals and even his crashes seemed swallowed by the summer day. The flag team came running out in heavy makeup and skimpy outfits. They gyrated and twirled their flags in a sloppy cross between burlesque and drag. Central Park did not appear to be their ideal venue.

The next night though, at the Knitting Factory, they were in their element. The band quickly abandoned the stage to play in the middle of the crowd and were met with howls of approval and wild dancing. Zack was smirking and bare-chested, his biceps bulging, the black of his hat matching the rest of his black outfit—leather wristbands, corduroys, and boots. The flag team looked glamorous and sexy in the dark, threading their way through the chaos, stopping to harass people who weren't moving to the beat, or dirty dancing with the occasional victim. There was something primal in the drumming and the horns coming over the top, something that pulled me to dance in a way I didn't normally dance, to move in synch with strangers. I felt free in a singular way. An unjudged, uninhibited, unlikely way, considering The Predicament boiling away on a back burner. Zack and I went back to our Hasidic Jewish hotel and made love with the lights on.

August 2005: Camp Roberts, CA

Drill weekend finally jolted me back into the real world. I got up at 6:00 a.m., showered, and put on my uniform. It felt like a snakeskin I had shed long ago. I took the turns through the hills as fast as I could, eager for the next afternoon when I could race through the turns from the opposite direction and cast off the snakeskin for another month. I dreaded acting like nothing was up, lying to my friends' faces. Strange friends, yes. But people I liked and respected, especially Sergeant Morgan. This might be the last drill they would see me as the feisty kid sister, the daughter eager to learn.

Our new captain was the first to congratulate me. "Del Duca, I hear you passed LDAC with flying colors." The captain was pale and short, with a long, horselike face. He launched into how fantastic it would be when I made Second Lieutenant. "I can pass you all the stuff I get bogged down with. I can't keep up, especially now that we're growing. We've recruited another four members. Pretty soon we can start working on repairing some of these roads."

I nodded, glad he'd picked something I could be honestly enthusiastic about—roads.

"Be alert during formation." He clapped me on the back and strode to his office on stubby legs.

I frowned after him. What did he mean?

During first formation the captain called me to the front. "Everyone give Cadet del Duca a big round of applause for finishing ROTC's Leadership Development and Assessment Course. Before long she'll be our Second Lieutenant."

The guys whooped and clapped. We broke formation to go inside, where Sergeant Morgan had set up donuts and punch. My heart folded into a small, brittle piece of origami. I forced a smile, wanting to hide, wanting to tell them, no, really, *really*, I did not deserve this.

• • •

I'd gotten in the habit of taking off most of my uniform soon after drill's final formation. A few miles outside Camp Roberts I'd pull over, tear off my cap and jacket, whip my brown-green shirt over my head, and put on a tank top. But that night I wanted to feel the wrongness all the way home. I kept my uniform on, taking the canyon turns in a storm of conflict. I threw my car into park before it came to a complete stop, raced up the stairs, and dug out the thick packet of information "Andy" had sent me. I'd only skimmed it before. I climbed onto my bed and began to read.

The Department of Defense Directive defined conscientious objection as "a firm, fixed and sincere objection to participation in war in any form or the bearing of arms, by reason of religious training and belief." The sentence sent barbs into the lining of my stomach. I didn't know if I objected to *any and all forms* of war. And did an objection to the bearing of arms mean that I had to be against gun ownership? Or the right of people to defend themselves? Then there was the religion part. I was an agnostic with no religious training. Zilch. I read on, slogging through dense explanations.

Paragraph 4.2 of the POLICY section read:

Because of the personal and subjective nature of conscientious objection, the existence, honesty and sincerity of asserted conscientious objection beliefs cannot be routinely ascertained by applying inflexible objective standards and measurements on an "across-the-board" basis. Requests for discharge or assignment to noncombatant training or service based on conscientious objection will, therefore, be handled on an individual basis with final determination made at the Headquarters of the Military Service concerned in accordance with the facts and circumstances in the particular case and the policy and procedures set forth herein.

What? I read the paragraph again slowly before moving on to CRITERIA:

5.1.1 Consistent with the national policy to recognize the claims of bona fide Conscientious Objectors in the Military Service, an application for classification as a Conscientious Objector may be approved (subject to the limitations of paragraph 4.1) for any individual:

5.1.1.1 Who is conscientiously opposed to participation in war in any form.
5.1.1.2 Whose opposition is found on religious training and belief; and
5.1.1.3 Whose position is sincere and deeply held.

5.2 War In Any Form. The clause "war in any form" should be interpreted in the following manner:

5.2.1 An individual who desires to choose the war in which he will participate is not a Conscientious Objector under the law. His objection must be to all wars rather than a specific war.
5.2.2 A belief in a theocratic or spiritual war between the powers of good and evil does not constitute a willingness to participate in "war" within the meaning of this Directive.

Let me get this straight. You could get a discharge if you believed in angels and devils waging war, but if you could picture yourself fighting in World War II you were out of luck? The consistent use of the pronoun "he" irked me too. I kept reading, the sentences piling up like a brick wall I would have to scale with nothing but my fingernails:

*In order to find that an applicant's moral and ethical beliefs are against participation in war in any form and are held with the strength of traditional religious convictions, the applicants must show that these moral and ethical convictions, once acquired, have directed his life in the way traditional religious convictions of equal strength, depth and duration have directed the lives of those whose beliefs are clearly found in traditional religious convictions.

*Great care must be exercised in seeking to determine whether asserted beliefs are honestly and genuinely held. Sincerity is determined by an impartial evaluation of the applicant's thinking and living in its totality, past and present.

*Relevant factors that should be considered in determining an applicant's claim of conscientious objection include: whether ethical or moral convictions were gained through training, study, contemplation, or other activity comparable in rigor and dedication to the processes by which traditional religious convictions are formulated.

*Commanders will appoint an officer in the grade of O-3 or higher to investigate the applicant's claim. During the course of his investigation, the investigating officer will obtain all necessary legal advice from the local Staff Judge Advocate or legal officer.

*Applicants may be disciplined for violations of the Uniform Code of Military Justice while awaiting action on their applications.

By the time I finished the twenty-page document and twenty-page appendix, it was dark outside, and the breeze coming in my windows was cold. I'd taken off my boots and BDU jacket and burrowed under the covers, sinking lower and lower in my cocoon as I read. There was a very good possibility I was screwed.

I listened to the foghorns blowing down at the marina and watched the red lights on the power plant towers wink. I usually liked the red blinking—I found it calming in a hypnotic way—but tonight the tips of the towers looked like blazing eyes putting out a warning: *mess with the powerful and get burned.* I dropped the papers off the side of the bed and pulled the covers over my head.

2. ADMISSIONS

August 2005: Morro Bay, CA

You would think I was applying to be a member of the CIA. The application began by asking for addresses and corresponding dates of every single place I'd ever lived, names and addresses of every school I'd ever attended, every job I'd ever had, and information about my parents, including their religious denominations. It was time to call my mom.

I stepped out of my apartment and leaned my elbows on the white-flecked wood railing. A salty wind was blowing up from the bay. I closed my eyes and let the air cool my face and sweaty palms. I saw my mother smiling from behind the camera in our Fromberg living room, me in my new uniform. I saw her at that Ft. Jackson picnic table, turning, beaming as I raced to her. I remembered how she'd drunk in my training stories and rattled them off when people asked about me, how she kept mentioning the guy at her work who was also in the National Guard, how she wished me a happy Veterans Day every year.

My breathing heavy in my ears, I dialed my mother's number. I played coy at first, asking for addresses and dates for "Army paperwork." Turns out I'd moved eleven times, about once every two years of my life.

"Anything else?" she asked.

"..."

"Ro? Are you there?"

"There's something I need to tell you."

Silence on the line again, but from her end.

"It's been going on for a while," I said.

"This is something I have no clue about?" she asked.

"I haven't told you because I'm not sure how you're going to react."

"You're scaring me now."

I stalled. Maybe I could still explain this away. Maybe—

"Are you pregnant? Because if you are, I'm not going to be mad."

"What? No! I'm not pregnant." It would be easy to tell her I'd gotten pregnant.

She waited me out.

"I need something from you. A letter."

The line sounded dead, but I knew she was there. She was putting me on the spot, no more prompts. "It's a letter of support. For an application I'm putting together."

"Ro, just tell me the whole story. I'm not sure what you're trying to say."

"I don't want to be in the Army anymore. I can't." My voice caught. "I'm applying to be a conscientious objector."

"Okay." She paused. "If you need a letter from me, it would help if you explained what that means, and why you're doing what you're doing." She kept her voice devoid of emotion.

I explained what it meant to be a CO in the modern military. Then, clutching the paint-peeling railing with my free hand, I let loose a deluge. "The more I think about the Army and war, the more it makes me sick that I'm a part of the military. We haven't been in a Just War since World War II, maybe Korea. Take—"

"Wait," she said. "What do you mean by Just War? I've never heard that before."

"It's this checklist experts and diplomats and thinkers came up with, of when it's right to enter a war. The list says the reason for going to war needs to be ethical and can't be solely for recapturing things or punishing people who have done wrong. Innocent life must be in imminent danger. Force should only be used when the basic human rights of whole populations are being violated. Not true for Vietnam. Not true for Desert Storm and not true for Iraq or Afghanistan. It talks about how Just Wars can only be started by political systems that have distinctions of justice. We do, but Bush steamrolled them. He acted like our checks and balances weren't even there. If we had a real justice system he would be in jail for concocting an illegal war!" I found myself nearly shouting and took a deep breath.

"Sounds like you've thought about this a lot," my mother said.

I took her reaction as encouragement and forged ahead. By now I was pacing the length of the balcony. "It talks about last resorts, too. Force should only be used after all other peaceful alternatives have been exhausted. What did we do to try and prevent a war in Vietnam or Iraq? Practically nothing. And last but not least, the benefits of waging the war should be proportionate to its harms. Korea, Vietnam, Afghanistan, and Iraq all had huge harmful effects. The Cold War. Agent Orange. Civilian murders. Atrocities. We should have never been in Vietnam just like we shouldn't be in Iraq or Afghanistan right now."

"This all seems very big picture. Why do you personally want to get out? Isn't that what they're going to ask you?"

I let out a sigh. "It *should* be about the big picture. It's *all* about the big picture. If everyone thought small-scale, like, 'I'm not part of the war, all I do is order supplies,' or 'all I do is heal soldiers so they can go back to their jobs'..." I trailed off. I wanted so badly to explain exactly how I felt. "I'm not doing this because I'm a wimp or spoiled. What we're doing is wrong. Not just for me, for everybody, on both sides. Iraq is in a civil war because of us. I know I don't matter in the grand scheme of things, but I don't want to look back on this decades from now and regret not doing the right thing."

Silence on the line. What if she thought I was overreacting? What if she thought I was making a mistake? What if she didn't believe me?

I stopped pacing and leaned my forehead against my front door. The carpet under my feet seemed electric blue, almost blinding in the sun. "Are you ashamed of me? Aren't you disappointed?"

"Of course not. Why would you say that?"

"Because you're proud that I'm in the military. You addressed all your letters to me 'Dear Army Warrior Chick.'"

"Honey, no. Listen. I am proud of you because whatever you do, you do well. You say you want to write for the town paper in high school and the next thing I know you're publishing articles. You join track and you make it to state. I show up to your boot camp graduation and you're leading the platoon. If you don't want to be in the Army, you shouldn't be in the Army. I feel awful this has been going on for so long and you didn't feel like you could tell me."

Of course I could have told her, but what could she have done? Especially from a thousand miles away. Besides, I couldn't pile more weight on her. She had her own baggage.

I jogged down the stairs and hit the parking lot. I didn't want my neighbors or my landlord hearing or seeing me lose it, if it came to that. "What are you going to tell people?" I asked. "They're not going to understand." I hated that my mother would be judged for my traitorous decision too.

"What people?"

"People who ask about me."

"It's none of their business. Why are you worried about what strangers think of you?"

"Because! And it's not just strangers. Grandma, Aunt Bev, Uncle Skip, *people*. I look like friggin' Benedict Arnold. Like a coward. Even if they say they're not, they're going to make assumptions. They're going to think I've acted like an idiot at the very least."

"You're human. We all make mistakes. If they don't understand that, they're not worth the time you'd take worrying about them."

I charged past the Morro Hilltop Motel sign, straight toward the bay. She made it sound so easy.

"You know, it surprised me when you wanted to join," she said. "I honestly thought that if you thought about it a couple weeks you would change your mind. I remember asking Alura and Leila, 'Can you picture Rosa taking orders?' But you've always been the unpredictable one."

I stewed on this. Christ, she'd been right all along. Here I was, refusing orders. I reached the staircase that led down to the Embarcadero. I loved going down those stairs because the hillside was covered in ice plants, their thick green tendrils fat like aloe vera, their pink and yellow flowers wide open and saturated with color.

"There's something else I need to tell you, Mom." I sat down on the steps. "I'm supposed to tell people who write letters of support about the main parts of my application."

"Isn't that what you just did?"

For the hundredth time I considered stopping. Changing the subject. She didn't have to know. But I was afraid if I didn't tell her she would learn about it from Leila or Alura and be even more hurt. "Mom, the Army thing—" I'd been about to say "it gets me really down." The same wording I'd used at fifteen years old, trying to tell her I'd started to hurt myself. When she hadn't believed me. Just like she hadn't believed me when I told her Wayne was molesting me. The memories sparked just enough anger to blurt out, "I cut myself sometimes. I started therapy. I'm on antidepressants. My application talks about it, so you need to know." I regretted it immediately.

"*What*? Why didn't you tell me any of this?"

My chest burned. "Because you're my mom. I don't want you worrying about me."

"Rosa, who better to worry about you? That's my job. How long has this been going on?"

I found myself squirming and forced my body still. "Since high school." I remembered telling her I'd fallen into brambles hiking the first time she'd seen the cuts. The second and last time she noticed them, I blamed the cuts on the jagged doorway to a fictional abandoned house I told her I'd explored.

"How bad is it?"

I ripped an ice plant flower off its stem and started shredding it. "Not bad. And before you ask, I'm not suicidal. It's not a big deal. The only reason I told you is so you can make your letter as accurate as possible."

"Why are you keeping these huge things secret? You know you can call me whenever you're upset."

"Yep." I wanted to hang up.

"Was that a yep or a nope? I couldn't tell."

"Yesss," I said, sounding like some cartoon snake.

"And to be clear, you're saying being in the Army is making you depressed."

"Yes."

"So why were you cutting yourself in high school?"

Julie called it "situational depression," the crap with Wayne and Dad and us moving away from Missoula to live in the boonies. Situations my mother would feel responsible for creating. "I don't know. I've always been moody," I said.

This was a family truism. While Alura and Leila could have bad moods, I was known as "the moody one."

"Are you okay now?"

"I'm fine." I tossed the destroyed flower down the stairs and reached for a stem, slicing it open with my thumbnail and peeling off the delicate green skin.

My mother cleared her throat. "I'm sorry all this is happening. If I had known…" She cleared her throat again. "Don't take this the wrong way, but now that we're being completely honest with each other, it did bother me at first. You joining the military. I didn't want you to."

I froze. "Why didn't you say anything?"

"I wanted to let you make your own decisions. And I thought if I said no you'd wait until you were eighteen and do it anyway. You were an adult."

"I wasn't! I was a moron."

"You were anything but a moron. You were valedictorian. You were serious and responsible. You were clearly ready to take charge of your own life."

It was what every parent had to do at some point. Let their grown children make their own decisions. But high school Rosa had needed to be stonewalled. She'd needed deep discussions and perspective and confrontation. "Why didn't you try to talk me out of it?"

A sigh crackled the line. "Do you remember what you were like at seventeen? You leapt down my throat if I so much as asked whether you had homework you should be doing."

"But what if it was worth having a big fight about? I mean, six years is so long." I tossed the gutted stem down the stairs.

"I guess I should have told you how I felt. I just didn't want our relationship to…"

This didn't matter. It was only another crystal-clear snapshot, courtesy of hindsight. "It's okay, Mom. You're right. I probably would have waited until I was eighteen and done it anyway. I had everybody fooled, including myself." I made polite excuses about a project I needed to get started on.

"Well, thanks for callin'." She often ended phone calls with this line. It felt good to return to routine, even though I suspected that after we hung up she would rehash the ugly years with Wayne, drinking in blame and guilt, a sin-eater. Meanwhile I faced the task of calling the six other people on my Letter of Support list and admitting everything all over again, and again, and again. And as for finally taking a step toward my mother by spilling my guts, I didn't know. It seemed we were still just as far apart.

3. CITIZEN SOLDIER

September 2005: San Luis Obispo, CA

Classes started up again. On ROTC PT mornings, I drove to campus before the sun rose in my black Army shorts and gray T-shirt, two backpacks on the front seat next to me, one for Student Rosa, one for Army Rosa. That early, it was easy to find parking near campus. I strode straight to KCPR, stashed Student Rosa's backpack, went to the gym, did PT with the other cadets, then raced back to the station, changed into civilian clothes, and swapped Army Rosa's backpack with Student Rosa's backpack.

In military science class I struggled to keep up appearances. I was a shitty actor. The cadets started ribbing me—asking if I was mute, newly single, a cyborg, or just pissed I'd gotten an average LDAC score. Fleishman was the only one who didn't tease.

Thursdays were ROTC lab days, where the whole program got together around 4:00 p.m. for additional training, usually in Poly Canyon. We were supposed to use our rucksacks as backpacks and wear BDUs all day on Thursdays, but I remained Student Rosa as long as I could, wearing civvies to class and then dashing back to KCPR for my BDUs. I'd count the minutes through lab, hoping, *hoping* we would end early enough for me to change into normal clothes before my last class of the day. But we always ended on the dot, or a few minutes late, forcing me to trot straight across campus to Spanish class, bursting in the door like some swamp monster—

dirty, face smeared with camo, chest heaving under my uniform, my ruck hanging off my back, my civilian backpack hanging off my front. My classmates (and my teacher) tried not to stare as I took my seat.

After Spanish I headed to KCPR, my sanctuary. I'd taken to doing my homework there, partly because I didn't have a printer or internet at home, and partly to keep on task instead of crawling into bed. I'd taken to working on my application there too.

Staring into the computer screen, I thought and thought and thought. Taking a break meant flipping through books from my English, philosophy, and journalism classes for inspiration. I wrote about wars. I wrote about the Golden Rule and the responsibility we had as beings of higher intelligence. I wrote about the use of force, the court system, how at the beginning I was proud to wear the uniform, and how far downhill I'd slid. I wrote about my family and depression and guilt and literature. I deleted everything and wrote it again. I poured out what would become a twenty-page manifesto, apology, and public diary all rolled into one. The opening reads:

I believe it is morally wrong to be engaged in war. Since the beginning of time, human beings have had the tendency to solve their problems by killing people who disagree with them or don't act according to their own societal structure. War should not be an option in a world where economic, political and social influence can be used to resolve conflicts. It is a vicious behavior that destroys lives, cities, bonds, and even ways of life. Every war eventually has an end and the terms reached for peace could have been arrived at without killing countless people. Everyone loses in war.

I try to base my behavior on compassion, love, honesty, fairness, and intelligence. Although I have strong confidence in my own decision-making process, I listen to people with different opinions and am not above admitting I'm wrong.

I believe everyone should treat people as they would wish to be treated themselves. In other words, I take great effort to follow the Golden Rule. As humans are the only species in the world with higher intelligence, I also believe we have a responsibility to treat the earth with respect. Our wars not only affect people, but the whole ecosystem. Our weapons destroy habitats, pollute, and therefore, set in motion even more destruction. The earth is not here for us to use however we like. We have a responsibility to animal and plant life, as well as future generations, who will inherit whatever mess we create.

My beliefs about what it means to act morally and ethically prevent me from being involved in any war. There is no good reason wars are fought. They are never the last resort. The moral and ethical thing to do in every situation is to avoid loss of life at any cost. There are always alternatives to war. It is wrong not to consider them. Violence only breeds more violence, especially if it is as grand scale as war.

I feel as if I will suffocate if I remain part of the Army, an organization structured to follow the orders of the high ranking. I've come to realize that in times of war I cannot respect all orders, nor be expected to give them. It has been drilled into my head that every member of the military is a soldier first. We are all infantry when *needed. Even though infantry-type warfare is not likely what I would be doing, every single military job supports war, whether directly or indirectly. It's not right. The United States should not have moral authority over every single person in the military, and as the number one power in the world, the same authority over the world as well. I can't be expected to give orders during warfare when my conscience is so deeply against war. I cannot respect orders given to me that contradict my beliefs, my morality, and my ethics. War never creates any good and I need to make a stand before I go crazy agonizing that I am part of it.*

Later, there are kudos to my mother, reprimands for the Bush Administration:

My mother taught me that to lie was just about the worst thing someone could do. I still hold this belief and am angered at what I would consider lies our government told to rally public support for invading Iraq. I've come to believe that dishonesty is a huge part of warfare and violence in general.

There is a nod to Gene Roddenberry:

I grew up watching Star Trek: The Next Generation. *The crew is governed by the Prime Directive, which is a set of laws about non-intervention and keeping the peace. I didn't realize what important moral questions the show raised until I was a little older. For instance, is it right to ask someone to do something you would not do? When you are faced with a choice between two negative situations, how do you decide? It also taught me the importance of conferring with knowledgeable people when you have problems.*

There is a long section about higher education, which reads in part:

In college my beliefs expanded after taking thought-provoking classes in ethics, history, English and psychology. More and more I realized the harmful effects of dishonesty, violence, carelessness, pride, prejudice, stubbornness, and lack of critical information. People/countries/organizations with these traits are headed for disaster.

All literature is derived from conflict and every piece of writing has some problem presented to the protagonist(s). Several books in particular had a strong influence on my developing beliefs regarding morality, integrity, compassion, and fairness. Leo Tolstoy's The Death of Ivan Illyich *taught me to examine my life more carefully and live each day with purpose. John Steinbeck's* In Dubious Battle *made me question: How far are we willing to go to get what we want? Where do we draw the line? In this book it is clear how violence breeds violence, power corrupts, and social classes look down on classes below them. These are things we must overcome.* Narrative of the Life of Frederick Douglass, *a slave who eventually escaped to the north and became an influential person, details how no amount of hardship should keep someone from trying to accomplish what is right. Guy Sajer's* Forgotten Soldier *is the true story of a French teenager with a German father who joins the German army during WWII. It is filled with heart-wrenching, sickening, and desperate descriptions of what he and other soldiers went through. It showed me in utter clarity that no one ever gains anything from war. It showed me that war can leave deep national wounds that can breed further violence.*

And smack in the middle, there is the circular narrative arc. Or in this case, a 180-degree revolution:

When I joined the military I felt good that the Army had a set of values which I agreed with in principle. Loyalty, Duty, Respect, Selfless Service, Honor, Integrity, and Personal Courage are all admirable traits we should strive for. However, as time went on I saw that many people in the Army and the government did not exercise them and many regulations went against these values. I became more and more depressed and anxious about my involvement in the military. ROTC training brought out even stronger feelings against violence and war. Every lesson had overtones of what I would face as an officer in a time of war. Now, the Army values have come to mean something different to me. I must have loyalty to the human race over loyalty only to the Army and certain citizens of my country. I have a duty to do what I believe is right. I have respect for all life on this earth. Selfless service can be accomplished in many ways other than waging war. Honor stands for the pride you feel when you know you are doing what you feel is ethical and moral. I have integrity in that I am being honest with the military, my friends and family, and myself in that I don't belong in the armed services. I have never had as much personal courage as I have right now.

It's not just an essay. It's the process in which I became a writer in the real world. The world of consequence. And even if I did possess a type of innocent, hippie naiveté, and even if I did insist on using *Star*

Trek as an example of my moral training, it's perhaps the vessel I used to finally become an adult.

4. QUANDARIES

September 2005: San Luis Obispo, CA

I rediscovered the bolt cam pin I'd accidentally taken home from Boot Camp #2 after coming home from LDAC. It was sitting where I'd left it, in the bottom of a blue, heart-shaped, plastic jewelry box, surrounded by silver chains and forgotten earrings and rings with bands that were more oval than circular, thanks to all my fiddling. Rolling the bolt between my thumb and forefinger, I decided to finally return it. I didn't want part of an M16 in my apartment. It wasn't a cool souvenir anymore, but another reminder of what I was trying to escape. I plunked the piece of metal into an envelope and thought about where to send it. The address to my old Company back at Ft. Jackson was probably somewhere on the internet. Or I could mail it to Camp Roberts, anonymously. Or I could even bring it there in person, next drill.

But then there would be questions. *What are you doing with this? Why didn't you return it earlier?* And once they found out about my CO application, they'd probably assume I stole it—which, in a way, I had. I tipped the envelope, feeling the lump slide from one end to the other, weighing my little moral quandary.

Was I a thief? A petty criminal? Or did I have an obligation to keep the bolt? I was a conscientious objector. I needed to determine the most moral course of action and follow it. What would Aristotle do? Or Kant?

Return property to its rightful owner? Even if that owner's actions were deeply compromised? Here was an opportunity to keep a deadly weapon out of an Unjust War, at least symbolically. I'd like to think that both Aristotle and Kant would tell me to throw the pin into the ocean.

I ended up stringing the bolt on a thin metal chain and wearing it around my neck as a reminder. I showered with it. I slept with it. I liked when people asked about it, even though I didn't tell them what it meant, only what it was, which usually left them baffled. The only time I took the necklace off was when I put my uniform on. I didn't want my peers, my superiors, asking questions or taking it away. It signified One Less. One less rifle. One less soldier. Me.

At least, that's how I rationalized it.

There is a level of rationalization throughout my manifesto too. For instance, I still believe I would have been part of the war effort during WWII. But Andy was ready for concerns like these when I called him, frantic and sick at the thought of building a case of moral superiority on half-truths.

"It's a hypothetical," he said. "You don't have to address it. You *weren't* alive, so you don't know with certainty what you would have done. Don't even go there, especially if they ask you during the investigation."

• • •

"Do you think that's really ethical, though?" I asked DJ Sasquatch. We were on a hike to the big letter "P" on the hillside behind school. "What I ended up writing is that Congress and the president can't be trusted anymore to engage in only Just Wars. Both Democrats and

Republicans have abused their power for the last sixty years. I don't see things changing anytime soon. Therefore, I'm against all wars. Does that sound presumptuous?"

"What I don't get is why they would want to hold on to you when you don't agree with what they're doing," Sasquatch said. "Why would they want to keep someone like that?"

I shrugged. "I cost a lot of money to train. I made a promise. They can't just let everyone who has qualms about the war go."

"But that would be the ethical thing for them to do."

"But then there might not be an Army," I said.

"Then we might not get into really unpopular wars," he said, scratching his head through his mane of unkempt hair.

I stepped around poison oak blocking the trail. "I've been thinking about it more and more. What if we brought back the draft? And not just for men. Women too."

Sasquatch stopped. "That's a terrible idea. That goes against everything you stand for, right?"

"Think about it. The only way people will wake up and give a shit is if their family is directly involved. So many people are checked out because the war doesn't affect them in the slightest. If they had to think about being sent to war, they would be a hell of a lot more politically involved. There would be massive protests."

"Look at Vietnam, though. The draft was a disaster."

"No, the draft got people into the streets. It got them talking and burning draft cards. It helped us pull out of Vietnam. And then what happens? The government cuts out the general public from all military action. They end the draft and voilà, there's an all-volunteer military. Everyone's happy. The government can go bomb whoever, and people who voluntarily join aren't likely to say, 'Wait a minute, this isn't what I signed up for.'"

A lizard skittered across the trail ahead of us.

"And Congress!" I practically shouted. "They would have to really, really make a case for every war. There would be accountability to only take military action when absolutely necessary if there was a draft. It would change everything."

"That would never happen. People would riot if we brought the draft back."

"I should hope so. That's the point. People might finally open their eyes."

Sasquatch plucked a crushed beer can from the side of the trail and dropped it into his cargo pocket. Litter was his biggest pet peeve. "It was strange, registering for the draft when I turned eighteen. I remember being bitter that girls didn't have to worry about it."

"I don't blame you. It doesn't seem fair. Especially when all women want is to be treated as equals. Maybe that's part of the problem too. Not enough women involved in any of these decisions."

We hiked in silence, our boots crunching on the dust and rocks.

Looking back, I'm embarrassed by this exchange. Sasquatch was right. A draft went against what I stood for: sparing people, especially naive kids, from being forced into shitty positions. The usual suspects were behind the desire for such a cruel and selfish revenge: jealousy and anger. I wanted to smack some sense into all the people going about their lives like nothing was wrong. Even the media had sunk into complacency. The war barely made the news anymore.

"Am I completely boring you?" I asked.

"Not at all. This is how I pictured college. Having debates. You know, it's funny how that never happened for the most part. Guess that's what I get for going into Urban Planning."

I paused to catch my breath and looked out over campus. I could see the communications building, where the radio station was, and, across campus, the ROTC building. In a week I would march over there and break the news.

"I'm becoming obsessed with moral quandaries," I told Sasquatch.

"How so?"

"Ever since writing the application, I get tormented by the smallest things. Like, I go to work and I wonder if it's ethical to print school stuff on their printer. It's basically stealing. Or I wonder if it's ethical to ask Zack to park around the corner when he stays the night. My landlord says he wants an extra seventy-five dollars a month if Zack stays over more than once a week. Smuggling in Zack is dishonest. And last week, I hit the bumper of a parked truck and I didn't leave my information. I got out and didn't see any damage, but does that make me a hit-and-run driver?"

Sasquatch laughed. "Following the rules doesn't make you an ethical person. I think morality is about intent."

"Everything's so complicated when you burrow under the surface. Like printing at work. I'm employed by Clear Channel, which is basically an evil empire given how they're going around buying out unique local stations and turning them into Top 40 drones. And I worked there without any pay for three months as an intern. Maybe it's not right to use their printers. But what the hell am I doing working for another organization I don't respect? Day after day they let Rush Limbaugh and Sean Hannity spew hate and misinformation and beat the war drum. It's disgusting. What am I doing there?"

"It's a job. Everyone needs to make rent. You're so hard on yourself."

"I could make money doing something else."

"Your job has nothing to do with those shows."

I made a noncommittal noise. "And take the landlord. That's not cut-and-dried either. Do a few more showers cost seventy-five dollars a month? No way. He could have asked me to pay the utility bill difference instead, or mentioned the guest tax thing from the start. The dude comes off as a little shady. Three times now he's knocked on my door at like nine thirty at night with mail that got delivered to the main mailbox instead of my mailbox, and he lingers at the doorway, wondering *what I've done with the place*—you know, hovering, wanting to be let in."

"Creepy. You should stop answering the door."

"But he knows I'm there. My car is out front, my lights are on..."

"Stop."

"Stop what? Making excuses, or—"

Sasquatch grabbed my arm and pointed. "Rattlesnake. Under that bush, see it?"

The snake's brown and cream scales blended into the dried branches and dusty brown of the dirt. It sat coiled in a rough figure eight, staring at us.

"Should we try to get past him?" I asked.

Sasquatch made a face. "It's too steep. Let's turn around."

We picked our way down the trail, the conversation turning to his crush on a girl, to the radio station, to our plans to hike by the beach soon. Sasquatch knew a spot where you could see starfish at low tide.

Coming on the heels of our moral debate, I couldn't help but remember the starfish I'd plucked out of the ocean right after moving to Morro Bay. I'd taken it home because I wanted it as a decoration. I left it by the front door to dry out. I assumed it was like a fish—once out of water for a few minutes, it died. No. Our neighbor told us they could take a full twenty-four hours to die out of water. God, I was a terrible person sometimes.

5. DECLARATION

October 2005: San Luis Obispo, CA

"Are you here to make my life more difficult, Cadet del Duca?"

Eyes wide, I searched Major Taulk's face, panicked that he already knew what I'd come to say. We stood in ROTC's spacious main office. The secretary peered at paperwork through her thick glasses. The female captain who taught the first- and second-year cadets leaned against a filing cabinet, drinking coffee. Another captain pawed through the shelf of military manuals in the corner. Each one disliked me. The secretary had a knack for screwing up my paperwork so I was always asking her to fix it. The captains were constantly on my ass for missing PT because of work. They'd both pegged me as checked out, a troublemaker. Which, as it turned out, couldn't be more accurate.

"Actually, yes, sir," I told Major Taulk, glancing down. Taulk was the only person in the room I admired. He was smart and easygoing and fair. It made what I was about to do that much harder.

"Well, what is it?"

My hands clenching, my fingernails digging into my palms, I raised my chin. I could see Taulk recognize something was wrong. The others seemed suspicious, curious. "I really need to talk to you, sir," I said, flicking my eyes to his open door.

Taulk hesitated, but only for a moment. "Come on in then."

He closed the door and offered me a seat. Light sliced through the blinds above us and striped Taulk's massive metal desk. I couldn't bring myself to look him in the face, so I stared at the rank sewn on his collar.

"Sir, you're not going to like what I have to say, and I'm sorry that I couldn't tell you earlier, but I was advised not to." I took a deep breath. His jaw clenched at the word "advised." His posture was stiff now and he was alert. I could feel the barrier slam into place. Me vs. Them.

Tears filled the corners of my eyes and threatened to spill over. Tormented at losing my composure this early, at Taulk being the first to witness my traitor transformation, I struggled to force out my declaration like pushing words through glue. "I. Am. Applying—" I let out the breath I'd been holding and looked him in the eyes. "Sir, I am a conscientious objector."

The Major stared at me, his brows knitting tighter and tighter together. "I don't understand," he said.

I stared back, then dropped my gaze to my long fingers spread over my camouflaged knees. I felt like I'd launched a popsicle-stick dinghy into the churning waters of the open ocean. No going back now.

"I'm against the war in Iraq and I'm seeking a discharge from ROTC and the National Guard on the basis that I'm a conscientious objector. Sir."

Taulk didn't seem angry. He seemed at a loss. Fed up in a fatalistic way. I could feel my face twisting and I clutched at my legs through my BDU pants, trying to claw away the tears.

"What do you want me to do?" he asked.

It was my turn for speechlessness. "I don't know. I was advised to tell you first, and then the National Guard. I'm not sure how it works."

He shook his head and gave a little shrug. "What do you mean, you were advised? Do you have a lawyer?"

"An organization is helping me put my application together. They know about the process…" I trailed off and dug in my backpack for my application binder. Inside was my manifesto. I planned on adding the letters of support in a week, when I got back revisions. Andy was a stickler for presentation. He'd even told me to throw out the letter from my dad for being too political and off-topic.

"Wait, wait, wait. Hold on a minute." Taulk held his hands up, eyeing the binder like it was a claymore. "Are you sure you want to do this?"

"Absolutely positive, sir."

He leaned back in his chair and rubbed at his temples. "Put that thing away. I need to do some research. I imagine we need to brief you on your rights and the process before we accept your application. And I'm not sure if ROTC handles these types of things. I would think the National Guard side handles it. Let me make some calls and get back to you."

I hesitantly stood up. "Is there anything else you want me to do?"

He didn't look at me. "Go to class and lab. Go to drill. Nothing changes for now."

I'd been hoping he'd suspend me right away. "Yes, sir."

I paused at the door, wanting to ask him if our meeting had been confidential, but felt the question was selfish. And of course it wouldn't be confidential. It would spread among the instructors like wildfire. And then it would leak to the cadets. I fled, head down. Outside, I fumbled for my sunglasses to hide my watery eyes, slapped my face, and walked to my car. I drove like a zombie back to Morro Bay, all the way down to the jetty. I picked my way over the rocks and sat down to watch the waves crash, the birds wheel—the setting a curious manifestation of my churning embarrassment and dread, and the soaring sense of relief above. *Well, it's all downhill from here*, I thought.

6. WRITING, IN AND OUT OF UNIFORM

October 2005: Camp San Luis Obispo, CA

In a twist of irony, the National Guard assigned me to journalism projects because of my conscientious objector application. Instead of drilling at Camp Roberts as usual, I did makeup drills at Camp San Luis Obispo, just ten minutes from campus. On my first drill there, I was ordered to take pictures of a new training course and write an article for their news flyer and possibly for the website they were building. Sergeant Morgan, my squad leader, my National Guard dad, was assigned to oversee my drill.

I met him outside Camp SLO headquarters, my eyes down.

"Morning," he said.

"Good morning."

When I didn't say anything more he announced, "I'm driving."

I followed Morgan to his truck. We got inside. He turned on the radio. Classic rock.

"How have you been?" he asked.

My eyebrows rose. "Okay, I guess. How about you?"

"Fine." He drove to the back of base, past all the buildings and parking lots, and hung a left on an empty road.

I couldn't contain my curiosity. "Do you know about my application?"

"I do."

I thought about apologizing, saying it had nothing to do with him, with our engineering unit, but I didn't know how to phrase my explanation. Maybe because it wasn't an explanation so much as a stand, and a stand I suspected he would see as a cop-out.

Morgan took the curves slowly. The area off to our right was exotically pretty and leafy, out of place for the rest of the dusty base. I wondered if there was a creek nearby allowing things to grow. We idled at a stop sign.

"I don't understand why you're filing that application. You seemed like you enjoyed what you were doing," Morgan said.

"I did like it, but I don't support the war," I said. "To be honest, I never should have joined the military."

Morgan nodded his head and eased the truck forward. We barely spoke the rest of the day. I took my pictures and conducted interviews. We ate an awkward lunch with two other sergeants who asked a lot about me. None of their questions required that I reveal my CO status, but I imagined Morgan biting his tongue through all my vague, off-kilter answers. Half an hour before we were free to leave for the day, Morgan came into the room where I was typing up the frame of my article.

"Major White wants to see you," he said.

"He's here?" Major White was part of Cal Poly's ROTC program. I was currently enrolled in one of his military science classes.

"He's got an office here. You didn't know he works at Camp SLO when he's not at Poly?"

I shook my head.

"I'll take you there."

Following Morgan, I braced myself. This couldn't be good. Then again, White seemed like an intelligent, soft-spoken guy. Maybe he only wanted to understand. Or maybe he would try to reason with me. Maybe, just maybe, this had nothing to do with my application.

"What the hell do you think you're doing?" White barked as soon as Morgan closed the door, leaving us alone. He was sitting at an angle, his chair tilted way back. I almost expected him to kick his feet up on the desk.

"By declaring myself—?"

He cut me off and leaned forward. "Sit down and shut up. I have a few things I'd like to say to you."

I lowered myself into one of the chairs in front of his desk. I stared at the row of books on the edge of his desk. Military histories. Training handbooks. He had given me a book called *Writing Under Fire* last year after finding out I was a journalism major.

"To say I was surprised about your little stunt is an understatement. I'm shocked. You signed a contract with us a year ago. One year later you're suddenly a conscientious objector?"

I stared at the book bindings.

"Answer me!"

The voices and movement from the other side of the wall halted.

I gripped the edge of my seat. "I didn't know I could be in the military and apply for CO until after I joined. I didn't plan for this to happen this way."

He stood, pressing his hands flat on his desk. "Think I believe that? Think I believe a word you say? I trusted you. I had respect for you. The whole cadre's disgusted. I want you to know I take this very personally. Your application is like spitting in my face."

I glanced at his red face, his blue eyes sharp with anger. I thought about the years of turmoil it had taken for me to stand up for myself.

He leaned a few inches closer. "It's a big 'fuck you, Major White.'"

I wanted to disappear. "I'm sorry you feel that way, sir."

"You're sorry? Damn right you are."

The silence stretched. I stared at his mug of camo pens. "I do respect you," I said. "But it won't change what I'm doing."

"You knowingly and willingly signed up to be an officer in this war. You swore an oath. Do you really want to be known as a liar? A failure? I would love to hear why you don't want to join the thousands of men and women doing their part in Iraq and Afghanistan, fighting terrorists, fighting for democracy."

I thought about clamming up. Waiting him out. He wasn't willing to hear an explanation. But he'd dared me to defend myself, so I launched the litany. "The war was built on lies. Hundreds of thousands of civilians have been killed. You can't force democracy on people who aren't ready. We don't have an exit strategy or—"

"Oh, so abandon your peers. Get your little degree and wash your hands of the real world. I expected more from you."

I kept my posture straight, looking past him to the back wall. He couldn't keep me here forever. Why did he suddenly care so much what I did? He barely knew me.

"Don't you have anything to say for yourself?"

"I'm not going to apologize, sir. I take my application very seriously."

He scoffed. "I take betrayal very seriously. Don't think anyone else will see it differently. Does George Ramos know about this?"

I shook my head and struggled to keep my back straight. After Ramos had called in to Dave Congalton's show, saying I reminded him of himself in college, we'd always exchanged smiles or waves in the hallway. Sometimes he asked about drill or ROTC. His office as Journalism Department Chair was steps from KCPR's door. I wanted to curl up in a ball.

"No? You left Ramos in the dark?"

I stared at the wall.

"I see one course of action for you. Have you filed your paperwork yet?"

I shook my head.

"Good. Don't. First thing Monday morning I want you to tell Major Taulk you withdraw your request. You won't be making a declaration. You can start earning back our respect from there."

"I'm not going to change my mind, sir."

"I think you've done a lot of changing your mind. Next time I see you, this better be over."

I stood up. "Am I free to leave, sir?"

He stuck a finger in my face. "You think about what you're doing."

"I have, sir."

His anger deepened. I saw a flicker of Wayne, like he wanted to hit me. And like with Wayne, I felt myself craving a blow so I could lord it over him. I saw a reflection of Drill Sergeant LaMonte the night he'd pulled

Santos and me into his office too: incredulity I wasn't following the script.

"Get out."

I flung open the door and strode into the hallway, pulling up short when I saw Sergeant Morgan waiting for me, his cap in his hands. From the look of chagrin he gave me, he'd heard everything. He reached out and gave my shoulder a squeeze. I flushed, the shame and regret White had been gunning for spilling over like bathwater left running.

• • •

At home, I found the article about me the *Tribune* had done the year before, the same week I'd been on the Congalton Show. "Education comes first" the headline read. "Cal Poly student defers call to active duty." There was a big picture of me inside one of the KCPR editing rooms, surrounded by posters and CDs and records, in front of a control board. A microphone hung in the foreground. I was looking away from the camera, a fist under my chin, wearing a half-smile of self-consciousness. Something about my face looked sad, but I couldn't pinpoint what.

```
Rosa del Duca had a difficult decision to make
recently, one the 21-year-old Cal Poly journalism
senior knew would alter the course of her life no
matter what she chose. The National Guard member
could either answer a call-up to active duty for
18 months, probably in Iraq, or she could defer
serving by at least two years and complete her
college education by enrolling in Cal Poly's ROTC
program. The seemingly obvious choice to finish
school first was complicated by the fact it would
require her to serve another four years in the
```

guard after graduation. It would also extend her college education by another year, in order to take the military science classes required by ROTC.

Del Duca chose to join ROTC, the option that gets her out of school quicker but keeps her in the military longer. The decision attracted the ire recently of some callers on a local talk radio program but also the support of a man who knows first-hand what she is facing. George Ramos, chairman of the journalism department, is confident del Duca will fulfill her duties after graduation.

"I don't know what her feelings are about the war in Iraq, but she's going to serve," he said. "That's a credit to her."

I stopped reading. White was right. I was a liar. And I'd made a liar out of Ramos. I replayed Dave's show in my mind. I'd proven to all those skeptics I was scum after all. What would Dave say when he found out? And Ramos? Even worse, what would Professor Madsen say? He kept nominating me for journalism department awards, raving about my work ethic and potential. And how were my ROTC classmates going to skewer me the rest of the school year? A dozen scenarios shot out like a waterfall. But then the current slowed, pooled. Even combined, the worst scenarios couldn't compete with the alternative. At least this lying scumbag wouldn't have blood on her hands.

7. BATTLE PLANS

November 2005: San Luis Obispo, CA

The conscientious objector application would be handled by ROTC, Major Taulk told me over the phone. "Come in as soon as you can."

I came that afternoon, slipping in the side entrance in hopes of avoiding everyone, especially Major White. The secretary shot me a cool look as I entered Taulk's office. We went through a small pile of paperwork: loss of VA benefits, a leave of absence from ROTC, possible disenrollment based on "information gathered," whatever that meant.

"Your first interview will be with a chaplain at Vandenberg Air Force Base," Taulk said in his new enigmatic voice—not necessarily robotic, but expressionless. "For the psychologist, you'll probably have to drive up to Monterey. And at some point they'll assign an investigating officer. That interview will be held here."

I found myself tensing my feet, my shoulders, my thighs. I knew all this. But now that it was happening, the anxiety wasn't somewhere overhead, but down around my ears.

In the hallway, I ran into Fleishman and Jones.

"Hey, del Duca. Can I swap spots on our book presentations?" Jones asked. "I need a couple days to finish."

I wondered if I should tell them I wouldn't be back to class. "Can't this time," I said, backing away.

"Please?" Jones called after me.

"Sorry, it's complicated. Gotta go."

Across campus, I met with my therapist. I was breaking the rules by seeing Julie for free this quarter. And to be honest, I felt both of us were only going through the motions. I didn't like her and she didn't seem to like me. I'd been hesitant to ask her to write a letter of support. I still suspected that she secretly disdained my trying to leave the Army. But at the end of our session she handed me a page printed on Cal Poly letterhead. It was short and to the point and included the line, "Although Ms. del Duca's current mood is more stable, it is my clinical judgment that continued military service puts her at risk of an exacerbation of depressive symptoms." I was grateful for the support.

My other ally at Health Services was Dr. Roan. I'd met him before LDAC, when Julie grudgingly referred me to him to see if I might benefit from medication as well as therapy. Unlike Julie, he'd been immediately sympathetic about the Army mess. He was the one who explained I could be suffering from "shark brain," a brain that operated on a muddled, primitive level emotionally, because of chemical imbalances. About a month after getting back from LDAC I'd gone on Celexa, courtesy samples he got for free. He knew I didn't have the money for a prescription and the samples were just sitting there in a drawer.

Roan burst into the exam room with a warm smile. "How are you holding up?"

My shoulders lowered. My hands stopped fidgeting. "Good. I'll probably submit my application next week. I have one last round of revisions, and then I need to get my letters of support notarized."

He scribbled something on his clipboard, then raised his eyebrows at me. "You know, I'm really impressed with you. This is a terrific response."

"What do you mean?"

"You've been on Celexa for a couple months now. I believe it has allowed you to act on your feelings."

I blinked. Could that be true? To be honest, I hadn't noticed a difference. If anything, I was experiencing one of the side effects: a drop in sexual drive and difficulty climaxing, not that I was going to admit that to Roan.

"I wrote about it in your letter of support, which I have ready for you today." He opened the top drawer of a small desk in the corner. He trailed a finger down the page and found his place. "'After starting her training with ROTC, Rosa started to experience more problems with depression. She sought professional counseling, but this brought up many issues from childhood and forced her to explore her personal feelings about participation in war. She started on medication and subsequently has been able to think clearly about her personal belief system and goals for her life. She is now able to clearly articulate her moral and personal beliefs, perhaps for the first time in her life.'" He looked at me over his glasses.

"Thank you for writing that." I felt like squirming and my shoulders had returned to their hunched position.

"You don't think it's true?"

Could a pill have been the final straw in launching my war against the war? I didn't want to give Celexa that much credit.

Roan folded the letter and handed it to me. "Let's talk about the challenges coming up. What are you most worried about?"

I tucked the letter into a textbook, where it wouldn't get crumpled. "The interviews. Especially the interrogation by the investigating officer."

"Why?"

"What if they assume I'm lying? Or what if I can't express myself the way I want to? And what if I turn into a crybaby?"

"You can't control other people. You can only control you. Let's practice. I'll pretend I'm the investigating officer. Ready?"

I thought about reminding him there was plenty of evidence I often couldn't control myself. But I steeled myself instead, picturing a furious major flanked by ROTC staff and cadets. "Okay, shoot."

November 2005: Morro Bay, CA

I reached under the table and lightly dragged my fingernails down Zack's knee. We were at our Mexican place in Morro Bay, waiting for taco bowls and margaritas. "Remember girlfriend points?" I asked.

"Girlfriend points? I don't know what you're talking about," Zack said, dipping a chip in the salsa bowl between us.

"Very funny. I think you should take me to the Bay Area sometime. Show me your shop."

"Introduce you to the Other Woman?" he said, twirling the ends of his mustache.

I pulled away and rested my chin on my fists. "I'm entitled to size up my competition." It was a running joke, him cheating on me with the old steam traction engine he'd bought. On weekends he was often in Oakland, building a crew to hook the engine up to turn a carousel. The plan was to take the whole operation to Burning Man—the first time he'd be running his own art installation. As usual, Zack's life was the opposite of mine.

"I settled on a name," he said. "Hortense."

"That's hideous."

"Take that back! Hortense is named after my grandmother."

The waitress plunked down our food and margaritas. I took a sip of my drink and shot Zack a glare over the rim of the glass. "I mean it. I'm cashing in. I want to see where your other half lives."

"Sure, doll. Whatever you want. I'll even come to your Army meetings."

I'd told him about having to be drilled by a psychologist and a chaplain, how I was dreading it.

"I'll sit there and give them the look. You know. Like a mob boss. A Rhinestone Cowboy. A bodyguard at least." Zack twisted the ends of his mustache again for effect.

I laughed. "I don't even know if that's allowed."

"It'll be a riot. We'll have you out of the Army in no time."

"You would take off work? The interviews are far away," I said, testing his resolve. Even if he waited in the car for me, it would mean the world, knowing I wasn't alone.

"Screw work," he said. "I want to be there. Consider it done."

8. INVESTIGATION

November 2005: Vandenberg Air Force Base, CA

I turned in my final application to Major Taulk and four days later I drove to Vandenberg Air Force Base to meet with a man named Chaplain Wong. Zack had pulled his usual stunt of canceling at the last minute.

The guards at the gate gave me a map of the base and explained that I could find Wong in the chapel. I pulled into the church parking lot and sat in the car for two full minutes, looking at the building. Wong's role in this, according to the Department of Defense Directive, was to "submit a written opinion as to the nature and basis of the applicant's claim, and as to the applicant's sincerity and depth of conviction." Telling a "man of God" about my very secular morals while inside his church couldn't go well.

Might as well get it over with, I thought, striding into the chapel and whipping my BDU cap off. A small, smiling Asian man sitting in the last pew turned toward me and stood.

"Cadet del Duca?"

"Yes, sir."

"Welcome." He was looking at me critically, as if there were messages hidden in the creases of my uniform. "We can talk here, or outside, where you might be more comfortable."

I eyed the pews and the stained glass windows. "I'm fine anywhere, sir."

He raised a hand toward the doorway.

We ended up on a bench under a tree with sprawling branches, the breeze making the shadows of the leaves dance across our uniforms and the sidewalk.

"I have read your application, but there are a few things I would like you to expand upon," Wong said. "First, why is it that you do not believe in God?"

I struggled to keep my face a mask. "I wasn't brought up that way, sir. My mother wanted us to come to a conclusion about God's existence on our own. Organized religion never made sense to me. No offense," I quickly added.

"And your father?"

"He wasn't around. But he's not religious either. At least not in the traditional sense. He's big into Native American spirituality, which appeals to me too. The way I feel about Mother Nature must be how some people feel about God. A sense of wonder and respect. Science, the universe, all the things we don't know yet... that's what's fascinating to me. That's what I believe in. The everything. Not stories people made up thousands of years ago to explain the everything."

Wong nodded. "But you have never gone to church?"

"I've been a few times."

"Are you judging something before you know it?"

I thought about the bizarre nature of this entire conversation. That not wanting to fight a war warranted an examination of my beliefs by someone who saw me as damned if I didn't accept Jesus Christ as my lord and savior. This was the twenty-first century. Couldn't I be trusted to think for myself? Wong was staring at me, waiting for an answer.

"What little I do know about the Bible and church doesn't make me want to know more. Religion seems responsible for as much harm as good. Take all the wars over religious differences. Skip forward to the US today, and religion is behind homophobia and hate crimes. It's sexist. Being judged by the twisted intentions of men who concocted the Bible back in ancient times has no appeal to me. I don't need the threat of hell or the promise of heaven to do the right thing. I think—"

Wong frowned down at his clasped hands. I closed my eyes. I was handling this about as well as the Army was. Suddenly it seemed like I was the bully and Wong the victim. I took a deep breath.

"I'm sorry. I don't mean to offend you. It's just that I don't associate religion with moral behavior. I probably would if I'd grown up going to church, but that's not what happened. Can I tell you about how my morals *did* form?"

Wong opened his hands, palms up. "Proceed."

December 2005: Monterey, CA

Three weeks later, I took Highway 1 north to Monterey, stomach churning in anticipation. Wong had seemed to believe me. That meant my application was two steps away from being complete. All I needed to do was meet with a Monterey psychologist and then endure whatever the investigating officer had in store. Without ROTC classes and PT sessions and labs out in Poly Canyon, I could taste freedom.

The road swooped low, a few hundred feet from the ocean's crashing waves, the sun illuminating foam on the sand that spun and met and parted like a kaleidoscope. *Freedom is not free* came the echo from boot camp, from AIT, from LDAC, from the many-limbed Green Machine. No, it wasn't. No matter what angle you looked at it from. The highway climbed up from the gleaming waves. My eyes lingered on the water, the surfers sliding down into the cradle of the waves, the pelicans gliding like mythical beings, never once flapping their wings.

I reached the Presidio of Monterey in a state of car-lulled optimism. This would probably all turn out fine. In a few months I'd be out of the Army. I'd join the anti-war movement. Our troops would come home. Maybe we would even learn. Evolve a little.

I turned onto the base and saw a roadblock ahead—a guard station flanked by men carrying M16s. I reached into my breast pocket for my military ID and eased the car forward.

"You need a new ID," the guard said, holding up my card. "This doesn't scan. Do you have any other form of identification?"

I passed my driver's license out the window.

"Why did you let your military identification expire?"

"I didn't know it was expired."

"It's got the date right here." The guard was no longer bored, but suspicious.

"I never use it. Where I drill, they don't check IDs at the gate."

"Why are you here?"

"I have a meeting with Dr. Linux at nine a.m." I could see from the clock on their wall it was ten minutes to nine.

"You're going to have to get a new ID card first."

"I'm only here for one day. I have the meeting, and then I won't be on another base for who knows how long. Can I take care of this back home?"

"Wait, why are you here?" He scanned my car, like he was looking for explosives, half-hidden weapons. He could see I didn't belong.

"I'm here to meet with Dr. Linux. He's an Army psychologist."

"Why?"

I flushed. "Sergeant, with all due respect, I don't see why the nature of the meeting is any of your business."

"We're going to need you to park right behind the guard tower. Bring your insurance and registration and any other identifying information. We're going to need Dr. Linux's phone number too, to verify the appointment."

They handled me like a dangerous suspect for half an hour before letting me go. Painfully late, all trace of optimism gone, I walked into an empty room that looked like a shared lobby. Several doors branched off, a large desk sat in one corner, and a water dispenser with paper cups was set up in another. In the center, there were chairs positioned around a low table with a couple magazines on top.

I sat down in one of the hard, plastic chairs and held my cap in my hands. None of the doors were marked with Linux's name and I didn't want to go knocking. When someone came out, *if* someone came out, I'd ask. That was all I had energy for. It felt like the old days—or the recent days, really—of moving through the world comatose. What was I doing here? Making another blind turn in the rat maze?

A noise like a coffee maker sighed and gurgled. After a few minutes I realized the sound was coming from a plastic contraption on the desk shaped like a giant sea shell. I wondered if it was supposed to sound like the ocean and why it was here. Maybe the walls were thin?

The blinds of a window next to one of the doors cracked and a tall man peeked at me. He disappeared, then emerged from the office. "You're here for nine a.m.?"

I stood, apologizing for being so late. The man looked at me, then looked toward the front door, like he wanted to leave.

"Have a seat in my office and I'll be right back. You want a soda?" He strode toward the door.

"No, thank you," I called after him.

His office had one of those psychiatrist chairs—more of a bed than a chair. I was eyeing it when Linux breezed past me, twisting open a bottle of Coke. I held out the thick folder of paperwork Taulk had told me to bring. "Do you want me to lie down on that thing?" I asked, looking at the chair bed.

"You don't have to. You can sit on the edge if you like. What's all this?" He flipped through the folder.

"Medical records. They had me bring copies of everything."

"I don't need any of this." He tossed the folder on his desk and took a gulp of soda. "Let's talk about your application. What I'd like to focus on is the depression issue, starting with the self-mutilation. Do you have scars?"

I sat down heavily. He didn't waste any time, did he? I unbuttoned my cuffs and rolled up my sleeves. Linux hovered over me as I pointed out my scars, most on my forearms.

He nodded, mouth in a little frown like he was mildly surprised. "Now, let's talk about your beliefs."

I told him my Army story. The happy-go-lucky start. The slow slide into suffocation. Getting called up. The blooming of a more mature conscience with two warring factions: one spurring me to join ROTC, the other driving me to the GI Rights Hotline.

Nearly an hour later, Linux had finished his soda and was twisting the cap on and off the empty bottle. A page of scribbled notes lay on the desk in front of him.

"I don't think you belong in uniform either," he said.

My chin jerked up in surprise. "You don't?"

"No. That seems clear."

"Are you going to tell them that?"

"That's not what I've been asked to evaluate."

I shook my head. "Right." According to the application, Linux was tasked with "a psychiatric evaluation indicating the presence or absence of any psychiatric disorder which would warrant treatment or disposition through medical channels, or such character or personality disorder as to warrant recommendation for appropriate administrative action."

"Is there anything you wish to add before we wrap up?" he asked.

I couldn't think of anything.

He stood and shook my hand. "You should keep going to therapy. I think you'll find it helpful," he said. And then he was ushering me out the door into the lobby with its sick ocean gurgle. Another doctor stood by his office door, urging his embarrassed patient to come back next week. Three soldiers waiting in chairs glanced at me and quickly jerked their eyes away. With the net of stigma sprung, I ducked my own head and scuttled to my car.

December 2005: San Luis Obispo, CA

The search for an investigating officer to handle my case dragged on for months.

"It can't be anyone from Cal Poly's ROTC program. It's got to be an officer above captain. And when you get that high, you're already handling a lot of work," Major Taulk explained to me. "They've got to read up on the regulations for the process, review your application and the reports from Wong and Linux, and get legal advice from the Staff Judge Advocate. It's a lot to take on. But we'll find someone. Be patient."

I went to class—Advanced Shakespeare, Spanish II, Feature Broadcast Reporting, Creative Writing. I started writing about the Army in first person but called it fiction. My professor went along with the game, encouraging me while at the same time writing comments like *make us understand the character's motivation here* in the margins. I avoided the ROTC side of campus. It seems childish now, but I even turned around and found a different way to class if I spotted BDUs ahead. I figured that by now, all the cadets knew. Someone had made a slip. Or someone had gossiped with the intention of it getting out. My former classmates had surely gotten together for a bashing session over beer and Jell-O shots. *She never said a damn thing*, they'd have said. By now, I was the enemy. The traitor. The cautionary tale.

I worked at KVEC as much as I could, rewriting stories from the newspaper into little briefs, recording updates to air throughout the day, screening calls for a health advice show on the weekends. Co-anchoring was over. They'd hired a replacement for Paul Kelly. I tried to avoid afternoons, when Professor Madsen and Dave came in. I didn't want to answer questions, didn't want to watch their opinions of me do a one-eighty.

Thanksgiving came and went. I flew home for Christmas and instituted a ban on Army questions. My mom kept us busy with Christmas cookie projects and board games and hikes in the snow. I kept drilling, writing cheery articles about the new climbing wall, the camp museum turning sixty years old, the graduation of high school ROTC cadets down in Santa Maria.

The year 2005 ended. The year 2006 began. KCPR's free trial of *Democracy Now!* ran out. I helped launch a fundraiser to keep it on air. Amy Goodman still seemed to be the only journalist talking about the wars in honest, complex terms. Saving her program might help cancel out taking home a paycheck from a Clear Channel station.

A new quarter brought new classes. A new batch of DJs started training. I took one under my wing. I kept very busy so I would barely have time to think about the military limbo I was stuck in.

In January, unusually big waves rolled into Morro Bay. Eight-footers. I'd always wanted to try my hand at real waves, not glorified shore break. I paddled out to the lineup one morning, the sea oddly like a lake, save for the giant curls. I'd been practicing dropping down into waves instead of letting them break behind me and hitching a ride on the tumult. This would be glorious. The day I finally proved myself as a surfer.

I watched the swells form on the horizon and float toward me—silent, arched perfectly, like mounds of undulating earth that stretched for miles. The swells lifted me high, lowered me down, and pushed on toward shore, cresting with a loud peal that grew into thunder. I was too far out. I lay down on the board and paddled a few strokes in. Craning my neck, I saw a giant looming behind me. I paddled like hell. The wave swept under me and drew me up. I leapt to my feet, but by then the nose of my board was pointing straight down. Not good. I took a deep breath and jumped away from my board. Under water, the wave spun and flipped my body until I couldn't sense which way was up. My leash pulled my ankle so hard I thought the line would snap. Frantic, I waited for the storm above to pass. It didn't. Instead, the wave dragged my board, which dragged me, toward shore. I beat back the instinct to take a breath and tried to claw at the Velcro around my ankle, but the water was too violent. The wave finally released me, but I still didn't know which way was up. I picked the direction easiest to swim in and broke the surface, gasping and heaving until a crash behind me turned my head. Another giant was bearing down. I ducked under the white water and let my leash drag me farther.

Body numb, I finally staggered out of the water with my board under one arm and flopped down to catch my breath. I couldn't help but compare the pummeling of the waves to the Army. Was this a sign the pushback was about to get bigger, stronger? Or that if I just clung on a little longer they would let me go?

I was still rattled that evening when Major Taulk called to let me know an investigating officer had been found for my interrogation.

"Does February 9 work for your hearing?"

Having escaped death that very morning, and having spent the afternoon examining what I'd done with my life so far and all that I still wanted to do, I said, "That sounds fantastic."

"Fantastic, huh?"

"Can't wait, sir."

February 2006: San Luis Obispo, CA

The interrogation was in a small conference room I hadn't known existed until Major Taulk pointed it out to me. I was five minutes late, my hand on the doorknob, when Fleishman came out of the men's bathroom down the hall.

"Hey, del Duca. Long time no see," he called.

I waved.

"Are you back?" he asked.

I was in BDUs after all, and it was Thursday, a lab day.

"I'm only here for a meeting."

He cocked his head. "What kind of meeting?"

I stalled. "It's like a review."

"Who with? Do we all have to get one?"

I shook my head, amazed he was acting like nothing had happened. Maybe my secret was safe after all. The doorknob turned from the other side. I took a step back, and Major Taulk poked his head out.

Fleishman looked from the major, to me, back to the major.

"Go to the computer lab and get that got-dang background check done for me, Fleishman," Taulk shouted.

Fleishman laughed and did an about-face. "Yes, sir!"

Walking into the conference room, I was surprised to see not only a strange man, who I assumed was Lieutenant Colonel Doan, my investigating officer, but Captain Rialtin, the only female on staff in the program. And instead of introducing me to Doan and leaving, Major Taulk reached for the phone at the end of the table and asked his secretary to make sure no one disturbed us.

The three of them had lined up on one side of the table. Jaw clenched, I made my way to the opposite side, knocking into the walls with my backpack. I dropped the pack and took out a notebook, pen, and the tape recorder I used for journalism interviews.

"I'd like to record the hearing," I said, my voice breathier than I would have liked.

The three officers exchanged uncomfortable looks.

"No," Doan said. He was younger than I'd expected. Probably in his thirties. He was thick, either with muscle, or because he was a little overweight under his Class A's. His blond hair was in a tight buzz cut and his eyes were a dull hazel.

"Sir, I believe I have the right to record the hearing."

"Where does it say that?"

I hesitated. I swore I had highlighted the words on some document. I just couldn't remember which.

"Well, Cadet, let's go over the directive," Doan said, paging through a thick binder.

"Why do you want to record the hearing in the first place?" Rialtin asked, her hands clasped on the tabletop.

"To have a record," I said. "In case…" I trailed off, struggling to express wanting proof without slinging the accusation that they might do or say something questionable. Why *wouldn't* I want to record the hearing? "And to be honest, ma'am, I feel a little ganged up on. Why are there three of you, against me? I was under the impression this was between me and the investigating officer."

Doan quirked an eyebrow but kept paging.

"It's not like that," Taulk said. "This is a hearing. I am acting as witness, and Captain Rialtin is here so there is another female in the room."

"You have the right to be represented by counsel," Doan said, glancing up from his book. "Do you want to reschedule the hearing at a time when your lawyer can be present?" He looked perturbed as hell. I wondered what program he was from, how far he'd traveled.

"I don't have a lawyer, sir."

"I thought you said you were being advised," Major Taulk said.

"I am, but it's by someone at a call center. I don't even know where he lives, or his real name. And he's not a lawyer."

Doan tapped a finger on the page he'd found. "Says here you may also present witnesses on your behalf."

"I don't have any witnesses, sir. Which is also why I would like to record the hearing."

He started reading from the binder. "'A verbatim record of the hearing is not required.'" He paused to look at me. "'If the applicant desires such a record and agrees to provide it at his own expense, he may do so. If he elects to provide such a record, he shall make a copy thereof available to the investigating officer, at no expense to the government.'" He dropped the book, spun it, and slid it across the table.

"I can easily make a copy of the tape and give it to you," I said.

"It didn't say anything about audio or video recording," Doan said.

"No, but it says a verbatim record of the hearing. That is what the tape recorder would capture, sir."

"They mean you can hire a person to record the hearing. Like a court stenographer."

"But a tape is more accurate. And it's free. And it's right here."

"Cadet, we have reviewed the regulations. It does not require me to allow you to record the hearing. Put that thing away. You may take notes."

My face burned. I stared at the recorder. It would be so easy to squeeze the record button when I put it back in my backpack. But then I imagined the tape running out and making a deafening, telltale "click" as the buttons popped back up. I thought about calling Zack or DJ Sasquatch and asking them to be a witness. But I couldn't ask them to drop everything and race over here. I reached for the recorder to put it away.

"You sure that thing's off?" Doan asked.

"There would be a red light if it was on," I said.

I could see Doan wanted to handle "the thing" himself. I slipped it in my bag, feeling a seed of sour satisfaction that I'd caused him a moment's unease.

Doan pushed his binder aside and picked up a small black book. The Bible. "First, you are required to swear in."

"I'm an agnostic. I'd rather not swear in on the Bible, sir."

Doan hesitated, clearly frustrated with me. "You have to. Or do you have a different holy book you want to use?"

"I don't believe in any organized religion. It doesn't mean anything to me," I said, enjoying being a pain in the ass.

"I think she can do an affirmation instead," Major Taulk said.

Doan glanced toward the massive binder but didn't pick it up. "You'll swear in twice. Once with the Bible, once with the affirmation. We're covered either way."

After the swearing in, Doan didn't waste any time settling into interrogation mode. Anyone watching would have guessed he was performing in front of a full courtroom with judge and jury.

"You joined the Army National Guard on November 20, 2000, correct?"

"Yes."

"Describe your motivations for doing so."

"I joined so I could pay for college and because the idea of fighting forest fires sounded fun and important."

"Money was your primary reason for joining?"

"You could put it that way. I was looking forward to a part-time job that would help pay for school."

"You saw the National Guard as a part-time job?"

"One weekend a month, two weeks a year is part time. The Guard itself calls its members citizen soldiers. I wouldn't have joined the regular Army."

"And why is that?"

"Because it was full time."

"Are you saying no one told you the National Guard could be full time?"

"That's not what I said at all, sir. I knew that National Guard units could get called up. But before September 11, it seemed incredibly unlikely I would get called up to do anything but help in a natural disaster."

"Unlikely, but not impossible," he said.

"Right."

"Because in your oath of enlistment you swore to support and defend the Constitution, the country and the state against all enemies, foreign and domestic. You swore to bear allegiance and obey the orders of the president and governor. Or didn't that oath mean anything to you because it ended with the words 'so help me God'?"

I paused, feeling my face prickle, his accusation causing an instant sunburn. "Are you implying that oaths and contracts mean nothing to me because I'm an agnostic?"

He squinted at me. "I'm not implying anything. As the investigating officer in this case I'm asking you questions."

"I took my oath and my contract very seriously," I said.

"Can you explain your reasons for breaking those oaths then?"

I wanted to ask him if he'd even read my application. It was all in there, expressed exactly how I wanted to express it. I wondered whether he was trying to undermine the whole thing by flustering me and making me change my answers. "I don't believe the wars in Iraq or Afghanistan are legitimate wars. I have come to believe that all war is unnecessary. And I refuse to participate in it."

A fire lit behind Doan's hazel eyes. He leaned forward and dug in. Before long, it was clear he was trying to establish a line of "aha" moments. Swearing disingenuous oaths. Lying on my initial paperwork. Joining ROTC to escape a tour of duty. Ripping off the military when I had no intention of honoring my contracts. It was a struggle to maintain my composure, to defend myself when he was the one in charge, demanding more information here, cutting me off there. My insides felt like a pot of water left on a raging gas burner—simmering, then roiling, then spilling over, ending up empty, brittle, and cracking with dry heat.

"Is there anything you would like to add?" he asked, apparently done with his show of disgust. His raised eyebrows dared me to correct the conclusions he'd come to.

"Yes," I said.

He let out an audible sigh. We'd been in the room for an hour and a half now. But I'd be damned if I didn't speak my mind at my own hearing.

"I didn't plan for this to happen. I didn't hatch some master scheme to take advantage of the Army to go to college. I've been struggling with this for years because I can't stand the thought of making a promise and then breaking it. It'd be nice if the US government had the same qualms. But they didn't hesitate for a second to start a war based on lies, send tens of thousands of soldiers to occupy a country that's descended into civil war, and—" I stopped. Doan was giving me a dull, heavy-lidded look. Taulk's jaw was clenched. Rialtin was outright glaring at me. There was that divide, wide as the Grand Canyon. I couldn't help but wonder how things would have been different if my application had been based on a simple answer: The Bible. Jesus Christ. The Lord Almighty. There was no arguing with that.

"Anything else?" Doan asked.

What was the point?

9. CODE PINK

March 2006: Oakland, CA

I replayed the hearing in my head for weeks. After nearly a month with no word, I emailed Major Taulk, asking about the status of my application. He didn't write back. So I threw myself into distractions: creative writing, KCPR, learning folk songs on the guitar, and Zack, when I could.

Zack did end up taking me to meet his other woman, Hortense. We drove up on a Friday, hitting a wall of traffic around San Jose. Half an hour into the mess I asked, "What's going on?"

"What do you mean?"

"This huge traffic jam."

"It's rush hour. It's always like this," Zack said.

"People just sit on the freeway for hours? Are there accidents or something?"

He smiled his Cheshire Cat smile. "You are adorable. It's like the time we were on a plane and you thought the individual video screens were mirrors."

I blushed. Not ten minutes before, I'd pointed out the window at a billboard, shouting "Did you see that? It changed! It moved to a whole different picture."

"You can take the girl out of Montana..." Zack said.

The West Oakland warehouse where Hortense lived was filthy. The concrete floors were smeared with dirt and grease. Junked cars and twisted metal lay in heaps. Cargo containers were stacked along the walls. Zack led me past a grungy communal kitchen, past a tower of wood pallets, to Hortense. She was impressive—an engine without a train with four enormous wheels that looked like they belonged on a medieval king's carriage. Zack showed me how she worked, beaming like a proud father. But the months of pent-up annoyance at his chronic disappearing acts hardened instead of softened. This was what he'd rather spend time with?

We wove our way past platforms and contraptions and a line of mutilated motorcycles to a set of stairs leading to his second-floor cargo containers, connected by a catwalk. Inside the containers, it was surprisingly like an apartment—a tiny kitchen, a tiny living room, an office, and a bed he'd commandeered from an old semi truck. He had a separate, soundproofed container for his drum kit.

"What do you think?" He was self-satisfied as hell.

"It's pretty awesome," I had to admit.

"I'm working on getting water up here. Then I can put in some kind of shower. Sadly, a toilet can never happen."

"Where do you use the bathroom?"

"At the front of the warehouse. It's pretty nasty though. I shower at the gym."

We'd been dating for almost two years. But the more I craved a life together, the more it seemed Zack slid into extreme bachelor mode. Was I doing something wrong?

"I should tell you," he said, his voice serious, all affect gone. "I've been looking for work up here. I want to move to a bigger market. All my friends are in the Bay, Hortense is in the Bay, the band is here. You're about to graduate. Maybe you could look for work up here too."

Heavy metal started blasting outside, and I could hear the beep of some machine backing up. I looked at the mini fridge and the tiny table and thought about how often I had to pee in the middle of the night. Zack's life here didn't look like it could squeeze in a goldfish, let alone a girlfriend.

March 2006: San Luis Obispo, CA

I was still hosting my children's show on KCPR with Aaron. It was called "Down the Rabbit Hole," a reference to *Alice's Adventures in Wonderland*, but probably not the best name for a kid's show now that I think about it. Aaron and I had settled into an easy, firm friendship, something I really needed and something I also knew was temporary. He was thinking about moving to Pismo Beach or way up to Arcata. I would probably end up in the Bay Area after graduation in a few months. I cherished the time we hung out at KCPR, and even though the show was about to come to an end, we decided to make a push to gain an audience. The show seemed to be popular with the DJs, but we weren't sure any kids were listening. Aaron had drawn a flyer, and I'd printed up a batch to post around town.

One day I drove downtown with a stack of flyers. I parked in the garage across from the independent movie theater, hurried down the concrete steps, and spotted a dozen women in pink shirts holding signs: "Women for Peace," "Stop Funding the War," "US out of Iraq."

Code Pink in San Luis Obispo? I knew all about Code Pink from *Democracy Now!*, but both SLO and Cal Poly seemed immune to protests in general. I smiled and flashed a peace sign passing them, earning a few meek cheers.

"Wait! You want a button?" a woman called after me. She was wearing a pink feather boa.

I turned around and took the pin she was holding out. "Thanks. I really admire what you're doing."

I had all their attention now. An older woman in a baseball cap squinted at me. "You're against the wars?"

"Completely. I'm a conscientious objector."

"Are you? You should join us then," said Pink Boa.

"What do you do around here?" asked another.

"I go to school. And I'm trying to get out of the National Guard, actually."

The circle around me tightened. "You're doing this all on your own?" asked Ball Cap.

"I'm getting advice from the GI Rights Hotline."

The women nodded in approval.

"We can help," said Pink Boa. "There's a lawyer in town who knows how to fight these cases."

"Oh, I think I'll be fine," I said. "I should hear back about my application any day now." The letters had come back from Chaplain Wong and Dr. Linux. Both were in my favor.

Ball Cap put her hand on my arm. "Just in case, honey. Let us give you his contact info. You never know."

10. CODE RED

March 2006: Morro Bay, CA

Toward the end of March, as the rainstorms tapered off and the days grew longer, I got a letter in the mail from Cal Poly's ROTC department. A copy of the investigating officer's report. I read it cross-legged on the floor as soon as I stepped inside my apartment.

The first sentence had me floating a foot off the ground: *I found Cadet del Duca's claim as CO convincing.*

Then, a crash landing. Accusations came flying off the page:

After looking at the evidence, it is apparent she joined the program for all the wrong reasons. Rosa's true intentions may be a lesson learned for all ROTC programs as reservists come knocking on the door when they are alerted to deploy.

Her failure to disclose any pre-existing depression issues is in violation of Article 107 of the UCMJ and thus viewed as grounds for disciplinary action in the National Guard and/or breach of her ROTC contract. Her CO status is now secondary to her depression issue as it falls under misconduct,—the more serious of the two.

The Army should disenroll her from ROTC, recoup all Army financial benefits she received while contracted, to include all National Guard Tuition Assistance funds for this misconduct. Her case should be forwarded to the California National Guard for UCMJ for further administrative action.

I felt like I was back on that wave, the nose of my board vertical, a wall of water poised to toss me like a ragdoll. Tears rolled down my cheeks. Was being depressed by war really a crime in this country? What did "further administrative action for misconduct" mean? Would they garnish my peanut wages to get that tuition money back? I hadn't filed for tuition assistance since becoming a conscientious objector. I didn't think it was right. Which meant I had a couple hundred dollars left in my bank account. Not even enough for the next month's rent until payday.

I wanted to curl up in a ball. I stood at the kitchen sink, splashing cold water on my face.

"They said no," I told Zack later over the phone, and read him the last paragraph of the report. I was in bed, the blinds to my picture window up. The power plant towers blinked a muted red through the fog.

"You want me to give them a talking-to?"

My eyes swollen and sore, my homework unfinished, a plate of untouched spaghetti in the kitchen, I was in no mood for jokes. "Am I a criminal? I did lie about depression, even though it wasn't really depression to begin with."

"Look, you're not a person to them. You're some number. They want their money back, that's all."

"Maybe I should pay them back then. I'd need to get a huge loan somewhere, but maybe that's the right thing to do."

"After the bullshit they put you through? What's that worth?"

I sat up in bed and wiped my wet cheeks. I'd never really known if Zack agreed with me, if he even cared about what I was going through. "I hate this feeling. Like I'm half traitor, half crusader. Like I'm fighting with my hands tied. They have their own justice system for Chrissake. How can I get a fair shot?"

A racket started up in the background. Grinding of metal on metal. "Can't you just tell them you're gay?" Zack shouted. "They'll drop you like a hot potato."

I'd thought about this when I first got called up, just like I'd thought about getting pregnant. "I can't be morally opposed to war and then turn around and lie to the government to get what I want."

"Why not? They took advantage of you."

"As much as I disagree with their rules for discharge, I want to follow them. I want to show them my morals are unbreakable. Let *them* be the unethical ones. My case stands on its own. Even the investigating officer agreed that I'm a convincing conscientious objector. If they don't give me a discharge, it's clear they can't even follow their own slanted regulations."

The noise behind Zack grew louder, then softer, like he'd cupped a hand around his phone. "Well don't give them a red cent unless you have to. Sounds like even if you pay them off they could still throw you in jail, or kick you out with a dishonorable discharge."

"What are you doing over there?" I asked.

"Hortense improvements. I'm about to run off to band practice too. How about I call you tomorrow?"

"Thank you."

"For what?"

"For supporting me. I know I'm not the most fun girlfriend, preoccupied with military crap half the time."

"I like that you're serious. All the rest of my friends are goofballs. Later, beautiful."

I got out of bed to close the blinds but ended up standing there watching the red lights of the old power plant. The tips of the smoke stacks flared and died like eyes opening and shutting, like lungs, like a threat shouted, then taken back. Not even the fog could stifle them from pounding out a warning for a defunct building. I remembered how they'd seemed to flash a warning the night I read through the Conscientious Objector Directive. *Mess with the powerful and get burned.* What was a power plant doing here in the first place? I imagined how gorgeous Morro Bay would be without the stacks looming over the beach. The view from the harbor, cuddling its flock of bobbing sailboats and fishing vessels, would sweep to Morro Rock, rising out of the sea like a mythical mountain, and glide down the length of the curved beach—a grand, stunning vista.

I marched to the bed, snatched the letter, and slapped it down on my desk by the window. I composed a response to Doan's report. The words poured out in a cool fury, aided by the blink, blink, blink from the towers.

I wrote and revised until midnight. I wished I had Doan's address so I could stand on his lawn with a bullhorn and read it to him. Instead, on a whim, I called DJ Sasquatch.

"I know it's late, but I don't think I'll be able to sleep anytime soon. Are you up for an adventure?"

"An adventure?" he said. "Sounds interesting. Say, have you ever been to the Madonna Inn?"

"What is it? Just a hotel? I think I've passed it on the highway."

"Just a hotel? No, no, no, no. It's a historic landmark. It's a destination. It has hot pink, heart-shaped dining booths and indoor rose bushes to match the rose carpets. It might just be the most kitschy, hideous hotel ever built. You at least have to see the men's bathroom."

We crashed the Madonna Inn's bathrooms, giggling like maniacs at the gaudy trappings, which included piles of fake grapes, gilded mirrors, swaths of pink, and lacquered wood bathroom stalls. The highlight was the men's communal urinal. It looked like an immense rock fireplace.

We raved about the comedy of the inn all the way to Avila Beach, where we slipped under a chain-link fence and climbed a cliff, tripping over rocks and pushing through bushes. We crept to the edge and sat with our feet dangling, admiring how the foam on the waves below seemed to glow in the moonlight, how we were poised on the end of the continent, how only the curvature of the earth and the limits of our eyesight kept us from seeing the people on the beaches of Japan gazing back at us.

I felt large and small at the same time. Grounded but free. Determined. This fight was not over.

March 2006: San Luis Obispo, CA

Lee Sunner, the Code Pink lawyer, seemed suspicious about how I'd gotten his number. He wasn't sure if he would take my case. But because I was a struggling student, he would offer me his discounted rate: one hundred dollars an hour.

Two days after getting the investigating officer's report, I drove to Sunner's house by the soccer fields in San Luis Obispo. I did homework in his sunny sitting room while he read through everything in his office. He emerged an hour later and pushed his delicate reading glasses up into his shock of gray hair.

"Ordinarily, I don't take cases like these anymore," he said. "Ordinarily, it's a waste of time. But you're different. You can write."

I raised my eyebrows, pleased to the core.

He cracked a hint of a smile. "And you have a strong case."

"Does that mean you'll take me on?"

Sunner sat down in a cushioned rocker. "I think I can help. This Doan, he made a mistake."

He had? I ran through his report in my mind.

"He went well beyond his authority. He was not tasked with investigating your medical records. He was tasked with evaluating the sincerity of your conscientious objector claim, nothing else. He pretty much ignored that and did a hack investigation of your medical history and initial enlistment. Now he's gotten himself in real trouble. We'll point this all out in the rebuttal. You have a response you'd like me to look over?"

I handed him my tirade from the other night. He plucked his glasses out of his hair and settled them on his nose, reading the pages slowly, ticking off checks in the margins.

"This is a good start," he said. "It's got all the bones. You were never seen for depression until recently, and both of your doctors agree it's situational. The situation is clear. And your recruiter really told you that? To brush over any physical concerns during your initial physical?"

"Yeah, if we thought they were minor. If we thought they didn't matter."

Sunner scoffed. "That's another point against them. But the real biggie is springing all this on you without any prior warning. You can't fight an argument you haven't heard yet."

Over the next week we composed a response that thrilled me in the same way watching the end of *Swiss Family Robinson* did—when the pirates fell into all the carefully constructed booby traps. Man, was it awesome to have a lawyer, even if he charged a hundred dollars an hour, even if he smiled once a week, and even if he insisted I use far too many exclamation points:

(1) The Investigating Officer has exceeded the express authority given to him under the terms of his orders.

Specifically, those instructions appointed the IO to "conduct an investigation and make determinations which include the following:

   a. The underlying basis of the cadet's professed conscientious objection

   b. The time period in which the cadet's belief became fixed

   c. Whether the belief constitutes conscientious objection under AR 600-43

d. The sincerity of the cadet."

No other authorization was granted!

(2) The Report and Recommendations made by the Investigating Officer violate the express terms of AR 600-43.

First, the IO admits in the opening paragraph of his report that he is to make a determination based on, among other criteria, "the sincerity of the cadet in her claim."

Yet in no place in his Report does the IO mention the sincerity of my claim or make any determination thereon.

Second, the IO fails to make any recommendation concerning the disposition of my case. Regulation specifies:

"(6) The actions recommended *will be limited* (emphasis mine) to the following:

(a) Denial of any classification as a conscientious objector.

(b) Classification as 1-A-O conscientious objector.

(c) Classification as 1-O conscientious objector."

No such recommendation was ever made!

Third, during the course of his investigation, the IO proceeded to look into matters of "misconduct" and/or "fraudulent enlistment," an investigation which he was neither qualified nor authorized to conduct and which ultimately resulted in his recommendations for punitive action.

(3) Since I had no prior notification that the Investigating Officer intended to expand his investigation beyond the bounds specified in his instructions, I had no opportunity to present evidence on my behalf.

First, since pre-existing medical conditions were to figure so prominently in the investigation, I would have provided medical evidence as to the nature of my present afflictions. I had never been seen, let alone been diagnosed or treated for minor depression until I started seeing a school counselor at Cal Poly in April of 2005. Being ignorant of the need for such evidence, I did not produce it!

Second, since the conditions of my original enlistment were to prove so important, I would have produced evidence of the representations made to me at the time of enlistment by my Army Recruiter to the effect that it would only complicate the speedy processing of my case for me to mention at my enlistment physical any prior minor irritations or complaints (such as acne, periodic backaches, occasional feelings of depression, etc.). Being ignorant of the need for such evidence, I did not produce it!

Third, since legal questions regarding the meaning of such phrases in the Army Regulations as "material misrepresentation" and "misconduct" and "pre-existing medical condition" were to figure so prominently in the IO's Report, I would have sought legal advice regarding my response. Being ignorant of the need for such advice, I did not seek it!

Fourth, since a recommendation was to be made by the IO concerning a payback of any educational benefits, I had no opportunity to address that issue with evidence of my willingness to repay appropriate amounts. Being ignorant of the need for such evidence, I did not produce it!

(4) The Investigating Officer made a number of errors and misstatements in his Report, all of which substantially prejudice my claim.

One. At numerous places in the Report, including four times in the Recommendations alone, the IO refers to my "misconduct" as a reason for disciplinary proceedings.

"Misconduct" is clearly defined in DoD Directive 1332.14 as either "a pattern of conduct consisting solely of minor infractions," "disreputable involvement with civilian or military authorities," "commission of a serious offence, or civilian conviction."

None of these apply to my case!

In fact, my record of military service, as evidenced by my Evaluation Report, is one of exemplary performance and behavior.

Two. The IO in his Recommendations accuses me of "failing to disclose a pre-existing and later an existing medical condition (depression and self-mutilation)."

Yet he also finds that "the most credible evidence" in the case is that presented by the two Cal Poly physicians with whom I've consulted about my feelings. Each of them issued a report agreeing unanimously that my condition is clearly situational, having been, as Dr. Julie Hoth put it in her report, "exacerbated by her military status and is at odds with her own personal values." She diagnoses my condition as 300.4 Dysthymic Disorder, Early Onset.

The IO accepts this diagnosis and admits in his Report that my "condition worsened in April 2005."

He then goes on to define the disease as a "*non-severe* situational depressed mood." He also approvingly quotes the findings of USAF Dr. Linux, who interviewed me for the military, that I do "not suffer from a psychological disease, defect or personality disorder of *sufficient severity* (emphasis mine) to warrant disposition through military channels."

Clearly, then, my present medical condition is, as all the experts have agreed, purely situational arising from the necessity of continuing my current military service while it is in violation of all my deepest principles and beliefs. By no means does it reach the level of "deliberate material misrepresentation" required for Fraudulent Enlistment.

Three. The IO in his Report maligns my entry into the ROTC Program by noting that, "after looking at the evidence, it is apparent she joined the program for all the wrong reasons."

Studying all the evidence in the case, one reaches exactly the opposite conclusion!

In regard to my specific enlistment in ROTC, it came about due to an unsolicited telephone call from Major Bate of the Cal Poly ROTC Program, who had heard of my deployment to Iraq and who advised me that ROTC offered a way to finish my degree and to become an officer before going to war. I accepted his reasoning and entered into the new program, agreeing to additional years of military service in order to secure what seemed to me to be clear educational and career advantages.

If such motivations denote acting for "all the wrong reasons," then it is only fair that I be allowed the opportunity to present evidence that these motivations are indeed the motivations of most, if not all, of the students currently enrolled in the ROTC Program.

III. CONCLUSION

To end this Rebuttal on a personal note, I would like to say that I feel deeply that the conduct of the IO's investigation and the recommendations he has made has betrayed the trust I placed both in him and in the military system to conduct a fair and impartial investigation of my claim as a Conscientious Objector. Based upon that trust, I entered into the process in a good-faith attempt to provide as honest and as open an account of my situation as was possible and cooperated fully.

Worse, I feel the Investigating Officer has also betrayed the trust placed in him by the United States Military to conduct a fair and equitable review of a sincere Conscientious Objector claim.

Instead of the fair review, the Investigating Officer entered upon a private witch hunt, searching assiduously for evidence of wrongdoing in my past which he then used not only to discredit my long and honorable service record, but also to defame and punish me as an individual.

Such a procedure has damaged more than just my own character and career. It has subverted and undermined the military review process, whose clear purpose and intent is to prevent the abuses here displayed.

For the above reasons, I respectfully request that my claim for discharge as a Conscientious Objector 1-O be approved. I further respectfully request that all other findings and recommendations not pertinent to my claim as a Conscientious Objector be denied and stricken from the record.

I printed the final draft of the letter at KCPR, folded it carefully, and carried it across campus to Major Taulk's office like I was carrying a hot coal.

"My rebuttal, sir," I said, handing the coal over. I half expected his desk to burst into flames.

11. THE LONG WAIT

April 2006–March 2007

The investigating officer felt it his duty to defend his original findings, which triggered a second rebuttal to defend my original rebuttal. Basically, we kept screaming the same things at each other.

By this time it was mid-April, two months before I was due to graduate with a bachelor's degree in journalism and a minor in English. I decided I didn't want to go through the ceremony. Here I was at the end of college having made one good friend: DJ Sasquatch, who wouldn't graduate for another year or two. Asking Sasquatch or Aaron or even Zack to come to the ceremony would be lame and weird. On the family side, Alura was almost nine months pregnant, and Leila was swamped with art school and even more broke than I was. It seemed silly to ask my mother to sit in the bleachers by herself while I walked across the stage with a bunch of near strangers.

"I'll come if you want me to," she said. "It's a big accomplishment."

I told her not to come, to help Alura get ready for the baby instead. The college degree came second to a bigger rite of passage. While my peers were celebrating all this classroom knowledge and gearing up to start their adult lives in earnest, I had been through a wringer of a course that dealt in real-world problems, not hypotheticals posed by some textbook. I'd made a bad decision and been hounded by that choice for five years. I'd developed complex political beliefs, confronted my demons, questioned my assumptions, acknowledged my flaws, and accepted the source of my depression, which I'd been in denial about. I'd been branded a fraud and offender, hired a lawyer, revolted against the establishment, and faced humiliation from people I respected. It did not come with a handshake and a piece of paper and a walk across a stage. And as proud as I was about how far I'd come, it wasn't over.

On graduation Saturday, I hung out at KCPR, burning CDs like crazy and thinking about how much I'd miss the station and Morro Bay and DJ Sasquatch and Aaron. I'd decided to move north to the San Francisco Bay Area with Zack over the summer. I just wanted an answer from the Army first. Taulk had said that answer was coming any day now.

He was wrong. The waiting continued, accompanied by a persistent, lurking feeling of *wrongness*—something in between waking up in a strange place and being jolted by a phone call in the middle of the night. The feeling followed me to my last drill, which I barely remember. It must have been in May or June at Camp SLO. The only thing I remember from that drill is eating chow by myself and walking back to the main part of camp. I still had cadet rank on my collar, the black circles, and three passing soldiers saluted me, one by one. I saluted them back, feeling like the biggest dirtbag on the planet. I didn't tell Sergeant Morgan goodbye.

The feeling followed me north to West Oakland where I moved into Zack's cargo containers. Zack had taken a "big boy" job in Sacramento, doing the same radio engineer work he'd been doing on the Central Coast but for a lot more money. In honor of my arrival, he installed a makeshift shower in his makeshift kitchen and bought a camping toilet. "Rosa's first potty," we called it.

I lived there for a month, applying to every journalism job I could find and hiding out in the containers like a mouse. The surrounding neighborhood wasn't safe. I knew nothing about the Bay Area. I knew no one. And Zack was a whirlwind of work, Hortense, the Extra Action Marching Band, and now a rock band too, where the other three members were lesbians, one of whom spun fire between violin solos. I was in jealous awe, firmly stuck on the outside. One day, perhaps feeling guilty, Zack pawned me off on a friend, who spent two hours showing me around San Francisco, pointing out landmarks on a laminated map.

"Now you won't get lost exploring by yourself," he said.

I managed a smile even though I had little desire to tackle the maze of hills and one-way streets myself. Even the transit system was intimidating. All those lines and colors. And what was the point? To reach someplace new, where I was just as alone?

The feeling of wrongness traveled to Oregon with me in early July, where Alura gave birth to a beautiful baby girl with olive skin and dark hair and eyes. For some reason, I am wearing a brown Army T-shirt in the only picture of me holding my newborn niece, Cira.

Zack and I had no business moving into a bright, one-bedroom apartment together across the bay from San Francisco. No business at all, considering we were emotionally oceans apart. But we did anyway.

Soon after the move, I landed a job writing for the web at KCBS in San Francisco. I'd broken into a major market—at twenty-three years old! Even getting there felt glamorous. I took BART to the New Montgomery station and walked ten blocks through the financial district, mixing in with the crowds of well-dressed businessmen and women, the bike couriers, the coffee shop crowd. The only thing that dampened my sense of accomplishment was when, every month or so, the security guard who worked the elevator asked how my internship was going.

In late July, I got a letter from the National Committee considering my CO claim. They wanted all medical documentation pertaining to my crime of depression. I drafted a letter back and ran it by Sunner:

Your request both concerns me and leads me to wonder if you have read my file, particularly the rebuttal dated 30 March. There is no medical history or documentation in regard to minor depression other than the two letters from Cal Poly physicians, both of which are included in my CO packet. Therefore I have no documents to add to my file. However, I will take the opportunity to inquire on the status of my claim. I have had no word since the claim was sent to you in April. Will the committee have a decision soon?

The committee did not feel the need to respond. The long wait continued.

In August I tagged along to Burning Man. Hortense performed gloriously, turning a carousel of giant insects to the delight of anyone who wandered by her corner of the desert. Zack (surprise, surprise) was too enamored with the project to do much of anything with me. But after a few days of moping around camp, unsure of what Burning Man even was, I got on my bike and started to discover for myself. I fell in love with the dusty people, the massive art installations, the Mad Hatter city bursting at the seams with strange and charged ideas, the open invitation to do and say and feel and *be* whatever I wanted to be.

Burning Man slowly revealed itself as something that fit Aristotle's concept of synergy perfectly. The whole was greater than the sum of its parts, not just in stark physical terms—a fully functional city rising from a void—but in ideological terms. Nothing was black and white here in this sea of freedom and frenetic individuality and unlikely unity. Everything was multifaceted underneath that layer of fine playa dust. That was the point. Burning Man drove curiosity and engagement, just like the strange mix of people, who called for you to get off your bike and stay a while in whatever bizarre camp they'd built from scratch.

An awakening of sorts began. The girl who'd spent her time hiding in her apartment, going back and forth to work with no deviations and waiting for her oddball boyfriend to come home to the sorry dinner she'd cooked, started to disassemble in Black Rock City. Her shell began to crack and flake off. Some of that shell is still in the desert, buried underneath layers of pale, silty soil.

• • •

Summer turned to fall. Still no word on my CO application. And still no word on what National Guard unit I was supposed to transfer into. I'd told my unit that I was moving and that I needed to know where to show up for drill. They had not responded.

The next letter from the Army came in November, more than a year after originally filing my CO claim. The form ordered me to report to an upcoming Readiness Training Weekend. The thought of putting on a pair of BDUs and going through the motions, which I hadn't done in four months now, seemed like a surrender after a year stuck treading water. More than that, it seemed like a lie. I was no soldier.

"Legally, I'm already AWOL, right?" I asked Sunner over the phone, the letter in my hand. "So skipping this training would make me doubly AWOL. Seems like I'd be daring them to come after me. Should I go?"

"I can't tell you not to go to the training. But I will say this. Other reserve soldiers have failed to show up at these weekends, and so far, the Army hasn't come after them."

How comforting. "This paper also shows my Estimated Time of Separation as November 20, 2006. That's six years to the day after I enlisted. Do you think that means they've forgotten about my ROTC contract extension?"

"It's possible. Although you don't want to remind them. Here's what you do. Write a letter, not an email, to your old unit commander. Give him your new address. Ask him again where to drill. Tell him your ETS is in a few weeks. Ask him how to proceed on that date. And ask him about the status of your application. It's been at the national committee for seven months now."

I wrote the letter. And waited. And waited. I kept having dreams that I was back in the ROTC program and my secret was out, or that military police were at my door and I was trying to find a way out our third-story windows, or that because of my misconduct, the Army was sending me to Iraq immediately. I had one day to pack and say goodbye to my family.

Zack grew more and more distant, saying he'd be home at seven and getting there at nine or not at all. Days when we did eat dinner together he'd stay for an hour, then head to West Oakland. He'd sleep in his cargo container half the time, claiming the next day he'd been too tired to drive the ten minutes home. I wondered if he was cheating on me. Our fights escalated in frequency and intensity. All I thought I wanted was him. I didn't know what the hell he wanted, but it was increasingly apparent it wasn't me. I clung on anyway. With Army Limbo stretching into oblivion, I couldn't lose my one beam of support.

Winter came. I spent the months working, exploring the bike paths on Alameda and Bay Farm Island, and writing moody songs on my guitar. I let the TV keep me company, watching idiotic reality shows and bad dramas. I applied to a creative writing master's program and was rejected. I watched my scars, planning to cut myself over the old marks so I wouldn't have new ones. I did not continue therapy like the Army doctor had suggested—not because I didn't think it would be helpful, but because I saw it as an expensive extravagance. I did not stay on antidepressants, partly because I wasn't sure they worked, and by this time I was uninsured. I started calling my mom and my sisters every weekend instead.

In March I got a call from ROTC, letting me know the decision had arrived. They wouldn't tell me the ruling over the phone. I could come get the letter, or they could mail it to me. Zack had some work to do at the Central Coast stations, so we headed south.

Zack rolled right past a sign reading "authorized vehicles only" and parked in a red zone outside Dexter Hall. I looked out the window and fidgeted with the ring on my pointer finger, working it over the knuckle and back down without thinking.

"Want me to go get it for you?" Zack asked.

I didn't want to face any of them, no matter what the decision was. I'd been coddled these past nine months, ever since my last drill—no hiding or pretending, no being lectured or yelled at, no tightrope walk between two conflicting ideas of the "right thing to do."

"I'll do it," Zack said. "Just tell me where to go."

"No, they already think I'm a coward. And I don't think they would give the letter to you anyway." I looked down at my hands. My knuckle was red and raw. I ripped off the ring and shoved it in my pocket. Outside, it was starting to rain. The campus seemed deserted. Maybe it was spring break. I opened the door to the building quietly and strode past the offices of the instructors. Major Bate's door was open. He glanced up as I passed. I heard footsteps behind me, then a knock on another door.

"She's here," I heard Bate murmur.

Perfect. I would have an audience. The dust devil in my stomach swelled to a full twister. I counted my steps to the office. Twenty-three.

Captain Rialtin was waiting there, along with Major Taulk and the secretary. Major Bate and Major White came in the office behind me.

"I'm here to pick up the decision," I said.

"You were denied," said Major Taulk.

I struggled to breathe evenly, wishing he could have given me the letter and let me find that out on my own. They stared. What were they here for? The satisfaction of seeing me have a meltdown?

"I'd like to know why," I said. I half didn't believe it.

Taulk ducked into his office and came back with a sheaf of papers. "The memorandum reads: 'The cadet did not present convincing evidence to warrant approval. Failure to accept a commission is a breach of her contract and may make her subject to recoupment of scholarship funds or involuntary call to active duty to fulfill her contractual obligations.'" He paused and looked up at me.

"That's it? That's all they said?" I asked, my voice growing thick.

"Just about," Major Taulk said, and continued reading. "'Inform the cadet of this decision and counsel her as to her obligation to commission in the United States Army. Advise the cadet that failure to accept a commission is a breach of her contract and may make her subject to involuntary call to active duty in an enlisted status.'" Taulk looked at me. "That's the end of the memo."

"Is there anything I can do?" I asked, struggling to process the words. "Can I appeal the decision?" What more convincing evidence did they want?

"The decision is final. There are no more appeals." Taulk flipped to the next page. "You have been formally disenrolled from ROTC. You *can* appeal that decision." He glanced up. "Do you plan to appeal? If so, I need to brief you on a few things."

Tears spilled down my cheeks. But when I heard my voice, I was surprised at how level it was. "You're asking if I want to fight to come back to a school I already graduated from to finish ROTC? No, I do not wish to appeal."

"In that case, you have the option to volunteer for active duty." He handed me a document. The first line read: *I, Cadet Rosa P. del Duca, having been found to be in breach of my contract, request to be ordered to active duty in an enlisted status in fulfillment of my contractual obligation.* Below was a line for my signature, and the signature of a witness. The paper blurred.

"Do I have to make a decision right now?" I asked.

Taulk frowned, hesitating. "No. I don't recall reading a deadline for your decision."

"Then can I pick up my documents and go?"

Taulk folded the papers in his hand and slid them into an envelope.

"You understand what this means, don't you?" Major White asked, his arms tightly crossed. "You can't just ignore this. All this follows you to the National Guard."

I took the envelope and left, straining to walk instead of run.

12. HABEAS CORPUS

April 2007: San Francisco, CA

I have never gotten more catcalls than during the short walk from the Powell Street BART station in San Francisco to the office of a lawyer considering taking my case in April of 2007. Sunner, my first lawyer, had said he couldn't help me from here. I needed to file something called a "habeas corpus proceeding" through a lawyer in my area.

"Hey baby, you don't gotta walk on past like that now."

"Damn, that is one long, long girl."

"Hold up, I think I know you. Rachel?"

Confused, I took an inventory of my outfit. Army boots, jeans, and a T-shirt. Nothing remotely provocative. I passed an alley and looked quickly away from a man peeing on a wall.

"Oh! You're killing me." A guy with greasy hair, pocked skin, and dirty clothes peeled himself off a chain-link fence and matched my stride. "Let me walk with you awhile."

I ignored him and walked faster. A group of guys lounging in an alcove, trash piled by their feet, laughed. A woman lying flat on the ground, missing a few teeth, shrieked with delight.

If I had asked anyone about the Tenderloin District beforehand, I would have known that this was normal—that the Tenderloin was home to the homeless, many of whom were battling drug addiction and mental illness.

They were largely harmless. But coming from Montana and the Central Coast, where homelessness was rare, I felt transported into a post-apocalyptic movie.

"What you lookin' for? I can help you find it," Grunge Man said, noticing me scanning the numbers on the buildings.

"Thanks, but I don't need any help," I said, ducking through a door hiding between two awnings and into a shabby lobby.

I took a narrow staircase up to Steve Collier's office, shoving down the impulse to twist the two rings I was wearing around and around and around. The skin was already chafed underneath them. I needed to stop wearing jewelry.

Collier shook my hand and introduced me to a young woman not much older than me. "This is Sonja. She'll be helping with your case."

My eyebrows raised. "Does that mean you've decided to take it?"

"Yes. We're going to take this on pro bono."

I'd heard this term. I had an inkling it meant something good.

"That means for free," Collier said, catching my blank look.

"Really? I can pay. I have a job."

Collier waved a hand and sat down at his desk, covered in neat stacks of paper. "There's a good chance this won't even turn into a case. Now, you've heard about the writ of habeas corpus?"

"I think so."

"Do you know what it means?" Sonja asked.

I studied the floor, wracking my brain. "I guess I don't," I said.

Sonja and Collier shared a long-suffering look. "It's a very old writ. One of the foundations of law in America," Collier said, waiting for this to ring a bell.

I flushed. No bell, no lightbulb.

Collier cleared his throat. "In simple terms, the writ of habeas corpus is a guarantee against any detention forbidden by law."

"How does it apply to me?"

"If the military comes after you—if they want to force you into active duty and you refuse because you are a conscientious objector—we will take on the government in Federal District Court. Habeas corpus is used to review the legality of the party's arrest, imprisonment, or detention."

"But the legality is clear," I said. "They don't recognize me as a conscientious objector. Therefore, I'm AWOL or in breach of contract or... a deserter."

Collier held up the memorandum I'd faxed him. "This is not an adequate explanation of why they denied your claim. They have just one line of reasoning in here." He flipped the paper around and read. "The cadet did not present convincing evidence to warrant approval." He looked over the top of the paper at me. "It's weak. There is no basis in fact, which is required by law. They can't deny you outright. They must present evidence *why*. Your essay was convincing. Your letters were convincing. Everyone who spoke to you found you convincing as a CO, even the investigating officer. You *are* a conscientious objector."

Hearing the words come from someone else felt like the sun on my back on a cold day. I wasn't delusional. I *was* a conscientious objector.

"We think they probably have a policy to deny almost all claims categorically," Sonja said. "Which is illegal, of course."

"What happens now?" I asked.

Collier leaned forward in his chair. "Don't do anything. You've tried to find a new unit to drill with. They didn't come after you for failing to show up for the Readiness Training Weekend. If they *do* pursue you, we will file a habeas corpus proceeding. In other words, we'll sue the federal government."

"For that to happen, would they need to arrest me first?" I still half-expected military police to come knocking on my door. By not accepting a commission, not volunteering for active duty, not even going to drill, the ball was in their court.

"It's possible. There's not a lot of precedent here."

Taking on the federal government in court? I was in way over my head. I thought about how military lawyers would spin the story. They'd latch on to the same things Doan had. They'd paint me as a lying, mercenary cutter girl who tried to split when the going got tough. But this time, the big Everyone would know. The public. My coworkers. The internet, where nothing ever died.

"Look, your case could be important. If this goes to court, you could be helping soldiers across the country in the same situation."

My fatigue and uncertainty leeched away. "Let's do it," I said.

Plunging back into the Tenderloin, I met the eyes of anyone who looked my way, a strategy that cut the catcalls in half. And as I walked through the heart of the city's pain and suffering, I saw how very lucky I was. How, in a screwy way, my one-woman war against the war was a privilege. How being *able* to fight was an advantage. I was able to fight because my mother had raised me with love. Because I'd gotten a good education. Because there were people who believed in me, who wanted to help me. I wasn't as alone as I felt most days. And as broken as I sometimes felt, deep down, I was whole in a way that suddenly seemed like a luxury.

13. ORDERS

June 2007: Alameda, CA

One day in early June I walked to the post office and found a letter from the Army. Goose bumps rose on my arms and the back of my neck. Standing in the lobby, I tore open the envelope and started to read:

YOU ARE ORDERED TO PERSONNEL ACCOUNTABILITY MUSTER DUTY.
PERIOD: 1 DAY
REPORT TO: MUSTER STATION, 2475 A WEST 12TH STREET, OAKLAND, CA 94607
REPORTING DATE: 01 AUG 2007 - 10 AUG 2007

WITHIN 72 HOURS OF RECEIPT OF NOTIFICATION, PLEASE CALL THE MUSTER STATION PHONE NUMBER PROVIDED TO CONFIRM RECEIPT OF YOUR ORDERS AND TO SCHEDULE YOUR MUSTER DUTY APPOINTMENT. YOU ARE ON MUSTER DUTY FOR ONE DAY ONLY AND WILL BE PAID A STIPEND OF $176. MUSTER DUTY MUST BE COMPLETED WITHIN THE TIME PERIOD INDICATED.

There was a list of things to bring and instructions on how to notify my employer. There was a reminder to come in civilian attire and a full page playing pussyfoot about what exactly muster was. Twice, in all caps, was the assurance: THIS IS NOT A MOBILIZATION MUSTER. There was also the threat: IF YOU ARE NOT PROPERLY EXCUSED FROM THIS MUSTER, YOU MAY BE SUBJECT TO

APPROPRIATE ADMINISTRATIVE ACTIONS WHICH MAY NEGATIVELY AFFECT YOUR MILITARY STATUS.

I hurried home and called Collier. "I don't know what to do."

"Who is it from? Is it from the Individual Ready Reserve?"

I scanned the pages, spread out on my kitchen table. "Yes, on the second page it says to 'bring this IRR muster order.'"

"Interesting."

"I'm not supposed to be in the IRR yet. That happens after your contracts are up."

"Maybe that letter you got in April wasn't a mistake after all."

In April, I'd gotten a letter thanking me for my "service to the Nation" and explaining what my duties were as a member of the Individual Ready Reserve. It had been equally vague: "The skills that you have acquired throughout your military career are invaluable as we continue to meet the demanding requirements of the Global War on Terror. In order to accomplish operational requirements and posture for the future, the Army's transformation efforts include developing an Individual Warrior population that will augment the Total Force in times of war or National emergency and improve the overall readiness of Warriors. All assigned IRR Soldiers are required to maintain satisfactory participation on an annual basis."

Clear as mud. Yet I knew exactly what they were getting at.

"Fax me those latest documents," Collier said. "I'd like to take a look at them and add them to your file."

"They don't say I have a choice about showing up, but do I?"

"You always have a choice."

Collier didn't say anything more and I remembered Sunner saying he couldn't legally advise me to go AWOL. When was this game of chicken going to finally end? "Do you think they'll come after me if I don't show up?"

"Again, it's possible. I personally think it's unlikely, especially since they made a point to say this isn't mobilization. But it is possible."

I gathered the papers, stuffed them in their original envelope, and grabbed my keys to find the closest fax machine.

"It's just one day," Collier went on. "It might be easier to go. Let me know what you decide and I'll make a note of it."

• • •

I decided not to answer the muster call on principle. I was a conscientious objector, damn it, whether the military admitted it or not. I didn't want to be paid for pretending otherwise. I certainly didn't want to explain my messy circumstances to someone who might dig a little deeper and discover how very AWOL I was. The seventy-two hours I'd been given to call the Army and schedule my muster passed. The days ticked by. Every time the phone rang a small bead of worry dripped into the pit of my stomach. But the Army was never on the other end. The true test would be in August, when I didn't show up.

A week or two after getting the muster letter, I made my daily trip to the post office and found a slip for a package too big to fit in my box. I stood in line. The postal clerk shoved a fat manila envelope under the glass. It was from the US Army.

I hurried out of the post office, staring at the return label, my mouth dry. This was it. This was a court summons. Or orders to report somewhere for active duty. I started jogging home, then stopped and ripped the envelope open. Inside was a thick, yellow folder I recognized as my medical records. A thicker, brown folder contained all my other records: contracts, orders, security clearance, everything. And there was a single sheet of loose paper. Orders with my name on them.

```
ORDERS 149-100129 MAY 2007
DELDUCA ROSA PACIFICA ###-##-#### SGT JFHQ-CA
(A01) CA ARNG 9800 GOETHE ROAD SACRAMENTO CA 95826-9101
You are discharged from the Army National Guard and assigned to the component indicated on the day following the effective date.
Reserve Assignment: USAR Control Group (Annual Training)
Effective Date: 20 NOV 2006
Type of Discharge: Honorable
Additional Instructions: Re-code (1) Records will be closed out and forwarded as required by NGR 600-200.
```

Not orders to report. Orders that said I had been honorably discharged since November.

I'd imagined this moment over and over. My victory. The conclusion to my Army story. In my imagination I had been euphoric, triumphant, jumping up and down, laughing, shouting, rushing to call my mom and my sisters and Sunner and Collier. In my imagination, after the giddy phone calls, I pictured myself blaring music and popping champagne with Zack and gorging myself on chocolate.

All that seemed distant and grotesque now. I crouched on the sidewalk, reading the paper three times, making sure there was no mistake. All the energy I'd spent striving and worrying and fighting and regretting slammed back on me. It was over. I was honorably discharged despite their denial of my conscientious objector application. That was why I was getting stuff from the Individual Ready Reserve. I cried all the way home, and for the next fifteen minutes. Not sobbing, but silent crying, slumped on the couch, arms flopped at my sides. I did not call anyone. I did not jump up and down. I did not turn on music or even try to figure out where Zack was. After wiping away the tears, I curled up under a blanket and tried to sort through my feelings.

Underneath the relief was a sense of hurt and betrayal that this had happened in the first place—that for the past six and a half years I'd paid for a mistake I'd made at seventeen, and the Army hadn't even had the decency to tell me I was discharged until six months after the fact. Six months that I had spent bracing for a court battle and jail time.

A small part of me felt robbed too. While I was finally free of the Army's grips, I had lost my one chance to make a difference. There would be no habeas corpus proceeding, no standing up to the Green Machine in court. They'd given me what I'd wanted from the start, but somewhere along the way the argument had morphed into something bigger than me. Now there was only fading back into civilian obscurity, leaving everyone else who was fighting one-man and one-woman wars against the war as alone as they ever were, as alone as I had been.

• • •

That night, as wonder and optimism started to replace all those negative feelings, anxiety swooped in, knocking everything back. Something wasn't right here. What about my contract extension? I wasn't supposed to enter the Ready Reserve until 2009.

I ran through the scenarios and came up with three theories. The first was The Mistake Theory. Somehow, I'd fallen through the cracks. The Army hadn't been able to keep up with me moving and joining ROTC and then filing a CO application and then moving and being disenrolled from ROTC. Maybe my contract extension had gotten lost in the shuffle.

The second theory, and my favorite, was that I was causing a bigger headache than I was worth. The Pain in the Ass Theory. Maybe the Army didn't want to waste any more time on me. Maybe they were afraid I'd take them to court and they didn't want the publicity.

The third and last theory was the Benevolent Army Theory, and the one I considered most unlikely. It was conceivable that my contract extension was annulled when I was disenrolled from ROTC, which would have kicked me back to my original contract, which ran out in 2006.

Whatever the case, I was not about to go poking around for answers. I would count myself extremely lucky. If I could just make it through August without them tracking me down and uncovering my rats' nest of paperwork, I'd be free for good. I tried to regain a sense

of enthusiasm, but my brain and my heart were worn out.
I went into hibernation mode.

14. MESSAGES IN THE WIND

June 2007: Alameda, CA

Four or five days after getting the discharge in the mail I took a long bike ride from my apartment in Alameda, through the state beach full of families and kite surfers, and all the way around Bay Farm Island, the wind off the bay whipping my short hair into tangles and whisking the heat of the sun off my skin. The wind in California could sometimes feel ominous or bullying, like the wind in Eastern Montana, but not that day. That day it felt packed with possibility and energy—like a puppy pulling at its leash, like a dare to join the kite surfers zipping across the water and leaping over the waves. It felt silly to stew over why I'd been discharged, or how. This was a victory. Time to spread the news.

My mother's exclamations were so loud I had to hold the phone away from my ear. Alura and Leila were more reserved, but just as happy. After my three phone calls, I celebrated by framing my discharge, buying a stack of used CDs and books, and making a pan of brownies. Then I threw my Army clothes into bags and drove to an Army Navy Surplus store.

"You might want to keep some of this," the cashier said, looking at the pile of green I'd dumped onto his floor for inspection. "Like the BDU pants. I can only offer you five bucks for those. The Oakland store might give you more."

"This is a purge," I said. "I don't want any of this in my house anymore."

The guy took a good look at my face. "Okay, I get it. Let me see what I can do for you."

I opened my mouth to explain no, it wasn't what he was thinking. I wasn't just back from a tour. But I bit my tongue before anything could come out.

• • •

The celebrations continued when Leila came to visit a week later.

"You know what I really want to do?" I asked. We were both buzzed on wine.

"Swim with dolphins," she said, eyes wide.

I giggled. "No. Well, yes. But no."

"Dress your cat up like a little astronaut? Get one of those cheesecakes with the graham cracker crust? Turn the lights out and start a rave? Slip into something more comfortable?" She waggled her eyebrows, winked, and nodded, all at the same time. She looked ridiculous.

"Yes!" I leapt to my feet and did a wacky little dance. We were listening to James Brown. "How did you know?"

We made up bad dance moves and howled with laughter until our eyes watered.

"Seriously," I said, collapsing onto the couch. "Do you know what I want to do?"

Leila flopped down next to me and took a deep breath. I clamped a hand over her mouth before she could rattle off another string of suggestions. "I want to burn all my Army papers in a fire pit down at the park, and roast s'mores over the flames."

Leila gasped when I took my hand off her mouth. "That is an excellent idea. Let's do it tomorrow."

We gathered supplies and headed to the beachfront park the next afternoon. It was another windy day, and hot. A few groups were scattered at the picnic areas, grilling burgers and hot dogs. Kids played in the water. Geese roamed. People whizzed past on bikes and Rollerblades. I built a small mountain of crumpled paper in the fire pit. Leila built a teepee of sticks around it.

"A moment of silence," Leila said.

I closed my eyes and thought about erasing the Army from my life. Letting it lift off my chest for good. I struck the match and held the flame to the paper. Leila hummed a long, clear note—the type of sound you'd hear in a movie when shipwrecked passengers spot land or when the long-suffering hero opens a treasure chest.

The fire burned for a full ten seconds before the wind whisked everything into a little ash cloud. Bits of burning paper landed on the picnic table and the bike path and in the grass. One landed on my arm. I slapped it off, leaving a black streak.

"What are you two doing? This is how brush fires start!"

Leila and I turned to see a dog-walker who had stopped to glare at us.

"We got it handled, thanks," Leila said.

The spandex-clad woman didn't budge. Her golden retriever grinned a sloppy dog grin at us. "Don't you know there's a red flag warning today?"

"We're using a fire pit," I said.

She shook her head and scoffed.

I didn't know what to do. I considered packing up and moving to another spot once the woman went on her way. Then again, she might follow us. I cleared my throat.

"Look, we'll be more careful. What else do you want us to say?"

"I want you to stop what you're doing. You don't even have any water to put out the fire if it gets out of hand." She peered from me to Leila, like she was memorizing our descriptions.

I looked at the bay, which was twenty feet away, and the swath of dirt surrounding the fire pit. It'd be almost impossible to start a brush fire here.

"Goodbye," Leila said pointedly. "I don't mean to be rude, but we're trying to have a moment here."

The woman finally started walking away, tugging at her retriever's leash. "I'm reporting you two when I get home."

The mood shattered, we turned back to our fire pit. The teepee had fallen over. All the embers were out. I rearranged the paper and sticks. I struck another match, irritated and unsettled. The wind blew out three matches before I could touch flame to paper. And again, the paper flared and the ashes lifted. Of course. The universe wouldn't make this easy, either. I threw back my head and let out a silent scream, hands balled into fists.

"It'll work," Leila said, her face set, her shoulders squared like she was ready to tackle anyone else who tried to interfere. "Let's find something to cover the top."

The wind reversed direction, sweeping my hair into my eyes and even my mouth. I opened my fists to fix my hair and then stared down at our small pile of litter. On second thought, it didn't seem like the universe was against me on this one. Maybe it was sending me a message: that I couldn't destroy the past and I shouldn't want to. The past made me who I was. Time to accept and embrace it. Otherwise how could I focus on the future?

"Forget it," I told Leila. "I'll buy a paper shredder. Let's go for some ice cream."

15. AFTERMATH

In the weeks and months that followed, a lot shifted. Zack acknowledged he was a terrible boyfriend during a terrible fight. Soon after he told me something was "really wrong with him" and that he'd started intensive therapy to try to figure it out.

"I think we should part ways," he said. "Here's the thing though, beautiful. I don't have the strength or the energy to be the one to end it."

It took me nearly two weeks to drum up the strength and energy myself. But once I did, it was a big liberation for both of us. August had come and gone with no word from the Army regarding my missed muster training. The freedom of release from the Guard coupled with release from a dysfunctional relationship spurred me to seek out communities of my own in the Bay Area. I started writing songs on the guitar and singing at an Alameda dive bar's open mic. I decided I wanted to live in Berkeley, home of the Free Speech Movement, where rumor had it people were still uppity and liberal and would embrace me as a CO. I was welcomed into a commune-type house where we split the grocery bills, shared everything in the fridge, gardened and composted out back, and cooked each other dinner one night a week (vegetarian, of course). If my coworkers invited me to have a beer with them when my shift was over, I started saying yes.

In my spare time, I began writing bits and pieces of my Army story, struggling to explain it, to understand it, to justify it in a way I could move beyond. Underneath the surface, just beyond rational thought, half of me felt like I was still tangled in loose ends, that I was still waiting for final word. I often dreamed I was back in the ROTC program, an outcast, the subject of ridicule, the cadets always asking *why*? Sometimes it spilled over to classmates, teachers, members of my Guard unit. *Why*? With each attempt to answer that question, the door on the long Army chapter of my life inched a little bit closer to shut.

Stretching my limbs in this new phase of self-discovery, I even posted a personal ad on Craigslist. The ad was up for twenty-four hours, during which time I received two requests to prove I was a woman, two cock shots, and about twenty-five messages from seemingly normal guys who were looking to date too. I deemed three of them worth meeting in person. On my first date post-Army and post-Zack, I met a sci-fi bookworm at the Berkeley Marina to fly kites. The attraction he'd had over email quickly evaporated. On my second date, I went hiking with a yoga and dog enthusiast in the Oakland hills. There was a spark, but nothing earth-shattering. And then, on my third date, I drove to a nearby café to have coffee with a guy named Nicholas. We'd emailed back and forth a bit, bonding over being writers, loving the outdoors, and digging folk music. He'd appreciated my characterization of Cat Stevens "going Tolstoy" later in his career, and then revealed that he taught English at a nearby college. And then there was that picture. Just an oddly cropped shot of his face, but the guy looked compelling and adventurous in a surfer, rock star kind of way. He was probably way out of my league.

September 2007: Berkeley, CA

Nicholas was sitting outside Roma Café at a small, wrought-iron table, wearing a blue T-shirt almost as bright as his blue eyes. With his shaggy blond hair and tan skin, he blended in with the California crowd, even though I knew he'd moved west from Minnesota. *I think I'm going to marry that guy*, I thought, before chastising myself, reminding my eager little heart it had a predictable penchant for infatuations that did not last long.

I ordered a mocha, which was delivered brimming to the top and with a towering blob of whipped cream that threatened to plunge right over the edge of the glass. Taking a sip would be like taking a pie to the face, but if the situation went ignored there'd be a mess on the table to deal with and there were no napkins in sight. I was headed for an awkward first impression at best. Nicholas looked at me expectantly, eyebrows high.

"How are you going to drink that?" he asked.

I laughed. "I have no idea."

He let me make a fool of myself, slurping off the whipped cream before it turned my glass into an oozing volcano. Then he asked me what it was like to work at a radio station, to grow up in Montana, to surf (turns out he'd never tried). I asked him what he wrote about.

"I'm writing young adult stuff right now," he said. "I just finished a manuscript about a seventeen-year-old kid who runs away from San Francisco to northern Minnesota. He's chasing a family secret. He found something that makes him suspect his parents aren't his real parents."

"Ooh, tell me more." I wrapped both hands around my warm glass so I wouldn't fidget.

"Most of the book is set in this tiny town where my great uncle ran a general store. I'm trying to capture the lonesome, wild, beautiful feel of the north woods at the same time I'm telling this coming-of-age story. I just wrote the end last week. The final page leaves the kid walking down the highway, right after he joins the Army."

My face fell. "Really?"

"Yeah, he's rocked by this tragedy, this big rift from his family's past, and the highway he's walking down marks the Continental Divide." Nicholas leaned forward, putting his elbows on the table and revealing a figure eight on one wrist—an infinity tattoo.

I pulled my own arms, marked by half a dozen ugly scars, into my lap. The last time I'd cut myself had been after that final blowout with Zack. But instead of forming their usual thin scabs and then fading, the cuts had raised up into thick, puffy red marks.

I weighed whether to say anything about the end of his book. I weighed too long. Nicholas looked into his empty coffee mug, perhaps thinking of a good excuse to leave.

"That's terrible," I finally said. "Does he have to join the Army?"

He considered. "I think he does. The book is a mix of comical and dark. I want the end to have the right tone. He's a lost kid, thinks he doesn't have any options. The Army's a kind of escape for him."

I shook my head, biting my lip. *What the hell.* "You know, I joined the Army National Guard when I was seventeen. It was the biggest mistake of my life."

• • •

If I am to be fair about my theories of trajectory, I have to credit the biggest mistake of my life leading me to the greatest love of my life. That day, after coffee, Nicholas and I walked around the block to linger in each other's company. We stopped to marvel at a tree that had grown around a metal pole. We've always remembered this tree because it represents what we would become—impossibly intertwined, thriving despite obstacles, something more together than apart.

Six years after that first date, in the middle of a DIY music tour from San Francisco to Minnesota, we stopped in the North Dakota badlands for a hike. It was sweltering and I was dragging ass from singing my heart out every night, crashing in our tiny camper, and then spending the next day driving to our next gig. Nicholas, as usual, had boundless amounts of energy despite setting up camp every night, serving as my roadie, and joining some songs on harmonica. Seeing a bench perched on an overlook, we clambered up a crumbling hillside and sank down to admire the labyrinth of multicolored sand mountains rising out of the desert floor.

Wheezing like an asthmatic, I blurted, "Hottie, I'm exhausted," in my best New Jersey accent.

"Will you marry me?" Nicholas asked, reaching into a bag I'd assumed held trail mix and pulling out a glass display case. Inside was a glossy, smooth, almost twisted piece of wood with two holes carved out of the middle.

"Are you serious? What is that?"

He laughed. "It's a ring sculpture I carved out of maple burl. The holes fit my ring ringer and your ring finger. I didn't want to pick out an engagement ring without you."

Of course my blue-eyed Minnesota wild man, who built chairs out of willow branches he hacked from nearby riverbeds, who could quote Nabokov, Neruda, and Salinger from memory, who had once written me a twenty-page love letter disguised as a short story, would propose with something extraordinarily out of the box. I reached for his face and kissed him, giggling at the absurdity of how the moment had unfolded, exhilarated to see where we would go from here.

I'd spent the last six years not only growing closer to Nicholas, but continuing to slowly come into my own, something I knew was a luxury, a privilege, as the wars dragged on, as the ripple effects spurred more terror cells, as more troops were called up again, and again, and again. I'd started to do the things I'd always pictured Future Rosa doing. I started a folk-rock band. I got into a graduate creative writing program and started writing and reading in earnest. When a position writing and producing newscasts for television opened up, I applied and got the job. I traveled to exotic places—the jungles of Northern Peru, ancient ruins peeking out from the undergrowth, and Greece, where antiquity stood in pristine restoration. I even taught college writing for a couple of years.

As for depression… Nicholas noticed my scars early on and bluntly asked what they were. I clumsily changed the subject. When I was ready for the conversation, he encouraged me to get laser scar revision for the worst few. The strange scar-zapping treatments didn't work, but after a year or two of looking angry, they finally flattened and faded, just like my bouts of depression ebbed into something manageable. I haven't cut myself since.

I haven't returned to therapy either—not because I don't believe in it or hold a grudge from my one experience with a therapist. But when I'm struggling, I do often return to a goal Julie gave me—advice I now know is industry standard. Instead of trying to outrun my emotions, or let them clutch me in a straightjacket, I try to observe the feelings as they come, recognize them, and accept them. I try like hell to be a little more zen, to ask exactly why I'm feeling what I am.

About a year after we got married, after reading an early version of this very book, Nicholas nudged me to stop ducking why and how I'd been discharged the way I had, to ferret out the real reason the military let me go.

"Don't you want to find out? Don't you think it matters?" he asked. We were sitting in our East Bay backyard, looking west toward the city. It was one of those clear days where you could make out the Transamerica building and Coit Tower across the water.

"Honestly, I don't want to draw any attention to it," I said. "What if my prying reopens the can of worms? What if they can still legally court-martial me or order me to serve the three-year contract extension?"

"Then you rehire that lawyer and go after them for habeas corpus. How can you not be curious about this? I mean, you're a journalist. This is what you do—follow stories to their end."

Rankled by the journalist comment, and increasingly doubtful the Army would go after me so long after the fact, I decided to track down Collier and see if he could shed some light on my case, and CO cases in general.

February 2015: San Francisco, CA

I took the train into the city and walked through the Tenderloin. The seedy, dangerous feel from 2007 was absent and I wondered if the city was different or if I was.

Collier's building looked especially run down. The tiny lobby had the ambiance of a nonprofit that didn't have the means or the time to bother with appearances. From behind stacks of paper, the receptionist told me to go upstairs. I clumped up the narrow, worn steps and loitered, unsure whether I should knock on one of the unmarked doors, when a tall, gaunt man came into the hallway.

"Are you Rosa?"

I hadn't remembered him being so tall and so thin. He towered over me. My first reaction was to hug him, but he didn't seem like a hugger, so I settled for a handshake.

He'd moved to a smaller office with a window facing the street. One wall was lined with books. The other had a few framed pictures, one a long quote about art.

"After taking a look at your old case, it sounds like they just kicked you back into the Guard," Collier said, hands clasped in front of him. He had a thick folder on his desk, presumably my old file.

"But what about the contract extension? That was with the National Guard." I passed him a copy of the extension. He spent a good five minutes frowning at it, and then paging through my file. I waited, listening to the sounds of the street coming in his cracked window. There was the airy rush of white noise and cabs honking and dollies rolling on the sidewalk. Conversations and clicking heels swelled and faded.

Collier finally looked up. "Maybe they didn't know about the extension."

It appeared he was in the slipping-through-the-cracks camp.

"You don't think I could have gotten out because I was causing too much trouble?"

Collier gave a slight shrug. "It's possible. But it seems to me when you were denied and disenrolled from ROTC the system threw you back into the Guard, and for some reason the contract extension was canceled. Annulled."

My eyebrows raised. "That seems extremely generous, judging from the rest of their behavior."

For the first time, Collier cracked a smile.

We circled around the issue a little more, but it was clear I wasn't going to get an "aha" moment. What I did get was a renewed sense of how very lucky I'd been. Collier explained that at the beginning of the war, the military and the courts weren't granting any conscientious objector cases. "They were using all sorts of excuses," he said. "But they were not legitimate or proper reasons as to why they were denying a lot of these cases. Once public opinion started to shift, they started granting more. Judges are human too. They started to have the same misgivings as the general public. Granting conscientious objection is often a political decision, not a legal decision."

He sounded like a professor. Like a philosopher. I remembered how he'd taken my case pro bono. I thought about the very humble state of his office. It looked like he helped a lot of people for free.

Before I left, Collier leaned forward and said, "You know by writing the book, you're waiving attorney-client privilege."

I waved my hand in half-forced, half-felt bravado. "Oh, I'm not worried about that. You don't think they'd make an example of me after all this time, do you?"

"It's highly unlikely," he assured me. "You've been out for..." He looked at the ceiling and did the math. "Eight years now? I know if they called me as a witness I can honestly say I remember nothing about your case. I don't remember you, or the paperwork, or the discussions."

I'd suspected as much. That he had no clue what an important figure he'd been in my minuscule war against the war. He'd been monumental. Willing to take on the federal government itself? The dude was a badass I'd never forget.

Collier's demeanor turned grim, like he was regretting reassuring me. "But then again, you never know the lengths the government will go to. I mean, you could be from the FBI for all I know." Collier was looking at his clasped hands. He was serious, afraid even. Something in my gut sharpened and I felt the blood drain from my face. A dim memory from 2007 came back. He'd asked some prying questions before that first meeting, apologizing by saying, "We just need to make sure you're not from the FBI or anything."

"That's something you legitimately have to worry about?" I asked.

He looked me in the face. "They're always trying to stop the work we do."

I waited, hoping he would go on, but his jaw was set and he looked uncomfortable. More than anything, I wanted to ask him what had happened, whether he'd had a case wrecked by the feds. Instead, I watched my journalistic pluck drain through the soles of my shoes onto the floorboards.

"I'm sorry," I faltered, gathering my things. I thought about whether I should give him the CDs I'd brought. It seemed hokey now. But I slid them across his desk before I could waffle further.

"What are these?"

"I started a band a couple years ago. Those are our first two CDs. We're not signed or anything, but we had a lot of fun making them." I blushed. *Why. Why did I bring them?*

Collier lifted the cover of the top CD case and read the inscription—a thank-you for all he'd done for me. His face lit up. "This is great. What else have you been up to? I never get to hear what happens to my clients after their cases end."

I felt my shoulders relax and told him, suddenly feeling like I was speaking not just for myself, but for all the soldiers who'd passed through Collier's office and managed to stumble into a happy ending.

• • •

When I got home I looked up a legal journal Collier had mentioned. It was written specifically for members of the Military Law Task Force, which he belonged to. I read through the habeas corpus CO cases and felt that old sense of claustrophobia spread across my chest. Take *Watson v. Geren*. Watson was a doctor who'd refused to treat wounded soldiers because he would be "weaponizing human beings." The Army was pissed when his case was upheld in court. But then the government turned right around and used Watson's argument against a doctor accused of treating terrorists, and therefore providing "material support" to al-Qaeda.

In *Kanai v. McHugh* a West Point cadet won his CO case in district court but went on to lose in the Fourth Circuit, despite complaints of bias and "procedural irregularities." Then there was Herbert Erickson, a Vietnam veteran who was denied CO status back in 1968 and convicted for it. Like me, he'd based his decision on personal ethics, not religion. Decades later he was kicked out of a program that offered in-home care because he had a felony conviction, despite President Carter pardoning all Vietnam draft resisters in 1977. A judge refused to expunge it.

One article was written by Collier himself. Back in 2011 he'd done some compiling and found that the military was beating conscientious objectors by a two-to-one margin. He called the odds "not bad," given how hard it was to win CO cases. The article came with advice and reminders for the other members of the Task Force. For instance, it was much better for COs to be religious than moral. The Fourth and DC Circuits should be avoided if at all possible because of how conservative they were—overturning even the strongest habeas petitions. And judges who made it clear they were skeptical of any CO claim now that we had an all-volunteer military should be handled with care.

Toward the end of Collier's article I found the closest thing to an "aha" moment I would get: "Applications submitted after deployment or activation orders were universally denied by the courts. Practitioners in the field know that timing issues are the shoals upon which CO claims founder, and recent case law bears this out." Waiting all that time, pushing down my doubts, trusting in the mysterious powers of the universe to end the war before I was called up—that was likely what had really done me in. I'd been doomed from the start. The narrative was that of a cut and dry turncoat: Girl volunteers to serve in the Army National Guard. Girl is called up to serve in war. Girl gets out of deployment by joining ROTC. Girl files a CO claim. It was damn hard to see it any other way—even from my soapbox, even from the small hill of moral high ground I always pictured myself standing on. At least, until you magnified the timeline of the narrative so that a living, breathing, feeling character emerged. Shame on the powerful to assume any story could be so simplistic. And shame on them for creating a labyrinthine, ridiculous process for conscientious objection under the guise that the process was meaningful and fair.

And as for finding answers? Nicholas calls it a "final little fuck-you" that I'll never know why they let me go when they did. Here I was, showing up again and again, playing by the rules, asking what hoops to jump through instead of spending my time looking for a loophole or running away to Canada. And they couldn't even manage to keep track of the details of my case. I've never been able to drum up anger about it. The feeling that sticks is more like heartbreak—an aching that the guys I'd gone through summer camp with couldn't see my perspective as legitimate, a disappointment that Cal Poly ROTC instructors and my investigating officer had taken my moral stand as a personal affront, and a burden that I'd forever be seen as a traitor by so many people, in and out of uniform.

16. PERCEPTION, ASSUMPTION, AFFIRMATION

I used to feel like I was confessing some crime, telling people I had been in the Guard, and telling them how I'd gotten out. This was partly due to my guilt and partly from having to defend myself to even the most thoughtful, open-minded people.

Usually, I let it slip at work because of some story we were running. A writer, producer, or anchor, uncertain about some detail, would shout across the newsroom:

"Anyone know if Marines can be called soldiers? Or are they sailors because they're part of the Navy?"

"Is a sergeant an officer?"

"What kind of gun is an AR-1?"

"If Obama says he's going to send non-combat troops that means they won't be in danger and won't fight, right?"

When I spoke up and answered these questions, all eyes would turn to me. I could read what they were thinking. *How would you know?*

"I used to be in the National Guard," I'd say. And once the scramble of getting the news on the air was over, people would approach me—curious, incredulous, suspicious.

"I can't picture you having ever been in the military," they'd say. "How long were you in?"

When I replied, "six years," they were always surprised. Which is why I couldn't stop there. I had to let them know: "Actually, six years is the standard National Guard contract. You can't sign up for less."

At this point, some would smile and offer quips like, "I could never handle that level of blind obedience," while others would say something like, "You know, my father fought in World War II," or "My uncle fought in Vietnam" or "My brother was in Desert Storm."

Uncomfortable at being pegged either a mindless grunt or a veteran, I'd tell them, "I ended up declaring myself a conscientious objector. I never went over," and wait for their reaction. This is when the most irritating things often emerged. For instance, "Well, you were in the National Guard, so you never would have gone over anyway," or "I wouldn't need to try to get out. They'd kick me out after a couple days," or "Couldn't you just say you were gay?" Some would suddenly become concerned about my character—"But you'd fight in World War II, right?"—or they would tell me more about what their fathers, uncles, brothers had done: "He was a bomber in the Pacific. He drove a tank. He got leukemia because of Agent Orange." Still others would offer praise mixed with a hint of disdain: "Oh, good for you. I never understood why your generation didn't throw a fit about the wars in Iraq and Afghanistan."

Unspoken assumptions flew. I saw their opinions of me crumble and reform. Many obviously thought I was dense and naive. That I was self-serving. Weak. A fool. Maybe even a disgrace. A few saw me as brave, a rebel. At the same time, I made new assumptions about them. I assumed that their patriotism was narrow minded. I assumed that despite their outspoken distrust of the government and disgust with the wars, they probably never did anything to instigate change—no marches or petitions or letter-writing campaigns. No discussions at work or the bar or during family get-togethers. I assumed they thought you didn't really need a conscience to declare yourself a conscientious objector—you need only lie, cheat, or flee the country. I assumed that by bringing up the people they knew who had served in the military, they were reminding me of the people I'd turned my back on. They were pointing out who I could thank for my freedoms as an American. Our assumptions reflected a divided and conflicted nation where somewhere between just one and two percent of its population wears the uniform.

During the Obama Administration, the world shifted. Military leaders and diplomats and politicians started writing books and giving talks about the stupidity of how we entered the war on terror, how we fought it, how we would be dealing with the repercussions for years to come. Everyone, regardless of political party, suddenly seemed to agree the wars were quagmires, disasters, horrible mistakes. Parallels were drawn to Vietnam.

With the election of Donald Trump, the fault lines shifted yet again—buckling and rending like never before. Patriotism was linked to more and more extreme behavior, like storming the US Capitol on January 6, 2021 to "stop the steal."

This second edition of Breaking Cadence is being published just a few months after President Biden declared the war in Afghanistan over, finally. (The Iraq war officially ended in 2011 but thousands of US troops remain. Deployment after deployment, we can't seem to extract ourselves.)

The chaotic, swift and deadly pullout from Afghanistan in August of 2021, almost exactly 20 years after we invaded, led to intense criticism from all sides. Suddenly everyone was concerned. Social media was flooded with Monday morning quarterbacks espousing advice, making demands, virtue signaling when for twenty years the public had largely been complacent, if not silent on the issue. Apparently, America had already forgotten the devastating revelations in the Afghanistan Papers, published in 2019. (The *Washington Post* investigation revealed that top US officials lied about the war year after year, hiding evidence that the hugely expensive mission in Afghanistan was not only "unwinnable" but deeply flawed and doomed from the start.)

On the 20th anniversary of the 9/11 attacks, I turned on NPR to hear former President Bush delivering a speech in Shanksville, Pennsylvania. Hearing his distinctive voice, I was transported back to those first years in uniform. It was a shock to the system that a man I considered a war criminal had been asked to commemorate the day. This time, social media didn't bat an eye. Neither did the mainstream media.

When Colin Powell died on October 18th, 2021, very few remembered that his speech to the United Nations in 2003, which was based on false intelligence of weapons and manufactured links between Al Qaeda and Iraq, paved the way for the Iraq War. In the weeks that followed, Powell was celebrated as a national hero.

It's a strange, fickle world we live in. So much has changed. And so much hasn't.

Consider this gem, which I hear every once in a while as I'm flipping through Top 40 radio stations:

"I'll never forget the first time I got the call," a young male voice says.

"They briefed us at the armory," says a female voice.

The young man continues, "The fire was getting dangerously close to homes. Helicopters started dropping water on the fire from above."

"It felt really good to help defend our community against the wildfire," the girl gushes.

The ad goes on to pitch the California National Guard as a great way to help your community and pay for college. It's like living in a time warp. And it's a lie. It is extremely rare for Guard members to be called up to fight a forest fire unless you happen to be an air tanker pilot. The ads on TV are worse, making joining the Marines seem like some heroic video game, or like you will be carrying out important humanitarian missions instead of killing people.

Who do they think they're fooling? Waves and waves of soldiers have come home and shared their horrendous stories of fighting in a dirty war. Many came home broken, only to be faced with a broken system. Some brought back a violent nature. But far more returned without the will to live. An estimated 18-21 veterans kill themselves in this country every single day.

"It's a shame this was so preventable," one of my coworkers said. Another soldier murder-suicide had just crossed the wires.

I squinted at her over the wall dividing our cubicles. "Preventable how? Like not starting wars?"

She looked annoyed, then pensive as she remembered I had been in the military. "No. Admitting that PTSD is an enormous problem and getting these guys treatment."

"That would be a good start," I said.

But let's get real. The only way to prevent post-traumatic stress is to eliminate the trauma. For some, that trauma starts in boot camp, where teenagers are trained to follow orders without question, to swallow complaints, to quash individuality, and to forfeit fundamental rights.

There is something insidious about the government pursuing legally binding contracts with teenagers, many of them low income teenagers. I've learned there is a term for this. The "economic draft." I've also learned that the US military spends six billion dollars every year on recruitment tactics.

In a country that strives to protect teens from cigarettes, alcohol, STDs, high interest on student loans and countless other risks, why do we not also protect teens from eight-year contracts that are virtually impossible to break without serious consequences? (I only recently learned that every military contract is actually *eight* years long. The inactive portion of these contracts can be made active at any time during those eight years.)

The United States is one of only three countries that have not signed on to the UN Convention on the Rights of the Child, which includes the right not to be recruited into the military. Instead, public schools in America are *required* to give military recruiters regular access to campus or risk losing their federal funding.

I often wonder who is signing their contract *right this very moment*. Who is swearing in today, or flying to boot camp, or trembling in the front leaning rest? What platoons are wolfing down food before hurtling through the bayonet assault course? At any given moment, thousands of young Americans are launching their military careers—getting that first buzz cut or marching to the gas chamber or sighting down their firing lane and pulling the trigger. Who will change their mind? Will they feel as lost and alone as I did? Will they find the book I wrote for them?

As for me, I don't see myself as a criminal anymore. I'm no hero, but I'm not ashamed of what I did. With the train cars of this rusting anti-war story all laid out, I can finally forgive, especially myself. Because forgiveness doesn't mean rolling over. It means moving on.

On these new train tracks, the future isn't mine so much as it is my children's. In late 2015, Nicholas and I became parents, naming our daughter Itasca, after a county deep in the north woods of Minnesota. In early 2018, our son, River, was born. We were both shocked, again, by how tiny and helpless newborns are, how they have the power to make you fall madly in love in a matter of minutes, how a mere startle reflex—teeny hands thrown in the air, grasping for something to hold on to—can suddenly seem like the most powerful of metaphors.

When I look at my mischievous, green-eyed, bookworm daughter and my sensitive, goofball son, growing and transforming at rocket speed, the sense of both hope and responsibility is overwhelming. The bigness I feel seems in direct contrast to the sense of responsibility the government lacks for members of the military.

It's not like Americans don't have a say. While criticizing the military and its leaders and even its members may seem taboo, it's not. Patriotism doesn't mean blindly following. It means believing in the greatness of our country—a country with the power to break cadence and build something better. We can say "no." We can say "stop." We can say "*this* way."

I know my war against the war is inconsequential in the grand scheme of things. And yet, maybe it isn't. Who knows how many people I can influence to think about things in a different way.

My vote doesn't directly elect a president. Your vote doesn't elect a president. My opinion, your opinion, doesn't change the world.

And yet it does.

The view from my window at the Morro Hilltop Motel, 2005.

My mother about to clobber me with the rolling pin, December 2005.

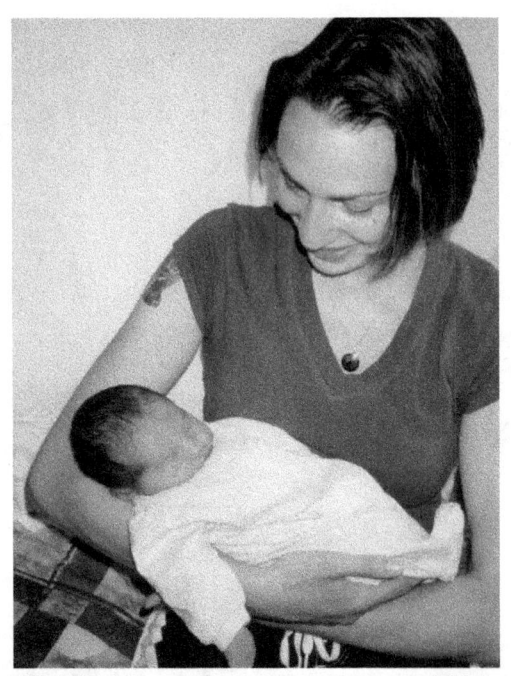
Holding my newborn niece, Summer 2006.

Zack driving Hortense on the playa at Burning Man, 2006.

My first glimpse of my future husband, Nicholas. He attached this picture of himself to his email responding to my personal ad.

Playing guitar soon after moving to Berkeley, CA in 2007.

Nick and I at our backyard wedding, June 2014.

Me holding baby Itasca, dressed up for Aaron's wedding in 2016.

The family, a few weeks after River was born in 2018.

Doing Truth in Recruitment work at Castro Valley High School, 2019. Recruiters from three branches of the military were on the other side of the gym.

ACKNOWLEDGEMENTS

Nicholas, Bandini, muse: when I write, you are, and always will be, the reader I strive to impress the most. This was all your idea in the first place. And now, I am indebted to you for the drafts you pored over and the hard questions you asked. Your never-wavering faith in me means more than you can imagine.

Mom, I am so proud and so grateful to be your daughter.

Thank you to Marilyn Abildskov, Lysley Tenorio, Rosemary Graham, Brenda Hillman, Glen David Gold, Matthew Zapruder, and Todd Pierce for making me a better writer and giving me the confidence I had the chops to tell this story in an affecting way.

Christine Baniewicz, John Engell, Juan Alvarado Valdivia, Dani Clark, Allison Landa, Christopher Cook, Jenny Bitner, Ian Hamill, and Tomas Moniz, your thoughtful feedback and moral support on this project is greatly appreciated.

To all the war resisters who came before me, thank you for standing up and speaking out, even if resisting the war meant running away, even if no one heard you say "no."

Thank you to Amy Goodman for covering the wars in Iraq and Afghanistan with journalistic integrity from the very start. Gratitude to Code Pink, Steve Collier, the GI Rights Hotline, and "Andy" (whoever you are). Your work is incredibly important and truly appreciated.

ABOUT THE AUTHOR

Rosa del Duca is a writer, journalist, teacher, and musician. She was born in Arizona and grew up in Montana, first in Missoula, and then in Fromberg. She has lived in California since 2003. Rosa's creative writing has appeared in *CALYX*, *River Teeth*, *Cutbank*, *Grain*, the *Los Angeles Review*, and other literary magazines. *Breaking Cadence: One Woman's War Against the War* is her first book.

In 2011, Rosa and Will Decher founded the band Hunters, which produced three albums: *White Lies*, *Treeline*, and *We All Go Up the Mountain Alone Together*. Rosa's most recent solo album is *Love Letters*.

Rosa lives in Castro Valley with her writer, professor, and craftsman husband, Nicholas Leither, and their two children.

To listen to the podcast Rosa created to explore topics related to this book, search *Breaking Cadence: Insights From a Modern-Day Conscientious Objector* wherever you get your podcasts. Since writing this book, Rosa has found a community of like-minded veterans in About Face: Veterans Against the War. Rosa has also joined Before Enlisting, a nonprofit seeking to make sure teens are as educated as possible before considering such a life-changing decision as joining the military. Learn more or schedule a presentation at beforeenlisting.org.

You can find out more about Rosa online at rosadelduca.com. You can reach her through breakingcadence@gmail.com.

READERS GUIDE

High School (Ages 14-18)

1. Why do you think the title "Breaking Cadence" was chosen? How does it fit in with larger themes in the memoir?
2. What recurring themes did you find throughout Breaking Cadence?
3. Is seventeen mature enough to enter into a military contract? Should our laws surrounding joining the military at 17 be reconsidered?
4. Do you think the recruiter was fair in how he pitched the National Guard to Rosa and her mom? What would you have done in her shoes?
5. Rosa spent six years feeling trapped in the National Guard. What techniques did she use to get herself through it? Were there positive and negative coping techniques? What makes a coping technique positive or negative?
6. What is Rosa's relationship to place? Do her relationships with Montana and California influence her choices?
7. The biggest decisions Rosa makes in Breaking Cadence are arguably her decisions to join the National Guard and then later to object to the war in Iraq. What or who influenced those decisions?
8. In what ways does Rosa demonstrate personal growth throughout the book? What steps did she take to achieve that growth?

University & Beyond (Ages 18+)

1. How would you characterize Rosa's life prior to meeting the recruiter? What about it made her susceptible to joining the National Guard as it was presented to her? Would you have made the same choice under similar circumstances?

2. In Part II, Chapter 3 ("Panic") Rosa writes in her journal that she is "officially activated" and shipping out October 15th. She states that she "cannot fight war" before joining the ROTC program. Should this be considered a breach of contract or should conscientious objection still apply?

3. How did Rosa's interpersonal relationships impact the decisions she made throughout Breaking Cadence?

4. In Part IV, Chapter 8 ("Investigation"), Rosa describes in detail Pastor Wong's required religious interrogation, part of the military's protocol when handling matters of conscientious objection. Was Wong fair in his questioning? Given that many Americans are not religious, is this a necessary line of questioning?

5. Rosa often feels claustrophobic and yet she is always in motion. How do you interpret Rosa's relationship to physical mobility and travel?

6. Rosa writes about fitting in with males in the military and how she felt she was viewed by them. How would you describe "fitting in" here? How did Rosa integrate into this world? What did she compromise?

7. In Part II Chapter 7 ("15 Minutes of Fame") caller Sam argues that in the Guard and Reserve the enlisted should have to serve their term of service before

receiving their college education. What would be the ramifications of requiring service before allowing individuals to receive their education? Is it morally wrong to enlist in order to receive a free education? If college was free to everyone, how would that affect the military?

8. Rosa feels isolated both in the civilian world and the military world. What contributes to these feelings? What internal and external factors make it challenging for her to connect?

www.ingramcontent.com/pod-product-compliance
Lightning Source LLC
Chambersburg PA
CBHW070949160426
43193CB00012B/1810